Cover photograph: A plastic "cast" of the lungs suggests the infinite detail of the body's structure and design.

Book Five   Health and Growth

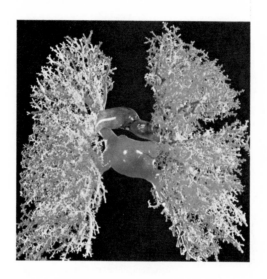

Julius B. Richmond, M.D.
Elenore T. Pounds, M.A.
Irma B. Fricke, R.N., M.S.
Dieter H. Sussdorf, Ph.D.

In consultation with
Orvis A. Harrelson, M.D., M.P.H.
Gladys Gardner Jenkins, M.A.
Norman H. Olsen, D.D.S.
Wallace Ann Wesley, Hs.D.

Designed by Norman Perman
Anatomical Art by Lou Barlow, AMI

Scott, Foresman and Company

Authors

Julius B. Richmond, M.D. Professor of Child Psychiatry and Human Development, Harvard University; Director, Judge Baker Guidance Center; Chief of Psychiatric Service, Children's Hospital, Medical Center; Professor and Chairman, Department of Social and Preventive Medicine, Harvard Medical School.

Elenore T. Pounds, M.A. Writer; lecturer; former Directing Editor, Health and Personal Development Program; classroom teacher; author of *Drugs and Your Safety* and other *Health and Growth Enrichment Booklets.*

Irma B. Fricke, R.N., M.S. Former Director of School Nursing, Evanston Public Schools, District 65, Evanston, Illinois; recipient of the 1971 William A. Howe Award in school health.

Dieter H. Sussdorf, Ph.D. Associate Professor of Microbiology and Immunology, Cornell University Medical College, New York, New York; coauthor of *Methods in Immunology.*

ISBN: 0-673-04324-X

Regional offices of Scott, Foresman and Company are located in Dallas, Texas; Glenview, Illinois; Oakland, New Jersey; Palo Alto, California; Tucker, Georgia; and Brighton, England.

Consultants

Orvis A. Harrelson, M.D., M.P.H. Director of Health Services, Tacoma Public Schools, Tacoma, Washington.

Gladys Gardner Jenkins, M.A. Lecturer in Education and Home Economics, University of Iowa, Iowa City, Iowa; former member National Advisory Council on Child Growth and Human Development; author of *Helping Children Reach Their Potential;* coauthor of *These Are Your Children.*

Norman H. Olsen, D.D.S. Chairman of the Department of Pedodontics and Dean of The Dental School, Northwestern University, Chicago, Illinois.

Wallace Ann Wesley, Hs.D. Director, Department of Health Education, American Medical Association, Chicago, Illinois; former teacher.

Advisors

Thea Flaum, B.A. Former editor, *Safety Education.* National Safety Council, Chicago, Illinois.

Willie D. Ford, Ph.D. Professor, Nutrition and Home Economics, Grambling College, Grambling, Louisiana.

Ruth Leverton, Ph.D. Science Advisor, Agricultural Research Service, United States Department of Agriculture, Washington, D.C.

Sara L. Meriwether. Elementary-school teacher, Marcy Elementary School, San Diego, California.

Joan S. Tillotson, Ph.D. Consultant in Movement Education; former teacher at elementary through college levels.

Walton Vincent, M.A. Fifth-grade teacher, Woodrow Wilson Elementary School, Denton, Texas.

Health Editorial Staff

Thelma H. Erickson, Executive Editor; Terse Stamos, Directing Editor; Jean Carr, Associate Editor; Patricia Siegert and Rosemary Peters, Assistant Editors.

Designer

Norman Perman, B.F.A. Graphic Designer, Chicago; Guest Lecturer, University of Illinois, Circle Campus, Chicago, Illinois; past President, Society of Typographic Arts.

Contents

6

1 How Does Your Brain Work?

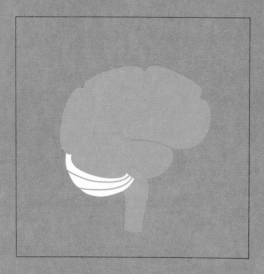

In this unit you will learn about that marvelous part of your body—your brain—which makes it possible for you to think, speak, hear, see, understand, remember, move, and do many other things. You will compare your brain with man-made "brains," such as electronic machines or computers, and find out how the human brain differs from, and how it excels, the man-made brains. And you will find why your brain is still the most remarkable structure in the world.

1. *What are some of the fascinating things the human brain can do?*

2. *How is the brain protected?*

3. *How would you describe the make-up, or structure, of the brain?*

4. *What are some things not yet known about the brain?*

5. *Could you see or hear without your brain?*

6. *What is the nervous system? How does it help you?*

7. *What are voluntary actions? Reflex actions? Involuntary actions?*

8. *How are human brains superior to man-made "brains" such as computers?*

What Is Amazing About Your Brain?

Something to Do

Look in the school or public library for books about the brain. Some books you might find are:

Cosgrove, Margaret. The Wonders Inside You *(Dodd, Mead).*

Elgin, Kathleen. The Human Body: The Brain *(Watts). Easy.*

Groch, Judith. You and Your Brain *(Harper). Advanced.*

Hyde, Margaret O. Your Brain: Master Computer *(McGraw-Hill). Advanced.*

Weart, Edith L. The Story of Your Brain and Nerves *(Coward).*

Inside that head of yours is a remarkable organ, the brain. Without it you could not read this book or understand any of the things that are going on around you.

You could not remember what you did yesterday or make plans for tomorrow. You could not play games, hear music, or talk to others. You could not imagine what things were like long ago or what they might be like in the future. Your brain does all these and countless other things as well. This activity is made possible by the billions of cells that make up the brain.

Scientists have estimated that if a computer could be built to contain the equipment in the human brain, that computer would have to be at least the size of a giant skyscraper.

What Has Been Learned About the Brain?

Hippocrates, a famous Greek physician who lived over two thousand years ago, was probably the first man to try to explain some of the wonderful things the brain can do. He felt sure that the brain helps us see, hear, smell, touch, and taste. He also believed that the brain is the part of the body that makes it possible for us to remember, forget, like or dislike, talk and write, and feel emotions such as fear and joy. He did not know how the brain did these things. But he did know that thinking was among its many amazing activities.

In the years since Hippocrates, scientists have puzzled over the process of thinking that goes on in the brain. In spite of all their work, there are still many unanswered questions about how the brain thinks. But answers to these questions will continue to be explored, and scientists will continue to add to their knowledge about the way the brain is made and how it works.

The Structure of the Brain

The brain is a soft, spongy mass of tissue that is covered by a protective coat, or *membrane*. Between this first membrane and a second one is a fluid. A third membrane covers the other two. The bones of the head, or *skull*, surround all three membranes. These bones protect the brain and help keep it from being injured by falls or blows.

During the early years of your life, your brain grew rapidly. It reached almost full size by the time you were about five years old. But it will continue to grow very slowly until you are about twenty years old or so.

When your brain reaches its full size, it will weigh about two and a half to three pounds. Only

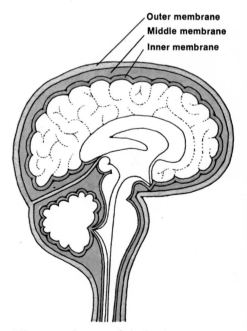

Outer membrane
Middle membrane
Inner membrane

Three membranes of the brain

two other creatures have brains that are larger. The brain of a full-grown elephant weighs about eight pounds, and the brain of an adult male whale weighs about five pounds. But *in proportion to body weight*, the human brain is larger than the brain of either the elephant or the whale.

Your brain has three main parts: the *cerebrum*, the *cerebellum*, and the *brain stem*. The lowest part of the brain stem is the *medulla oblongata*, which is connected to the spinal cord. Each part of the brain is connected by nerves with all other parts of it.

The Cerebrum

The cerebrum is the biggest part of the brain. It has a grayish-pink cover called the *cerebral cortex*. The cerebral cortex has deep wrinkles in it, which give more room for brain cells than a smooth cover would. Under this cover, the cerebrum is whitish. The whitish parts are nerve fibers that carry messages *to* and *from* all parts of the body.

The cerebrum is divided into two parts or halves, left and right. These two halves are connected by a band of nerves that joins them near the bottom. In each half, or *hemisphere*, of the cerebrum there are special places on the cortex where messages are received from various parts of the body. For example, there are centers for messages of hearing, seeing, touching, tasting, and smelling, which come from the main sense organs.

Messages traveling over the nerves from the eyes, for instance, are sent to the seeing, or vision, center in each half of the cerebrum.

There is a special center for speech and for each of the main senses in both halves of the cerebrum. When messages are received in these centers, the brain interprets them and decides what action to take, if any is needed.

Cat brain

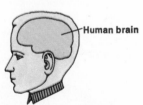
Human brain

Whale brain
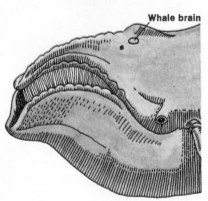

Size of cat brain, human brain, and whale brain—each in proportion to overall body weight

10

Each half of the cerebrum also has a motor center in it. It is from the motor centers that messages are sent from the brain to the muscles in your body —messages that make you move about. The right side of your brain controls the motion in the left side of your face and body. The left side of your brain controls the motion in the right side of your face and body.

One way in which scientists have found these special centers on the cerebral cortex is by studying people who have had brain injuries. For example, it was found that when a certain area in the back of the cerebral cortex was injured, the ability to see was affected. If an area near the top center of the cerebral cortex was injured, the legs might lose their ability to move, or become paralyzed.

A famous surgeon, Wilder Penfield, also made a major discovery. He found that when he was operating on a patient's brain and touched the nerve cells in the front part of the cerebral cortex, a remarkable thing happened. The patient could remember clearly experiences out of the past—experiences seemingly forgotten because there had been no need to recall them. This surgeon's work provided useful clues about where memory may be stored in the brain.

It is because of such studies that scientists have been able to make a "map" of the cerebral cortex. This map is the same for all people because all human brains are the same in their physical make-up. Large areas on the cerebral cortex are unmapped because their functions, if any, are not yet known. In fact, the function of about two thirds of the cerebral cortex is not yet understood.

Even after years of study, scientists are not sure just where thinking, reasoning, and remembering

Something to Do
Someone in your class might get from a butcher shop the brain of a pig or a cow. Then your class could examine the gray matter (cortex); the white matter (nerves); and the wrinkles, or grooves, in it.

11

go on. But they believe that these activities occur in the forward part of the cerebrum.

It is known for sure, though, which parts of the brain are receiving areas for the senses of sight, sound, touch, taste, and smell; it is also known where the speech and movement centers are.

A great part of the cerebral cortex that is as yet unmapped is thought to be made up of nerve cells that send messages within the brain from one part to another. These areas that are not yet mapped with certainty are called *association areas*. They are called this because they are believed to relate messages that come to the brain and make them more meaningful.

The vision center is at the back of the cerebral cortex. But you do not just *see* an object — a dog, for instance. You also recognize the dog as friendly, familiar, a collie, or none of these. You may become sad as you think of a dog you once owned or a story you have read about such a dog. Thus the seeing area draws upon other areas of the brain. It does this by means of a set of nerves connecting one part of the brain with another.

The Cerebellum

Lying under the cerebrum is the cerebellum. Look at the pictures on pages 17 – 19 and find the cerebellum. The cerebellum is about the size of your closed fist. Like the cerebrum, the cerebellum is divided into two halves, or hemispheres, connected by nerve tissue.

The cerebellum sees that your muscles work together so that you can walk, run, and move about. It also receives messages from the semicircular canals of the inner ear and helps you keep your balance. (See also pages 33 – 34 and 50 of this book to learn more about the semicircular canals.)

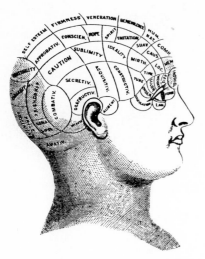

This brain "map" was made before any research had been done on the areas of the brain. You can see a scientific map on page 18.

After the decision is made that you are to move, your cerebellum takes over and keeps you moving.

Your cerebellum coördinates your muscle movements so that they are made smoothly and with precision. If your cerebellum is injured, control over your muscles is greatly disturbed.

The Brain Stem

The brain stem is a column of tissue that connects the cerebrum with the spinal cord. Nerves on their way to and from the higher centers of the brain pass through the brain stem.

This part of the brain does many important things. For example, the lowest part of the brain stem, the medulla oblongata, helps regulate such things as breathing, the digestion of food, and the circulation of blood throughout the body.

The Spinal Cord

The spinal cord is a long cord of nerve tissue that extends from the brain stem down the length of the back. This cord is enclosed and protected from injury by the chain of bones called the *backbone*, or the *spine*. Small, irregular bones called *vertebrae* make up the spine. The spinal cord is surrounded and protected by the same fluid that is around the brain. It is also surrounded by the same three layers of membranes that protect your brain.

The spinal cord provides a passageway for nerves. The *sensory nerves* carry messages from such sense organs as the eyes, ears, and skin, and they travel only *to* the brain. The *motor nerves*, which carry orders for action *from* the brain, travel to the muscles all over the body.

Cranial nerves, which are located in the brain, chiefly serve the head and face. Branching off from the spinal cord are *spinal nerves* that divide and subdivide until they reach all parts of the body.

Something to Do

Prepare a special report on the effects on the brain of alcohol and other drugs. A good reference book you might use is Drugs and You *by Arnold Madison (Messner).*

13

What Is the Nervous System?

Your nervous system is made up of your brain, your spinal cord, and the nerves that extend all over your body.

The brain is sometimes called the busiest place in the world. It is hard to imagine the number and kinds of messages that are being flashed all the time *to the brain* over the sensory nerves from the eyes, ears, skin, and so on. These messages are received in various parts of the brain, acted upon if necessary, or stored as memories.

It is also difficult to imagine the number and kinds of messages that are going all the time *from the brain* to the muscles over the motor nerves. These messages concern moving or not moving muscles, and so on.

The nerves are sometimes likened to telephone wires. Unlike telephone wires, however, nerves are made of living tissue.

The messages that travel over the nerves are all alike. It is impossible to tell one from another. What does set one message, or *impulse*, apart from another is the place where it is going. Thus if the message comes from the ears to the hearing center of the brain, you hear. If the message comes from the eyes to the visual center of the brain, you see. If the message comes from the brain to a muscle, you move that muscle.

The final stopping place of the message determines such things as whether we see, hear, taste, smell, move a muscle, or the like.

Some nerves in the body send messages at a speed of 20 feet per second. Others can send their messages at a rate of 400 feet per second—or over 300 miles an hour. Since distances are short in the

Something to Think About
When do you think the brain gets its best chance to rest?

14

human body, communication from one part to another takes place almost instantly.

No one knows how messages that start with sense organs such as eyes or ears change into thoughts, ideas, and memories in your brain. But we do know that these messages bring your brain the impressions of all you hear, see, touch, smell, and taste. These impressions are stored as memories that can be combined in millions of ways.

We do not know just how memory works. But we do know that it is important to store in your brain many kinds of experiences and knowledge upon which you can draw to work out a situation or to solve a problem.

Voluntary Actions

Most times when you think about your nervous system, you think of the actions you can direct. These are called *voluntary actions*. Whenever you want to do such things as walk or run or chew or talk, your brain sends messages over motor nerves to the correct muscles in your body. Then the muscles do what the messages tell them to do.

Reflex Actions

When thinking is required, your brain must do the work. However, there are times when an automatic reaction, which is called a *reflex*, occurs. Your eye blinks, for example, when a speck of dirt comes toward it. When you stumble, your arms are thrown out to break your fall. When the tendon just below the kneecap is tapped, the knee jerks.

These are all reflex actions, in which sensory nerves flash a message to the spinal cord. In turn, the spinal cord, acting as a relay center, flashes back a message to the muscles to move at once—and it also sends another message to the brain about the original message.

Reflex action of the knee tendon when the knee is tapped

15

The brain may send orders about a response to be made so that you say "Ouch!" But this takes place *after* the reflex action. Reflex actions, as you can see, are very useful in emergencies.

Some other reflex actions are these: coughing when something gets in your windpipe, sneezing when something irritates the inside of your nose, jumping when you hear a loud noise, and pulling your hand away if it touches a hot object.

Still another reflex action occurs when you enter a dark place; the pupils of your eyes grow larger to let more light into the eyes. When you go into a very well-lighted place, the pupils of your eyes grow smaller to let in less light.

Involuntary Actions

There are other actions that take place without orders from you. These actions are known as *involuntary actions*. Digestion of the food you eat, the beating of the heart, and breathing are largely involuntary actions.

The division of the nervous system that is in charge of involuntary actions is the *autonomic nervous system*. It controls organs of your body that cannot wait for you to think about them before they do their work. The autonomic nervous system sees that your heart, lungs, liver, stomach, intestines, kidneys, bladder, and various blood vessels function properly. (See the picture on page 21.)

There is a close connection between your emotions and the activities of your autonomic nervous system. If emotions such as fear, worry, joy, or excitement are aroused, nerve messages to many of the organs may speed up or slow down the work of these organs. For example, your heart may beat faster when you are excited. Or you may find that you breathe more rapidly.

Something to Try

The act of breathing is largely automatic. You can hold your breath—but only for a short period of time. Try holding your breath. How long does it take before your nervous system sees to it that breathing goes on?

16

The Human Brain and Man-Made "Brains"

Study the pictures of the human brain and the nervous system on pages 17-21. Then read the captions above the pictures of man-made "brains," or computers, on pages 22-24. Decide how the human brain is unique.

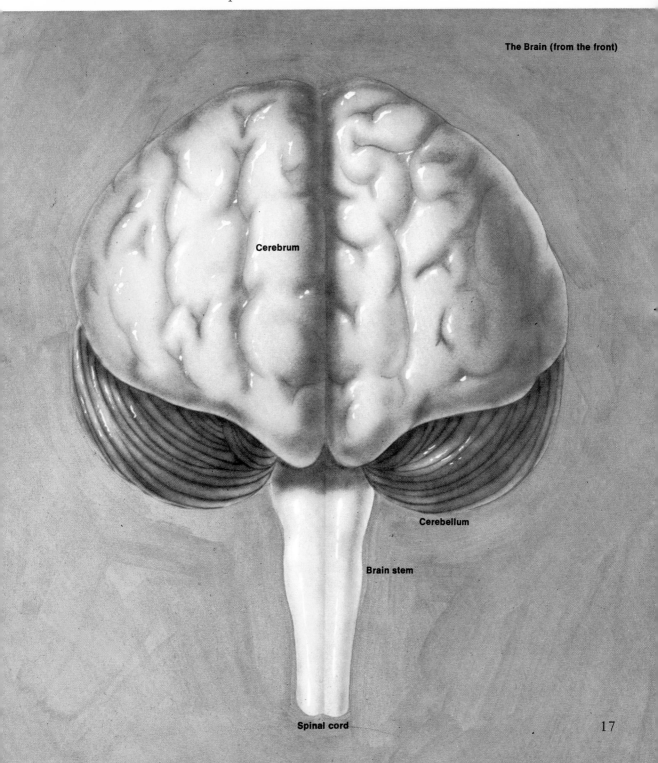

The Brain (from the front)

Cerebrum

Cerebellum

Brain stem

Spinal cord

17

The cerebrum is the biggest part of the brain. Notice the wrinkled cover called the cerebral cortex. *Can you find the special center for each of the five main senses? Can you find the motor center?*

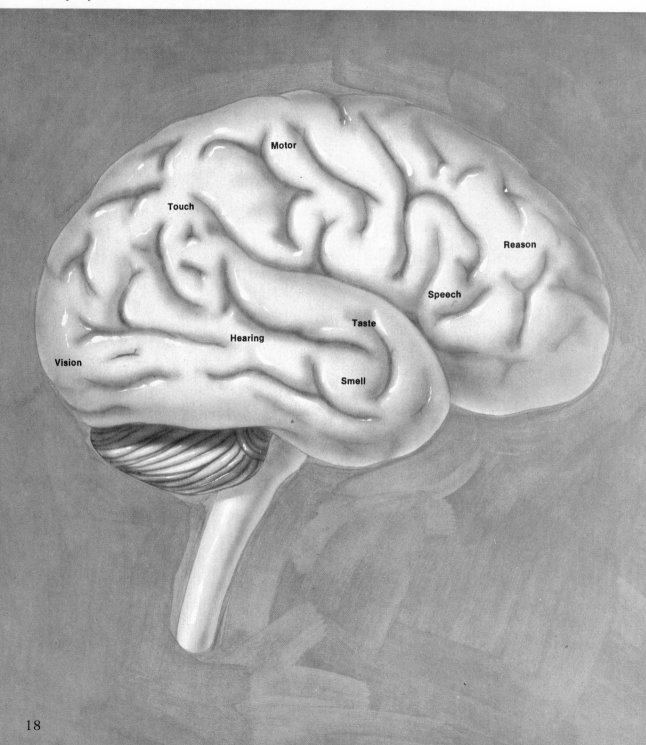

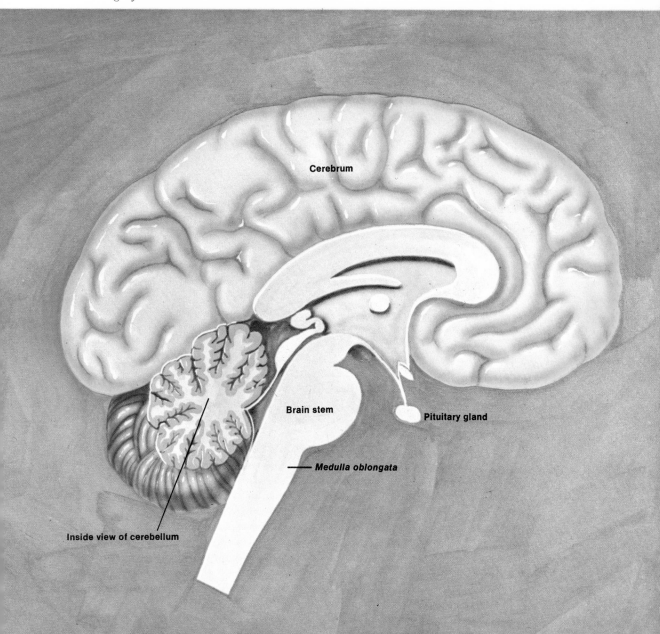

Cerebrum

Brain stem

Pituitary gland

Medulla oblongata

Inside view of cerebellum

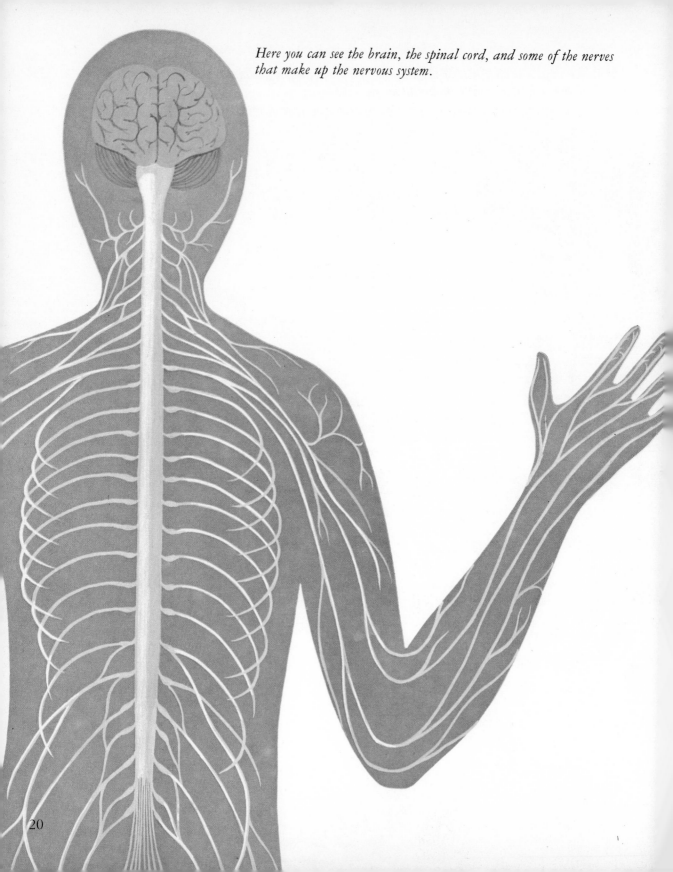

Here you can see the brain, the spinal cord, and some of the nerves that make up the nervous system.

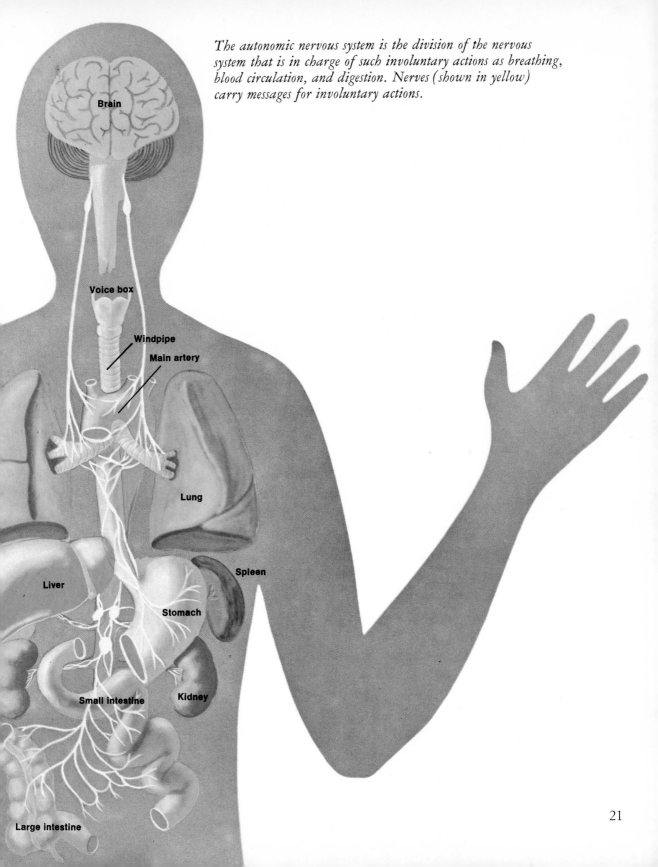

The autonomic nervous system is the division of the nervous system that is in charge of such involuntary actions as breathing, blood circulation, and digestion. Nerves (shown in yellow) carry messages for involuntary actions.

Brain

Voice box

Windpipe

Main artery

Lung

Spleen

Liver

Stomach

Small intestine

Kidney

Large intestine

21

Here you can see one type of man-made "brain," or computer. Computers can do many mechanical operations faster than can human brains.

This picture gives you a close-up view of the complex wiring on a computer control board. This intricate machine can relate, apply, store, and retrieve vast amounts of information.

23

Wonderful as computers are, the human brain still has to plan what is fed into them. Then the human brain uses the information obtained from the computer to solve difficult problems of modern life.

Health Questions Young People Often Ask

Here are some questions young people your age sometimes ask about the brain and how it works. Can you answer them?

1. Do smart people have bigger brains than other people?

2. What is the mind?

3. What are brain waves?

4. If the brain is inside the skull, how can it grow?

5. How can you make your brain work better for you?

Check your answers with the ones below and on pages 26 – 27. Then think of some questions about the brain that *you* would like to have answered.

How might you find answers to the questions you have raised?

Do Smart People Have Bigger Brains Than Other People?

Scientists have studied this question over the years. They have examined the brains of very smart people as well as those of other people. As a rule it can be said that very smart people — like all other people — may have small, average-sized, or large brains.

What Is the Mind?

"Mind" is just another word for the thought processes carried on by the human brain. Among these processes are reasoning, judging, imagining, and creating.

What Are Brain Waves?

Brain cells in your brain give off electrical discharges, or *brain waves*, at regular intervals.

A machine has been invented that can measure and record these brain waves. It is called the *electro-encephalograph*. It picks up the electrical discharges,

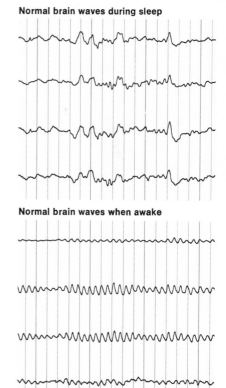

Normal brain waves during sleep

Normal brain waves when awake

Here you can see normal brain waves when a person is asleep and when he is awake.

or brain waves, and records them in the form of wavy lines on a continuous roll of paper. This tracing of brain waves is called an *electroencephalogram*, or EEG. An EEG is made by taping wires to a person's head at certain spots. These wires, which carry the electrical discharges from the brain, plug into a special box. From this box, the discharges travel to the recording part of the machine.

If the Brain Is Inside the Skull, How Can It Grow?

The design of the skull permits growth of the brain as an individual matures. In the first place, the skull is made up of more than one bone. In a newborn baby, several bones that make up the skull have rather wide spaces between them. Such places are called "soft spots." As a child grows older, the bones grow until they close up. But they do not close entirely until the brain is fully grown. Then they become so tightly closed that they cannot be pulled apart without breaking the skull.

How Can You Make Your Brain Work Better for You?

The more you really *use* your brain through having interesting experiences, taking trips, reading books, seeing worth-while TV programs, talking things over with others, trying to solve problems, the more efficient your brain can become.

At school, and all around you, you have many chances to learn. But it is *you* yourself who must make the effort to learn. Here are some ideas you may find helpful.

Pay Attention

Paying attention is a great aid to helping you learn well. This means keeping your mind on the work at hand. Try to be aware of what it is you are to learn.

Often your teacher "cues you in" on what you are to learn. Thus she may suggest that you are to

Reminders

1. Don't forget that the encyclopedia is a good source for finding answers to many of your questions.

2. Another reference book you may find in the school or public library is The Question and Answer Book About the Human Body *by Ann McGovern (Random).*

3. Remember that continued deep sniffing of glue used for airplane models is dangerous. It can damage the brain and other parts of the body.

26

find out what the three parts of the brain are and what each part does. Or your textbook or reference book may start out by suggesting what important things you are to find out. (Notice the sections in this book, for example, called "Read to Find Out." These sections are at the beginning of each unit.)

Be an Active Learner

If you keep what you are to learn in mind, you are more likely to be an active learner. Your attention is kept on seeking important ideas. Otherwise you may be a passive learner who does not separate important from unimportant ideas.

Also watch for signals in what you read or hear. Authors of books or speakers on TV or radio often help you with such statements as "The three main causes are. . . ."

Look for headings in books, too. These headings tell you beforehand what each section is about.

Be a Good Listener

Many of the things you learn come through listening. Try to follow carefully what the teacher, your classmates, or other speakers are saying so that at any point you can ask a question of your own or try to answer a question asked of you.

Learn How to Memorize

There may be important factors or formulas in schoolwork that you must memorize. There are ways you can improve your ability to memorize.

1. Read the material silently and think about what it means.

2. Repeat the material to yourself, looking back at the copy only when you have to.

3. Try writing the material; check from time to time to see if you are correct.

4. Space your learning periods so that you do not try to learn all the material at any one time.

Did You Know?

1. We can all improve the way our brains function. It has been estimated that everyone has more ability than he or she uses.

2. The use of alcoholic drinks can affect the way the brain works. Thus alcoholic drinks can interfere with a person's normal ability to understand, to reason, and to make decisions.

1. Look back at the questions on page 8. How would you answer them now?

2. Why do you think the brain might be called a central exchange?

3. What would happen if a person's cerebellum was injured?

4. Which side of the brain controls motion in the right arm and leg?

5. How would you explain this statement: "What we know about the brain is small compared with what is yet to be learned about it"?

6. Do you think the day will ever come when electronic brains will take over *all* our thinking for us? Explain your answer.

7. How do reflex actions help protect the body?

8. How would you explain this statement: "Even if we did not need the brain for thinking, we would need it to keep us alive"?

9. How might a person lose the power of speech even though his vocal cords were in good condition and there was no injury to the muscles used in speaking?

10. What are some things you learned in this unit that you had not known before?

Things to Do

1. Prepare a short talk on some things you can do to help make your brain work more efficiently.

2. Write a short paragraph telling the various ways the brain is protected.

3. Tell what each of these terms means:

  a. brain wave   d. spine

  b. cerebral cortex   e. vertebrae

  c. EEG   f. voluntary action

4. Be ready to tell about the work of the autonomic nervous system.

5. Make a list of some of the amazing things the human brain can do.

6. Describe what happens in your nervous system when you hear your telephone ring and then you answer it.

Special Research

1. Find out if these simple animals have nervous systems: the *amoeba*, the *sponge*, the *earthworm*. Then make some comparisons with the human nervous system.

2. Look in an encyclopedia or another reference book for comparisons of sizes of the brains of such animals as monkeys, dogs, birds, and dolphins.

Self-Help Review

Use a ruler or a strip of paper to cover the answer column at the right. Read the first item and write the missing word or words on a piece of paper. Then move your ruler or paper strip down to uncover the answer and see if you are right. Go on in the same way with each of the other items. Do not write in this book.

The numbers by the answers show the pages in this book that give information about the subject. For the items you miss, go back and review this information.

1. When your brain reaches full size, it weighs about _____ to _____ pounds.

2 1/2 to 3
9

2. The cerebrum is covered by the cerebral _____.

cortex 10

3. Messages are sent from the _____ center in your cerebrum to the muscles to make them move.

motor 11

4. The spinal cord is enclosed and protected by bones of the _____.

spine 13

5. Your nervous system is made up of your _____, your spinal cord, and your _____.

brain
nerves 14

6. Actions in your body such as breathing are called _____ actions.

involuntary 16

7. Brain waves are _____ discharges given off by the brain.

electrical 25

8. The part of the brain that helps your muscles work together smoothly is the _____.

cerebellum 12

Health Test for Unit One

Part I

Copy each number on a piece of paper. After the number write the correct answer, *true* or *false*.

1. The cerebrum is the smallest part of the brain.

2. Fear, excitement, or anger can affect the way some body organs work.

3. The cerebral cortex is always very smooth in an adult.

4. The brain is protected by three surrounding membranes, some fluid, and the bony skull.

5. The cerebrum is divided into two halves, or hemispheres.

6. Messages from the ears go to the vision center of the brain.

7. The brain stem connects the cerebrum with the spinal cord.

8. The spinal cord is six inches long.

9. The medulla oblongata helps regulate such things as breathing.

10. Scientists have learned all there is to know about the brain.

11. The brain directs a reflex action.

12. A brain wave is the same thing as a wrinkle or groove on the brain.

Part II

Copy each number in List A and after it write the letter of the item in List B that best answers the description.

List A

13. largest part of brain
14. backbone
15. grayish-pink covering of cerebrum
16. part of brain that helps make muscle movements smooth
17. nerve tissue that extends from brain stem down the length of the back
18. nerves that carry messages to muscles
19. part of brain stem that helps control such functions as digestion
20. bones of the head

List B

  a. cerebral cortex
  b. motor nerves
  c. cerebellum
  d. spine
  e. skull
  f. cerebrum
  g. medulla oblongata
  h. spinal cord

Number of Answers   20

Number Right   _____

Score (Number Right x 5)   _____

2 How Do Your Senses Help You?

In the first unit of this book you learned many things about how your brain works. Now you will find out more about how information is received from the five main sense organs—the eyes, ears, nose, tongue, and skin—and how this information is passed along to your brain. You will also learn about some other senses that are not so well known —senses that are often called "deep senses."

Read to Find Out

1. What is the major task performed by each of the five main senses?

2. What do you think the "deep senses" might be?

3. What happens to make you see things?

4. How do you hear sounds?

5. Which two senses work more closely together than any other pair?

6. What are the four main tastes?

7. Which of the senses might be called the "chemical senses"? Why?

8. What can your sense of touch tell you?

9. What does it mean to be color-blind?

How Many Senses Do You Have?

Something to Do
Look in the school or public library for books like these about the human senses:

Barker, Eric J., and Millard, W. F. Science Projects and Experiments —The Five Senses (*Arco*).

Froman, Robert. The Many Human Senses (*Little, Brown*). *Advanced.*

Gilmour, Ann B. and James A. Understanding Your Senses: Easy Experiments for Young People (*Warne*).

Liberty, Gene. The First Book of the Human Senses (*Watts*).

White, Anne Terry, and Lietz, Gerald S. Windows on the World (*Garrard*).

For many years the senses that people have known about — and the ones doctors and other scientists have studied about — are those of *seeing, hearing, smelling, tasting,* and *touching.* These five senses are the ones that help you know what is going on in the world about you. They are sometimes called *special senses* or *main senses.* But in this unit you will find out about some additional "deep senses."

The "Deep Senses"

Nowadays it is known that the five main senses are not the only ones you have. Deep within your body there are some sensory nerves that tell you of your body's needs. Such senses let you know when it is time to eat, when you have had too much to eat, when you are thirsty, when you need more fresh air to breathe, when the bladder needs to be emptied, and so on.

Your Muscle Sense or Kinesthetic Sense

You have a *muscle sense*, or kinesthetic sense, too. It helps you know about such things as weight and movement. For instance, if you lift two boxes of the same size, your muscle sense tells you if one is heavier than the other.

This sense also makes it possible for you to carry out movements almost automatically. Usually you do not pay much attention to this sense until you are trying to learn a new muscle skill, such as throwing or catching a baseball. Then, for a time, you pay attention to what your different muscles and joints are doing. Once a skill is mastered, though, it becomes automatic. For instance, you walk now without paying attention to doing it. But actually this is a very difficult skill, requiring great coördination of movements. This skill took lots of practice when you first learned to walk.

Your muscle sense, aided by your sense of direction, helps you know about left and right, up and down, backward and forward. These senses are useful as you do such things as walk, ride a bicycle, play games like dodge ball, and perform stunts.

Your Sense of Balance

You also have a sense of *balance*. In your inner ear are some hollow loops called the *semicircular canals*. These parts have nothing to do with hearing. Instead, they help you keep your balance. Without them, you could not keep your balance when you walk, stand, or sit. See the pictures of the semicircular canals on pages 52-53 and 54.

The semicircular canals are filled with liquid. When the liquid is violently shaken up, you may feel dizzy or unsteady for a short time. This is what happens when you have been whirling around for a few minutes. Some people are more affected

Something to Do

Have you ever been aware that you were losing your sense of balance? Tell about it and why you think it happened.

33

than others by the shaking up of this fluid. They may develop *motion sickness*. This sickness may result from riding in an auto, airplane, ship, or train. Once a person becomes used to various motions, he can usually adapt to motion sickness. For those people who cannot adapt, there are motion-sickness medicines.

Tests for astronauts include some that judge the degree and the duration of the dizziness they experience after being violently shaken up. Why do you think such tests are important?

Research on the Senses

While much is known about the human senses, there are many things yet to be learned. And there is much scientific research still taking place — some of it on the senses that are not so well known. For instance, some people have what are sometimes called "internal clocks." That is, they wake up a few moments before the alarm clock goes off. Or they do not even set a clock. They just wake up when they want to wake up. Scientists are studying people with this special sense to try to find out more about it.

One thing that is known for sure, though, is that people differ in the way they sense the same things. Thus a number of individuals may taste exactly the same food. To some the food may taste somewhat bitter; others may find it a bit salty; and a few may say it is rather sweet. Individual differences are to be expected in the way people sense things just as there are individual differences in all other human reactions.

Although there are many senses, this unit will discuss chiefly the five special, or main, senses. These senses, as you know, are the senses of seeing, hearing, tasting, smelling, and touching.

Something to Do
Make a list of ways some of your various senses have helped you since you woke up this morning.

34

How Do You See?

Of all your senses, the sense of sight tells you most about the world around you. Through your eyes you see people and things. You can read books and signs and learn from them. You can see things near to you. Or you can see faraway things like the sun and stars that are millions of miles away.

Light to See By

Since your eyes need light to see by, you must know something about light before you can understand how you see.

Suppose you are in a completely dark room. Your eyes may be open, but you will not see anything. Then suppose you turn on a flashlight. When the flashlight goes on, you will see things in the room. For example, you may see a table nearby.

The light from your flashlight shines on the table, but it cannot go through the table. So the light bounces back from it. This light that bounces back from the table is *reflected light*.

To see the table, your eyes and the table are not enough. There has to be light, too. When the light hits the table, some of it is reflected into your eyes and only then do messages of sight go from the eyes to the seeing area of the brain.

Almost everything you see is by reflected light. The light is reflected from such things as the sun, the stars, electric light, or gaslight.

The Front of the Eye

Now that you know something about light, you are ready to learn about your eyes and their part in helping you see.

You know such parts of the eyes as the *eyelids* and the *eyelashes*, don't you? But do you know how these parts help protect your eyes? When bits of

What Do You Think?

Why is it a good idea to turn on a light before you walk across a completely dark room?

35

dirt are flying around, your eyelashes serve as screens to help keep out the dirt. Also when bits of dirt come near your eyes, your eyelids shut quickly to keep the dirt out.

The colored part of your eye is the *iris*, and the little opening in the middle of the iris is the *pupil*.

The iris is really a ring of muscles. It acts very quickly to change the size of the pupil in different lights. In this way the iris protects the sensitive back part of your eye from too much light. When you go into a brightly lit room, tiny muscles of the iris make the pupil smaller to let in less light.

When you go into a dark place, tiny muscles of the iris make your pupil larger. Then more light enters and you can see better.

In front of the pupil and the iris there is a cover called the *cornea*. The cornea is colorless, and it is transparent, so that you can see through it. The cornea keeps bits of dust and dirt from going through the pupil.

The Tear Gland in Each Eye

You may wonder what keeps the cornea from getting dusty and dirty. Keeping the cornea clean is the job of the *tear gland* in each eye.

The tear glands are located above the outer corner of each eye. Liquid from these glands washes the eye's surface and drains into tiny tubes, or *ducts*, at the inner corner of each eye. These ducts empty into a large duct which drains into the nose.

When you blink, the eyelids spread the tears over the front surface of the eye. The tears wash away the dust and leave the cornea moist. There is a substance in your tears, too, that helps destroy germs which may enter the eyes.

So far you have been reading mainly about the front of the eye. If you could see the complete

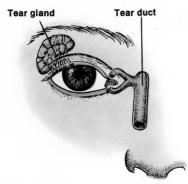

Tear gland   Tear duct

How do the tear glands help keep the eyes clean?

eye, or the *eyeball*, you would see that it looks something like the picture on page 41.

Your eyeball is set far enough back in your head to be protected by the bones of your cheeks and forehead. The eyeball is also protected by little cushions of fat.

On the outside of the eyeball is a strong white covering called the *sclera*. If you look into a mirror, you can see part of this white covering in your own eyes. You may have heard it called the "whites of your eyes."

There are muscles that can move your eyeballs up and down and sideways. Can you find them in the picture on page 38?

Inside the Eyeball

What is inside the eyeball? Let's follow a ray of light as it goes into the eye.

First the light hits the cornea. It passes easily through this colorless covering. Next the light goes through a clear watery liquid which is a weak salt solution.

The light passes on through the pupil and through the *lens*. This lens is a clear-looking part that can change in size. Tiny muscles pull the lens to make it *thinner* when you look at distant things. These muscles relax to make the lens *thicker* when you look at things nearby.

Then the light goes through another clear liquid in the center of the eyeball. This liquid is somewhat jellylike and keeps the rounded shape of the eyeball. It is mostly water with some protein in it. It is dark inside the eyeball because the eyeball has a dark inner lining.

Finally the light is focused on the *retina*. The retina is a thin filmlike tissue that lines the back of the eye. In the retina are some tiny parts of

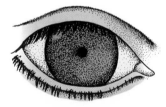
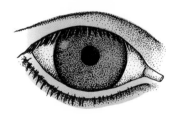

Here you can see how the pupil changes in size when it is in different light conditions.

37

cells that respond to light. Small *cone-shaped parts* are stimulated by bright light. When a bright or colored light falls on the *cones*, they send messages about color to the brain. The retina also contains many *rod-shaped parts*. They are in use only when you see black and white or shades of gray.

There are millions of connecting parts of cells in the retina, too. Such cell parts connect the rods and cones. They also connect with tiny thread-like nerves in the retina that come together to make the *optic nerve*. The optic nerve goes from the retina of each eye to the vision center on each side of the brain.

The Eyes and the Brain

Your eye works much like a camera works. When you look at something—a cat, for example—the likeness or image of the cat is carried by rays of light through the pupil of each eye, on through the lens, and then to the lining at the back, or retina.

When the image of the cat goes to the retina, a wonderful thing happens. The retina, which is like the film inside a camera, takes a picture of the cat. This picture, like all pictures on the retina, is upside down.

Since you have two eyes, you get two upside-down pictures—one with each eye. The nerve cells of each retina send messages about these pictures to your brain over the optic nerve in each eye.

When the messages reach the vision center in each side of your brain, the brain blends the two pictures into one. The brain also makes the upside-down picture right-side up and makes it clear what the picture is. In other words, the brain gives meaning to the picture. Then you think, "I see a cat."

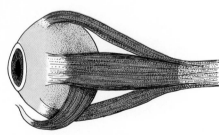

Eyeball seen from the side, showing the muscles of the eye

38

Why Do Some People Need Glasses?

One of the most wonderful things about the lens in each eye is the way it changes in size to help you see better. It can adjust to bring the light rays that come through the lens either closer together or keep them farther apart.

When you are looking at something far away, tiny muscles make the lens thinner. This thinner lens is the shape needed to bend the light rays so that they come to a point, or *focus*, on the retina of each eye.

When you are looking at something nearby, tiny muscles make the lens thicker. A thicker lens is needed to focus light rays from the nearby object on the retina.

The pictures at the right show how the lens in a normal eye changes in size to focus on things far away and on things up close.

How would you describe the shape of the lens when a faraway object is being viewed? When a nearby object is being viewed?

Near-Sightedness

Sometimes the eyeball is too long from front to back. This causes light rays to be brought to a focus in front of the retina. A person whose eyeball is too long from front to back is *near-sighted.* People with near-sighted eyes can see nearby things well, but they cannot see faraway objects clearly. See the diagrams on page 40.

Glasses of the right kind help a near-sighted person see as a person with normal eyes sees. Glasses can be made that will bend the light rays so that a clear picture is formed on the retina. Then the near-sighted person is able to see faraway things more clearly.

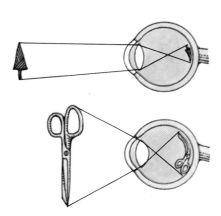

Top. *The lens bringing a faraway object into focus*
Bottom. *The lens bringing a nearby object into focus*

39

People who need very thick lenses or who find regular glasses a handicap may have *contact lenses* prescribed for them. Contact lenses are small, plastic lenses that fit over the cornea of the eye.

In the top picture at the left you can see how a normal eye focuses a picture on the retina. In the middle picture at the left you can see how a near-sighted eye focuses the same picture. In the near-sighted eye, where is the picture focused?

Far-Sightedness

An eye with a too-short eyeball makes a person *far-sighted*. People with far-sighted eyes can see things that are far away, but they cannot see nearby objects clearly. Nearby objects look blurred. In the far-sighted eye, the image is focused behind the retina.

Now look again at the pictures in the margin at the left. Which picture shows light rays entering a normal eye?

Which picture shows a far-sighted eye? How can you tell? Where is the picture focused in the far-sighted eye?

Astigmatism

Still another eye problem is *astigmatism*. This difficulty is caused by irregularities in the shape of the cornea or the lens. The result is blurred vision. Glasses that provide correction for the uneven shape of the cornea help a person with astigmatism see normally.

Strabismus

Strabismus results from certain muscle irregularities that cause the eyes to turn in toward the nose or to turn outward from the nose. Young children often have this problem. They should be under the care of an eye doctor who has ways of correcting the difficulty.

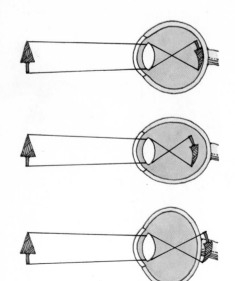

Top. *A normal eye*
Middle. *A near-sighted eye*
Bottom. *A far-sighted eye*

Some Interesting Parts of the Eye

What parts of the eye are pictured here? What can you tell about some of these parts?

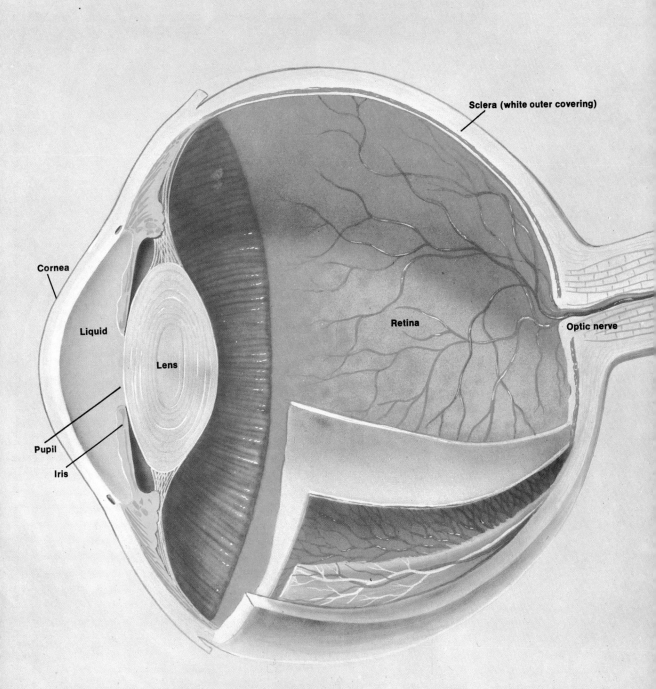

Sclera (white outer covering)

Cornea

Liquid

Retina

Optic nerve

Lens

Pupil

Iris

On these two pages you can see a close-up of a healthy retina. (The light-colored spot is the beginning of the optic nerve.) The rods and the cones, at the right, lie in the deepest layer of the retina. What do they do?

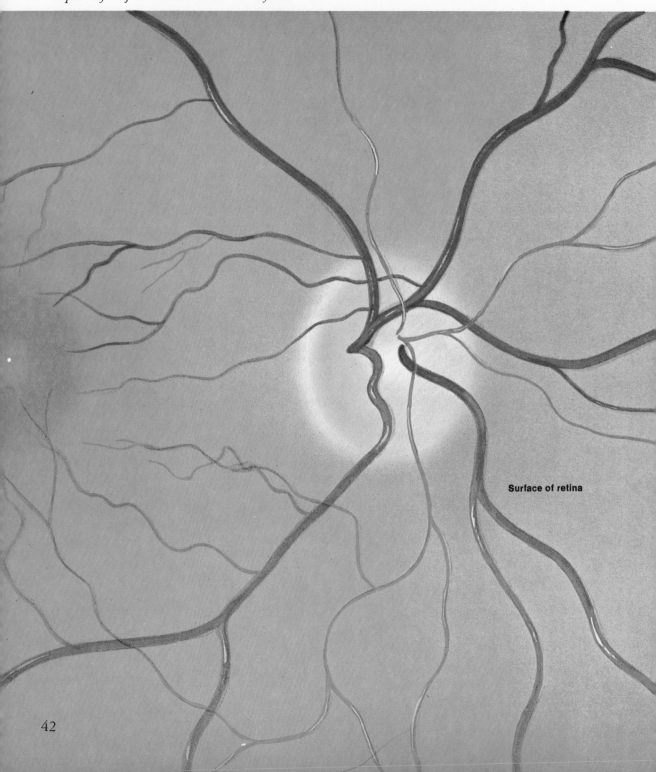

Surface of retina

42

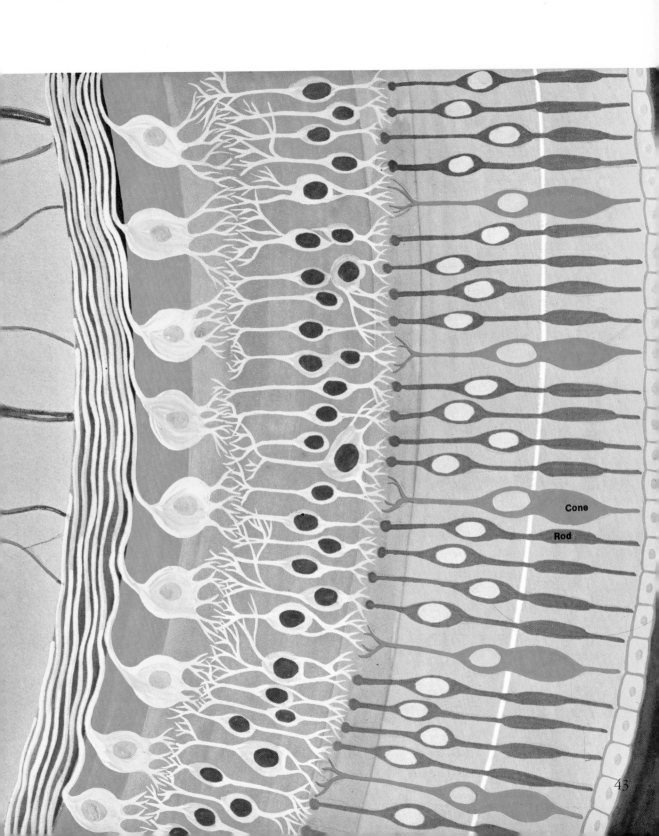

Cone

Rod

43

This is how the eye would see a scene if the person were near-sighted. Things that are near are clearly seen. The background is fuzzy.

This is how the eye would see a scene if the person were far-sighted. Things that are far away are clearly seen. Things close up are fuzzy.

Here you can see a scene as the normal eye would see it. Things both near and far can be seen clearly.

How Do You Hear?

Your sense of hearing is also very important in helping you know what is happening in the world around you. Your ears help you at school and, in a way, they are your antennae to the world. You learn many things by listening to others. You can hear beautiful music, and you can enjoy radio and television through your sense of hearing.

You are safer also because of your sense of hearing. For example, if you hear the honk of a car, you move quickly to keep out of its way. Or you may hear and obey the warning bell at a railroad crossing telling you that a train is coming.

How Sounds Get Started

You know that you hear sounds. But do you know just what sounds are? And do you know how sounds get started?

A good way to start learning about sounds is to try a demonstration. Take a ruler and hold one end of it on a table top. Make the other end of the ruler move back and forth.

When the ruler starts to move back and forth very fast, you hear the sound it makes. All sounds are caused in this same way. *There has to be something moving back and forth very fast to make a sound.* When something moves back and forth very rapidly, we say it is *vibrating*.

When you talk, your vocal cords vibrate and make sounds. You cannot see the vocal cords vibrate, but you can feel them by putting your hand on your throat while you are talking.

When anything vibrates, air is put into a wavelike motion. These wavelike motions move out in all directions in much the same way as do the ripples of water when you throw a stone into a pool.

Something to Do
Describe what you think your life would be like if you had no sense of hearing.

47

Your ears are made in such a way that they catch the wavelike motions known as *sound* and funnel them deeper into your ears. If the source of the sound is too far away, however, the sound waves die out before they reach your ears. Then you do not hear the sound.

The closer together the wavelike motions of the air are, or the more vibrations per second, the higher will be the *pitch* of the sound. Some sounds are too high for the human ear to hear. However, some animals hear sounds that people cannot hear, because their ears have a wider range of hearing.

Sounds often vary in *loudness* or intensity as well as in *pitch*. The stronger the vibrations are that reach your ears, the louder will be the sounds that you hear.

Most sound waves consist of air in motion. However, there are several other ways in which vibrations of sound can travel. Sounds can travel through *liquids* and through *solids* like wood, rock, and bone.

The Parts of the Ear

Now that you know how sounds are made, let's explore how your ears help you hear those sounds. You first need to know about the three main parts of the ear: *the outer ear, the middle ear,* and *the inner ear.*

The Outer Ear

The visible part which you tend to think of as your ear is really only the outer ear. This part is made up of the curved flap on the outside of the head and a short passageway that goes to the middle ear.

The curved flap of the outer ear is made of *cartilage*, a material that is harder than muscle but softer than bone. There is also some fat in the

What Do You Think?

Sometimes a person who is a little hard of hearing cups a hand around an ear. Why might the person do this?

48

lower, rounded part, or *lobe*, of the ear. Can you feel the fat in this area?

The passageway that leads from the outer ear to the middle ear is called the *auditory canal*. The first part of this auditory canal is lined with hairs as well as tiny glands that produce wax. The hairs and wax help keep dust and insects from going into the inner parts of the ear. See the pictures of the auditory canal on pages 52 – 53 and 54.

Sound waves are caught by the outer ear and started moving along into the auditory canal toward a skinlike part called the *eardrum*. Although the outer ear is helpful in hearing, you could get along without this part of the ear. The real hearing starts at the end of the canal — in the part known as the middle ear.

The Middle Ear

The middle ear is a small cavity between the outer ear and the inner ear. This middle-ear cavity is separated from the outer ear by the eardrum that stretches across the end of the auditory canal. This skinlike part looks like the covering of a drum. That is why it is called the eardrum.

The eardrum is attached to a chain of three little bones in the middle ear. This chain of bones extends across the cavity of the middle ear to the inner ear. See the pictures on pages 52 – 53 and 54.

When sounds strike the eardrum, it vibrates. The vibrations of the eardrum cause the bones in the middle ear to move. As these bones move, the vibrations are passed along and strengthened greatly.

The last bone in the chain of bones fits tightly against the thin skinlike cover of a small oval-shaped window. The oval window leads into the inner ear.

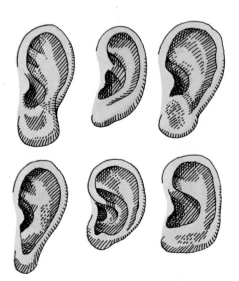

Here you can see a few of the many types of ear shapes.

49

There is also a tube that goes from the middle ear down into the throat. It is called the *Eustachian tube*. Find it in the pictures on pages 52-53 and 54. This tube lets air in and out of the middle ear and helps keep the air pressure the same on both sides of the eardrum.

The eardrum needs air on both sides of it to do its work well. And the air pressure on each side of the eardrum needs to be the same; otherwise you would have an unpleasant feeling in the ear.

The Inner Ear

The most important part of the ear is the snail-shaped part called the *cochlea*. Find the inner ear and cochlea in the pictures on pages 52-53 and 54.

Inside the snail-shaped cochlea are canals filled with liquid and nerves ending in soft hair cells. When the last bone of the chain in the middle ear pushes on the oval window, the fluid in the inner ear starts vibrating.

The vibrating fluid pushes and pulls on the soft hair cells which come together to form the hearing nerve, or the *auditory nerve*. The auditory nerve carries messages of sound to the special hearing area on each side of the brain.

Also in the inner ear are the semicircular canals that you read about earlier. (See pages 12, 33-34.) These parts of the ear have nothing to do with hearing. They help you keep your balance. You can see them in the pictures on pages 52-53 and 54.

When You Really Hear

To summarize how you hear and exactly *when* you hear a sound, let's follow some sound waves through the ear.

First the outer ear catches the sound waves and sends them down the auditory canal. When the sound waves reach the eardrum, it begins to

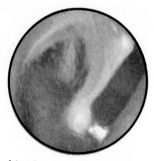

In this picture you can see how a normal ear looks when the doctor views it through the otoscope.

50

vibrate. The vibrations send the sound waves along the tiny chain of bones in the middle ear and at the same time strengthen the sound waves.

From the bones of the middle ear, the sound waves travel through the "second eardrum," or oval window, to the cochlea of the inner ear. As the sound waves pass through the liquid in the inner ear, they set the liquid moving. This moving liquid stimulates the tiny hairlike cells which come together to make the auditory nerve. The auditory nerve in each ear sends the message of sound to the hearing area of the brain. A hearing area is located on each side of the brain.

When these sound messages reach the hearing area, the brain makes it clear to you just what the sound messages are. At that point you *hear*.

What Can Cause a Hearing Loss

Sometimes a disease or defect of some part of the ear prevents the sound waves from traveling through the ear as they should. This results in a hearing loss. A hearing loss may be very slight or it may be very severe.

An instrument known as an *audiometer* is used to test for hearing loss. If a hearing loss is detected early enough, steps can often be taken to correct it or to keep it from getting worse.

Today there are hearing aids that can help people with certain difficulties hear better. One kind makes the sound waves stronger as they go along the usual path through the middle and inner ear. Another kind is placed on the bone just behind the ear. Sound waves are caught by this hearing aid and sent through the bone to the inner ear. There the sound waves start the liquid moving and cause messages of hearing to be sent to the brain over the auditory nerve.

Something to Try
To see how sounds can be carried through the bones of the head to the inner ear, place a large watch on a table. Next stuff your fingers into your ears. Then bend down and press the watch against your forehead. Do you hear the watch ticking?

51

The Parts of the Ear

You can use this diagram to help you tell the story of how we hear. What is the path that sound waves take through the ear?

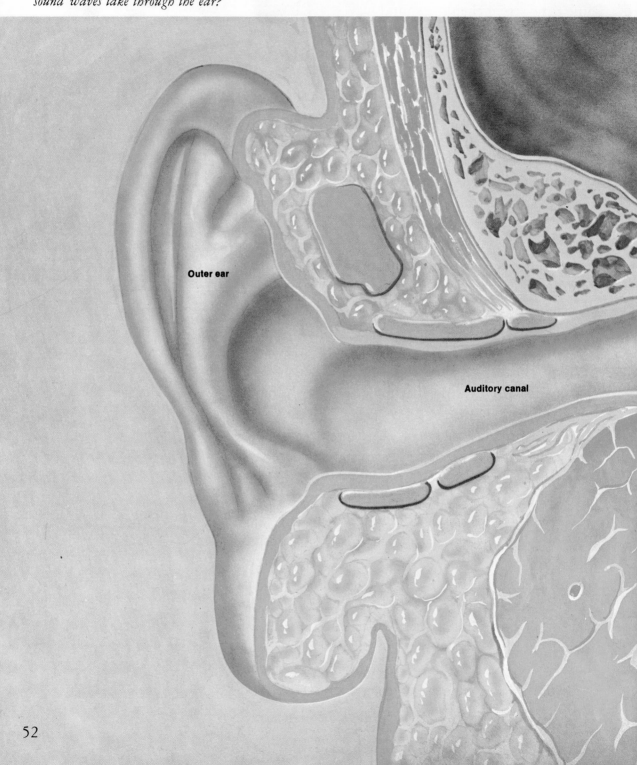

Outer ear

Auditory canal

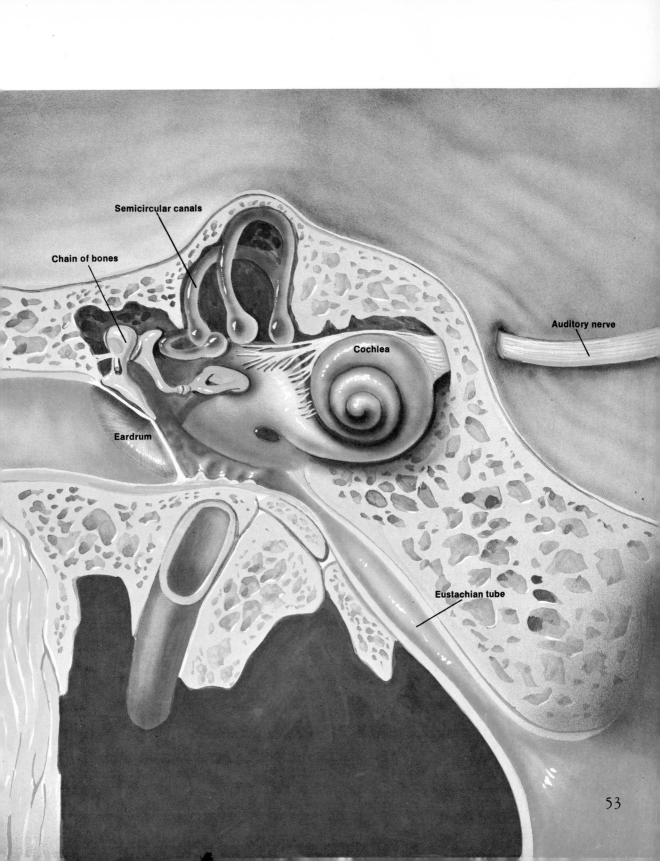

Semicircular canals

Chain of bones

Auditory nerve

Cochlea

Eardrum

Eustachian tube

53

Here you get a closer view of the middle and inner ear. What parts do you see?
Notice that there is a cutaway view of the snail-shaped cochlea.

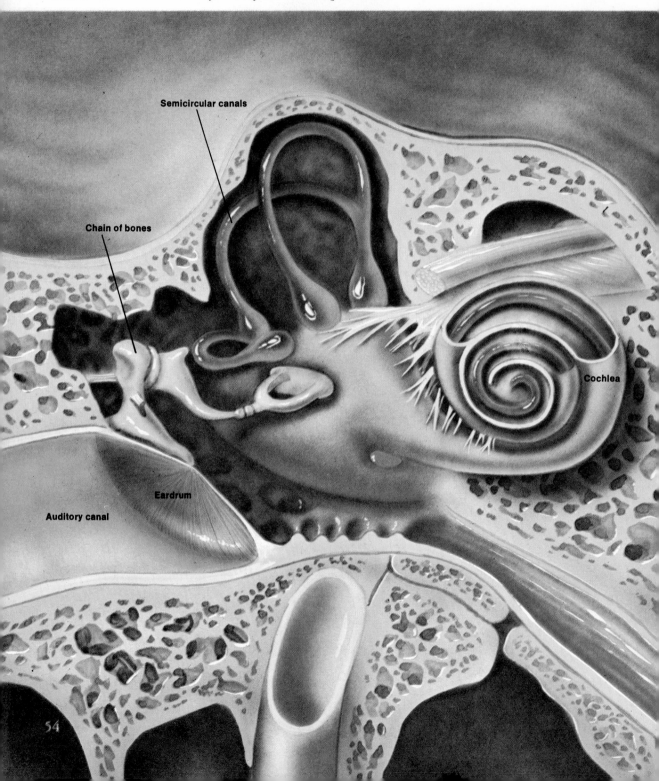

Semicircular canals

Chain of bones

Cochlea

Eardrum

Auditory canal

What Are the Senses of Taste and Smell?

Your senses of taste and smell are not so important to you as your senses of seeing and hearing. But without the senses of taste and smell your life would not be nearly so pleasant. Can you think of some ways in which these two senses add pleasure to your life?

These two senses work together most of the time. That is why you are studying about them together.

One way to find out how closely the two senses work together is to try this demonstration.

Shut your eyes and hold your nose. Then ask a classmate to feed you small bits of raw fruits and vegetables. See if you can tell what foods you are eating when you are not able to smell the food as you taste it.

Of course, without thinking about it, you have done this kind of thing many times. Do you remember the last time you had a bad cold and your nose was "stopped up"? How did your food taste to you then?

Four Main Tastes

The senses of taste and smell work closely together. But there are four basic tastes that do not depend on the sense of smell. You can taste these even when you cannot smell anything. Most other tastes are thought to result from a blending of these four tastes: *sweet, salty, sour, bitter*. Some research workers, however, think they are finding other basic tastes such as *metallic* and *astringent*, or *puckery*, tastes.

Your sense of taste is located chiefly in tiny parts on the surface of your tongue called *taste buds*. You will learn more about these taste buds later. But the taste buds do not pick up tastes evenly over the entire surface of the tongue. Instead, each of the four

Something to Try
Here is something to try. It shows how the sense of smell helps you taste. Blindfold a classmate. Put a piece of sliced onion under his nose, but give him a piece of carrot to eat. See what happens then.

55

main tastes has a center on the tongue where it is tasted more strongly than in other places. For example, a piece of candy tastes sweeter on the tip of your tongue than on other areas.

The bitter taste is strongest at the back. The salty taste is strongest at the front sides, and the sour taste is strongest at the back sides.

As you eat, however, you taste with your whole tongue. So you do not have to worry about pushing certain foods to a particular part of the tongue to taste them.

How You Taste Things

To understand how you taste, you have to know that the food you eat must be mixed with liquid. And you have to know about the parts of your tongue that pick up messages of taste and send them along to the taste area in your brain.

If you dry the tip of your tongue and then put a little sugar on it, you will not taste the sugar. Not until the saliva begins to dissolve the sugar will you taste the sweetness. *That is because sugar is a chemical* as are all the foods you eat. *These chemicals must be dissolved — in water or in the saliva in your mouth — if you are to taste anything.*

Chewing food well so that it is thoroughly mixed with saliva brings out the flavor and makes the food taste better.

If you look at your tongue in a mirror, you will see that there are little bumps on it. These bumps are called *papillae*, and inside them are the taste buds. The papillae at the back of your tongue are the biggest ones. Some of these papillae have as many as 200 taste buds in them. There are about 9000 taste buds in the papillae on your tongue. The picture at the left shows how papillae look under a microscope.

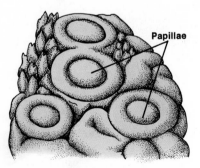

Papillae

The tiny bumps, or papillae, *on your tongue would look like this under a microscope.*

56

In the picture at the right you can see how a taste bud would look if you were viewing it under a microscope.

In each taste bud are taste cells. Each taste cell has a tiny hairlike part that comes out of an opening in the taste bud into little pits on the tongue. At the bottom of the taste bud is a nerve thread that gathers together with other threads into a large nerve. This large nerve carries messages to the taste area of the brain. See the tongue and taste nerves in the picture on page 58.

The tiny hairlike parts coming out of the taste buds are stimulated by the chemicals in the food you eat. These hairlike parts send messages through the taste cells and over nerves to the taste area of the brain. When the messages reach your brain, you know what it is you are tasting.

Your tongue does some other things besides sensing taste. The tongue also senses the heat and cold, the roughness and smoothness, the hardness and softness of what you are eating. For example, it is not only the taste of ice cream that you enjoy. You also enjoy its coldness and smoothness.

How You Smell Things

As you have learned, foods are made up of chemicals, which help make it possible for you to taste things. The chemicals also make it possible for you to *smell* them. That is why the senses of taste and smell might be called the "chemical senses."

Let's see, for instance, what happens when you smell a flower. The flower has certain chemicals in it. Tiny bits of these chemicals keep breaking away from the flower in the form of gases. These tiny bits that break away are called *molecules*. The molecules mix with the air and come into your nose with the air you breathe. *(Continued on page 60.)*

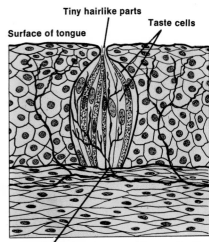

A taste bud (greatly enlarged)

Tiny hairlike parts

Taste cells

Surface of tongue

Nerve thread that connects with nerve leading to the brain

Here you see a close-up view of the tongue and the taste nerves. What must happen to the food you eat before you can taste it?

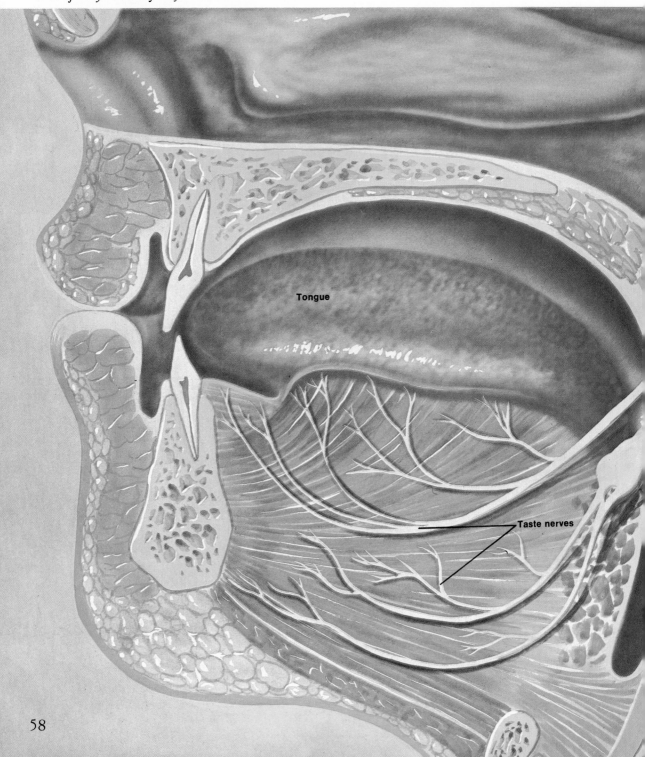

Tongue

Taste nerves

Here you see a close-up view of the inside of the nose. What happens to enable you to smell something like a hamburger cooking?

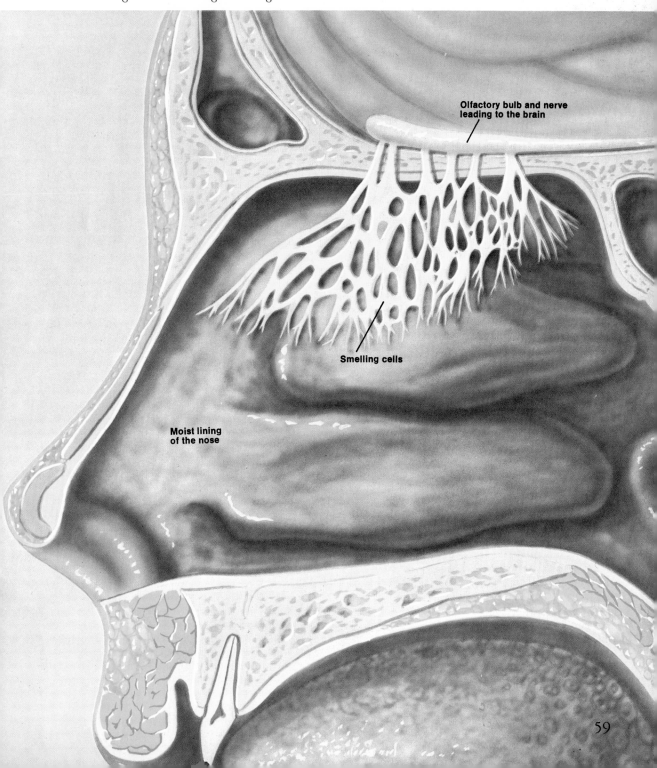

Olfactory bulb and nerve leading to the brain

Smelling cells

Moist lining of the nose

The chemicals dissolve in the moist lining of your nose. The dissolved chemicals reach the nerve endings, or smelling cells, located in the upper part of your nose. These nerve endings join the *olfactory nerve*, which carries the message to the smelling center on each side of the brain. The brain then interprets what it is you are smelling. Find the olfactory nerve on page 59.

However, just as individuals differ in how they react to various things tasted, so do they differ in the way they react to the things they smell. Thus, certain flowers smell more fragrant to some people than to others. And some few people can detect no odor at all in the very same flower that others find fragrant.

There is one peculiar thing about the sense of smell. The smelling cells in the nose quickly become used to one particular odor. When this happens, the nerve cells stop sending messages about that odor.

This is the reason why you soon become accustomed to an odor. You soon get used to it unless the substance causing the odor hurts the nose. Getting used to an odor helps people who have to live or work in places where there is an unpleasant odor. However, there can be a hazard involved in getting used to an unpleasant odor. The situation can be dangerous when the odor is a warning signal, as the odors of smoke and some gases are.

The nose may be sensitive to various particles in the air besides odors. For instance, when some people breathe in pollens from certain plants, they get what is known as an allergic reaction. The lining of the nose swells, the eyes water, and breathing becomes difficult — just as a person reacts when he is suffering from a cold.

Do You Know?

Cigarette smoke that is drawn into the mouth over a period of time can damage the taste buds. And cigarette smoke, when it is constantly drawn over the smelling cells in the nose, can damage these cells. Then the senses of taste and smell are dulled.

60

What Is Your Sense of Touch?

Since you get so many sensations through the skin, another good name for the sense of touch is the *skin sense*. There are five special skin senses: *touch, pressure, heat, cold,* and *pain*. Each has different nerve endings.

Touch and pressure are responsible for such sensations as roughness, hardness, softness, and smoothness. Pain, itch, and tickle are received by nerve endings for pain. And heat and cold each has its own *separate* nerve endings.

Nerve Endings in Your Skin

To understand how you feel things, you need to know more about your skin and about the nerve endings in the skin.

The outer part of the skin is called the *epidermis,* and it is made up of layers. The topmost part of the epidermis is mostly dried cells that are dead. These cells are constantly being rubbed off. The lower part of the epidermis has live, growing cells in it. As these cells grow and form new cells, they push the old cells upward to the topmost part of the epidermis. There are no nerve endings in the outer part of the epidermis.

Under the epidermis is the true skin, or *dermis*. In the dermis are many blood vessels and many different nerve endings.

Each tiny hair growing in the skin has a nerve around it. And there are many other kinds of nerve endings in the dermis. These nerve endings send messages to the brain about the things that touch the skin—about whether these things are hot or cold, smooth or rough, soft or hard, and so on. Special nerve endings also send messages of pain to the brain.

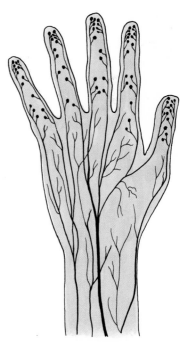

Nerve endings in the fingers. Why are your fingers particularly helpful in telling whether things are hot or cold, smooth or rough, and so on?

This key will help you find the nerve endings in the picture: A. deep pressure, B. pressure, C. warmth, D. touch, E. light touch, F. cold, G. pain.

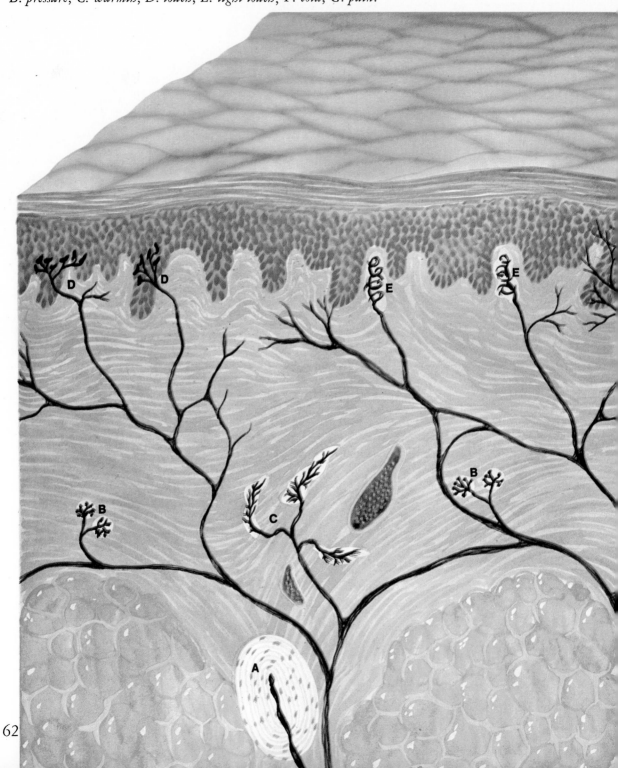

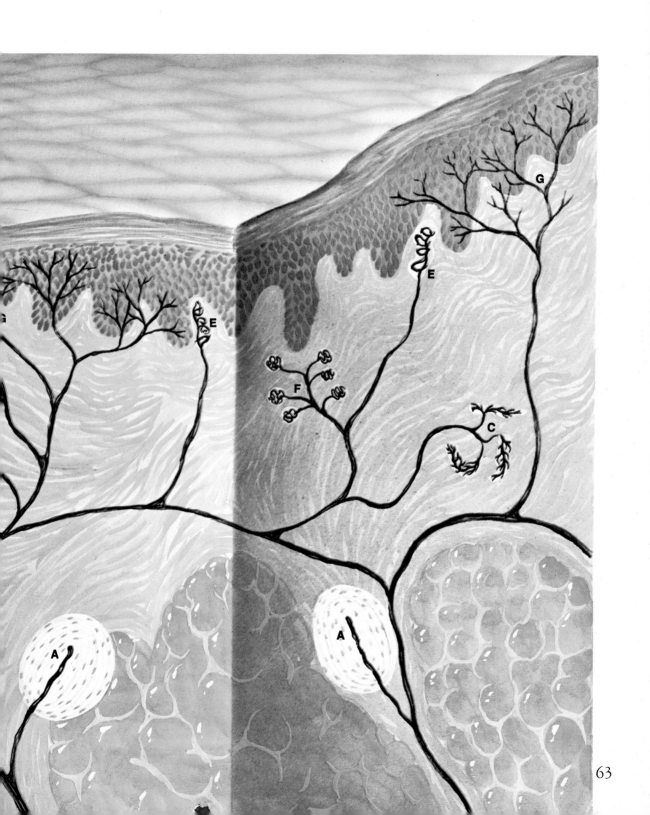

You have learned many interesting things about your senses, but you may still have questions you want answered.

Here are a few questions some boys and girls your age have wondered about. How would *you* answer each of these questions:

1. What does it mean to be color-blind?
2. What is an eye bank?
3. What are some signs that you may need glasses?
4. What are some signs of hearing trouble?

After you have tried to answer each question, check your answers with the ones given below and on page 65. Be ready, too, to suggest some questions of your own that you wonder about.

What Does It Mean to Be Color-Blind?

People who are color-blind cannot tell the difference between certain colors. Only a very few of these people are so completely color-blind that they see all colors as gray.

Most people who are color-blind have trouble seeing reds and greens but can see blues and yellows. A few color-blind people, though, cannot see blues and yellows.

Color-blindness is tested by charts which check a person's ability to tell the difference between dots of one color on a background of dots of another color. Two such charts are shown at the left. Can you see the patterns of red and of green?

Color-blindness is inherited, and it is much more common among men than among women. It has been estimated that one out of every 25 men have some form of color-blindness, while only one out of every 500 women is color-blind.

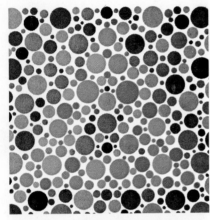

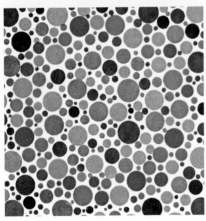

These are two of several charts used in color-blindness tests. If a person cannot distinguish red and green, he will not see the red dot pattern and the green dot pattern in these charts.

What Is an Eye Bank?

An "eye bank" is a medical storage place for healthy corneas from the eyes of people who have willed them to medical science after their death. These healthy, clear corneas are available to be transplanted, as soon as possible, in the eyes of persons who have developed scarred or clouded corneas. This replacement of clouded or scarred corneas with clear ones can prevent blindness among some people. It is not possible as yet to transplant whole eyes, however.

There are other types of organ and tissue "banks," as you will learn later. One of the best-known is the blood bank. What do you know about it?

What Are Some Signs That You May Need Glasses?

Look at the signs listed at the right. Is your answer *yes* to some of the signs of poor eyesight shown here? If so, tell your parents and your teacher about these signs. An examination by an *optometrist* or by an *ophthalmologist* can probably be arranged.

What Are Some Signs of Hearing Trouble?

Some obvious signs of ear trouble are these: having to ask people often what they have said; constantly turning the head to one side to listen; having a "running ear" with liquid coming out of it.

Sometimes a hearing loss is temporary and is caused by a cold or other infection or by an accumulation of wax in the ear. Prompt treatment by a doctor usually restores the hearing.

If the hearing loss is permanent, there are things that can be done to improve the situation. You read about some types of hearing aids on page 51. Special instruction in lip-reading may also be given. And in some cases surgery can restore or improve the ability to hear.

Some Signs of Eye Difficulties
Do you
often have red eyelids or sties?
frequently have watery eyes?
often have headaches?
usually squint when reading?
hold your book too close or too far away from your eyes?
tip your head to one side when reading?
frown as you read or write?
often lose the place when reading?

Check Yourself

1. Look back at the questions on page 32. How would you answer them now?

2. What are the five main senses? What are some other senses?

3. How would you describe each of these parts of the eye?

a. cornea	d. pupil
b. iris	e. retina
c. lens	f. rods and cones

4. What does it mean to be near-sighted? Far-sighted? To have astigmatism?

5. What is the auditory nerve? The optic nerve? The olfactory nerve?

6. How would you describe each of these parts of the ear?

a. auditory canal	d. inner ear
b. eardrum	e. middle ear
c. Eustachian tube	f. outer ear

7. How would you explain this statement: "You need your brain to see"?

8. Why do little children often roll the tips of their tongues over suckers?

9. How would you make a "map" of your tongue? What would you show on it?

10. Why do you get a tickly feeling if you touch a hair on your arm?

Things to Do

1. Here is a way to see how your sense of touch sends a message to your brain. Hold out the palm of your hand, close your eyes, and have a partner trace on your palm a letter or a number. Can you tell what the letter or number is?

2. Did you know that you have a "blind spot" in each eye? This is the spot at which the optic nerve leaves the eye to go to the brain. You cannot see an object if its image falls on this blind spot. Here is how you can test for your own blind spot.

On a piece of white tablet paper, draw a circle slightly smaller than a dime. Color the circle black.

About 1 3/4 inches to the *left* of the circle draw a cross. Each part of the cross should be about 1/2 inch long.

Close your right eye. Hold the piece of paper 12 inches in front of your left eye. Move the paper slowly toward you as you look steadily at the black circle. Does there come a time when you cannot see the cross out of the corner of your eye? When this happens, the image of the cross is falling on your blind spot.

More Things to Do

1. You might make an individual or a class scrapbook of poems that tell how your senses help make life more pleasant.

A poem that you might copy for your scrapbook is shown below.

What are some other poems you might put in the scrapbook?

Where might you look for poems for the scrapbook?

The world is full of wonderful smells[1]

The world is full of wonderful smells
And you have a nose that always tells
Of bread in the oven, hot and nice,
Of cake being baked with lots of spice,
Of a barn with fresh-cut hay in the mows,
Of horses and pigs and cats and cows,
Of a dog when he's warm and lies in the sun,
Of applesauce and chocolate and a sugar bun.
Wouldn't it be dreadful if you'd no nose
   to tell
Of every wonderful, wonderful smell?

[1]From *Jingle Jangle* by Zhenya Gay. Copyright 1953 by Zhenya Gay. Reprinted by permission of The Viking Press, Inc.

2. Write a paragraph or so on one of these topics:
How Sounds Are Produced
What It Means to Be Color-Blind
How the Sense of Touch Helps Us
How the Eyes Help Protect Themselves
Rods and Cones
The Chemical Senses
The Sense of Balance

Special Research

1. See if you can find out how a deaf child is taught to speak.

2. Find out about how blind people can read books written in what is called *Braille.* Where might you find such information?

3. Read the book *Seeing Fingers: The Story of Louis Braille* by Etta Degering (McKay). It tells the story of how Louis Braille invented a system for helping sightless people read.

Self-Help Review

Use a ruler or a strip of paper to cover the answer column at the right. Read the first item and write the missing word or words on a piece of paper. Then move your ruler or paper strip down to uncover the answer and see if you are right. Go on in the same way with each of the other items. Do not write in this book.

The numbers by the answers show the pages in this book that give information about the subject. For the items you miss, go back and review this information.

1. The five main senses are those of _____, _____, _____, _____, and _____.

seeing, hearing, smelling, tasting, touching 32

2. Without the sense of _____, you could not walk steadily.

balance 33

3. Besides your eyes and your brain, you need _____ if you are to see.

light 35

4. The opening in the iris is called the _____.

pupil 36

5. A sound is made by something that is _____.

vibrating 47

6. Before you really hear a sound, the sound messages must be sent to the _____.

brain 51

7. Two senses that work together are those of _____ and _____.

taste, smell 55

8. Before you can taste food, it must be _____ in saliva.

dissolved 56

9. Papillae are the tiny bumps on your _____.

tongue 56

10. Five skin sensations are *touch*, _____, _____, _____, and _____.

pressure, heat, cold, pain 61

Health Test for Unit Two

Part I

Copy each number on a piece of paper. After the number, write the letter that goes with the *best* answer choice.

1. Your semicircular canals help you
   a. see things clearly
   b. keep your balance
   c. hear sounds around you
2. The colored part of the eye is
   a. the iris
   b. the cornea
   c. the lens
3. The cornea of the eye is kept clean
   a. by the retina
   b. by tears
   c. by rods and cones
4. The main hearing nerve is called
   a. the olfactory nerve
   b. the auditory nerve
   c. the optic nerve
5. The part of your eye that is most like the film in a camera is
   a. the lens
   b. the iris
   c. the retina

6. If your eyes are near-sighted, you are able to
   a. see faraway things clearly
   b. see normally
   c. see nearby things clearly
7. You need your outer ears
   a. so you can learn to wiggle them
   b. to catch the sound waves
   c. to keep your sense of balance
8. When sounds strike the eardrum
   a. it vibrates
   b. it breaks in two
   c. you know at once what the sound is
9. Before you are able to taste food, the food must
   a. turn sour
   b. be something you like
   c. start to dissolve
10. You can smell the things in the world around you
   a. because of the cochlea
   b. because of the chemicals in them
   c. because of your papillae

Number of Answers   10
Number Right   _____
Score (Number Right x 10)   _____

69

Part II

Copy each number on a piece of paper. After the number, write the name for each part of the body described below.

1. colorless covering of the eye
2. small opening in the eye
3. part of eye that can bend light rays
4. colored part of the eye
5. passageway that leads from the outer ear to the middle ear
6. snail-shaped part of ear
7. liquid that helps dissolve food when you chew
8. outer part of the skin
9. bumps on the tongue
10. filmlike part of the eye

Part III

Copy each number on a piece of paper. After the number, write the correct answer, *true* or *false*.

11. When you go into a dark place, the pupils of your eyes become smaller.

12. Tears keep the cornea of the eye clean and moist.

13. The sclera is an important part of the human ear.

14. All sounds are caused by something moving back and forth.

15. If the air pressure on both sides of the eardrum is the same, an unpleasant feeling results in the ears.

16. You get most of your feelings of touch through the skin.

17. Special areas for each of the senses are in the brain.

18. Your senses of taste and smell rarely, if ever, work together.

19. The only senses that anyone knows about are the five main senses of seeing, hearing, tasting, touching, and smelling.

20. There is no known use for the eyelashes.

21. The bones of your head help protect your eyes.

22. The eyeball is filled with air.

23. There is a chain of bones in the middle ear.

24. Sounds can travel only through air.

25. An audiometer is used to check your eyes.

Number of Answers   _25_

Number Right   _____

Score (Number Right x 4)   _____

3 What Does Your Skin Do?

Perhaps you have never stopped to think much about your skin and its work. If so, you may be surprised to learn that the skin is one of the body's most complicated structures. It is far more than just a protective covering, as you will discover in this unit.

1. What important jobs are done by your skin?

2. What causes differences in skin color?

3. What causes "goose pimples"?

4. How can you help keep your skin healthy?

5. What are calluses? Corns? Warts? Moles? Hang-nails? Freckles?

6. Is each person's skin different in some ways from everyone else's?

What Is Known About the Skin?

Do you have any idea of how much skin you have? If your skin could be stretched out in one piece, how big do you think that piece might be?

A fairly accurate estimate is that in an average-sized ten- to eleven-year-old there might be as much as 10 square feet of skin on the body. That is why it is the body's largest organ.

The outer part of your skin, as you read on page 61, is called the *epidermis.* This outer part consists of some four or five layers of cells, one on top of another. One important thing the epidermis does is to serve as a cover that helps keep harmful bacteria out of your body.

What the Epidermis Is Like

If you could look at the skin on the back of your hand through a magnifying glass, you would learn many interesting things about the epidermis. First of all, you would notice that there are many little folds, or creases, in the skin. Then, if you closed your fist tightly, you would notice that these folds smooth out.

Something to Do

Several in your group might use old newspapers to make a "rug" that is ten feet square. That will help you visualize about how much skin a person has.

What do you think is the function of these folds, or creases, in your skin? What would it be like if your skin were really "skin tight" all over?

These folds, as you probably decided, make it possible for the skin to stretch easily when you move the different parts of your body.

These same folds, on the other hand, also provide lodging places for dirt. That is why it is important for you to wash and to take baths often.

Another thing you would see, if you looked at your skin under a magnifying glass, is many little hair pits out of which tiny hairs grow. Oil made by the oil glands in the deeper layers of the skin comes up through these pits and helps keep the skin soft and smooth. The oil also helps make your skin waterproof.

If you were observing your skin under a very strong magnifying glass, you would see many, many tiny openings called *pores*. Sweat, or *perspiration*, comes out of these pores, when you get very warm.

You would need more than a magnifying glass, however, to learn all about your epidermis. The live, growing cells in the lower part of the epidermis keep making new cells. These new cells push the cells above them upward. As the cells are pushed upward, they die and change into a dry, flaky material. Some cells of the outer layer of the epidermis become very hard. They grow outward to form fingernails and toenails.

The topmost layer of the skin is the part you see. You shed dead cells from it each day. You also rub off dead cells when you wash.

Your skin makes many millions of new cells each day. At the same time it is shedding millions of its dead cells.

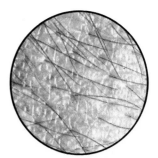

Here you can see a section of skin as seen under a magnifying glass.

73

When the top layer of cells is shed or washed away, it is replaced by the next layer of cells. Since you are always shedding dead skin cells, the outer skin you wear today is not the same skin you were wearing last year.

Pigments in the Skin

Another interesting thing about the epidermis is that it contains two different kinds of coloring matter, or *pigment*, which give the skin its color. One pigment gives the skin a yellow tinge; the other gives it a brown or black tinge. These two pigments, along with the rosy tinge from the blood vessels showing through the skin, give skin its various shadings.

Except for the *albino*, who lacks normal pigmentation, every person has some of both kinds of pigment in his skin. People with brown or black skin have more of one pigment. People with yellow skin have more of the other pigment. People with white skin have lesser amounts of each of the two pigments. Exposure to the sun causes the pigment in the skin to darken, which is especially noticeable in light skin.

Except for differing amounts of pigments in the epidermis, the skin of every human being has the same structure and the same jobs to do.

The Dermis

The *dermis*, or true skin, as you read in Unit 2, contains the nerve endings for your sense of touch. Look back at the nerve endings in the picture on pages 62–63. What different kinds of nerve endings do you find?

In addition to the nerve endings, the dermis is made up of live skin cells, fluid around the cells, blood vessels, and glands. Can you find some of these parts in the picture on pages 78–79?

Things to Do
1. Tell what you have learned up to now about how your skin functions.
2. Look for books like these at the library which are about the skin— or which have chapters in them about the skin.

Froman, Robert. The Many Human Senses (*Little, Brown*). *Advanced.*

McGovern, Ann. The Question and Answer Book About the Human Body (*Random*).

Showers, Paul. Your Skin and Mine (*Crowell*). *Easy.*

Blood Vessels in the Skin

There are many tiny blood vessels in the dermis. You realize this when you cut your finger and blood flows out from one of these opened blood vessels. Also, the rosy color in your nails and lips comes from the blood vessels showing through the thin layer of tissue.

Some of these blood vessels are *arteries*. The blood in the arteries carries oxygen and digested food in liquid form to all the cells in the body, including the skin cells. The oxygen and food keep the skin cells alive.

Some of the blood vessels in the dermis are *veins*. The blood in the veins carries away carbon dioxide and other waste substances from the skin cells and other cells of the body.

Tiny tubes called *capillaries* connect the arteries and veins. When the blood flows through the capillaries, an interesting thing happens. Food and oxygen for the cells pass out of the blood through the thin walls of the capillaries. And wastes made by the body cells pass into the blood through these same thin capillary walls.

Sweat Glands

The pores you see in your skin are really openings for tiny tubes, or *ducts*, that begin in sweat glands down in the dermis.

The sweat glands take in salty liquid from the spaces around the skin cells and send it up through the ducts to the surface of the skin. This salty liquid, which contains small amounts of waste material, is sweat, or *perspiration*. It leaves the body through the pores. Perspiration helps keep the skin soft and moist.

You are perspiring continually. But most of the time you do not see the perspiration because it

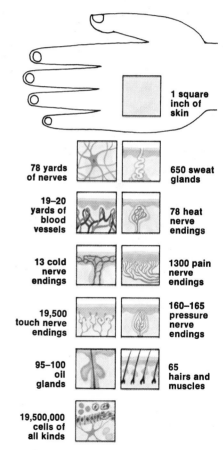

78 yards of nerves

19–20 yards of blood vessels

13 cold nerve endings

19,500 touch nerve endings

95–100 oil glands

19,500,000 cells of all kinds

1 square inch of skin

650 sweat glands

78 heat nerve endings

1300 pain nerve endings

160–165 pressure nerve endings

65 hairs and muscles

Believe it or not, just one square inch of skin contains what is shown in the diagram above.

evaporates, or goes into the air, shortly after it leaves the pores. When the weather is hot — or when you have been exercising — you perspire more than usual; then you can easily see the drops of perspiration standing out on your skin.

As the perspiration evaporates, the body is cooled. This is one of the ways the body has of keeping itself from getting too warm.

As you can see, perspiration serves more than one purpose. In addition to cooling the body, perspiration helps keep the skin from becoming too dry. Perspiration also carries off very small amounts of waste material.

Oil Glands

Besides perspiration, there is something else that comes out of the skin, and that is oil. The little pits out of which tiny hairs grow begin down in the dermis. From oil glands, near the roots of the hairs, oil flows up along the hair shafts to the skin surface. This oil helps keep the skin from getting too dry and from cracking.

Can you find the oil glands in the picture on pages 78 – 79? The amount of oil secreted by these glands varies with each person. Some people secrete a lot of oil, and they have very oily skin. Some other people secrete a very small amount of oil, and they have dry skin. Still others secrete neither a lot nor a small amount of oil, and they have skin that is considered normal.

Now look for the hair in the picture. At the root of each hair are tiny muscles. When your body gets cold — and sometimes when you are frightened — these tiny muscles contract, becoming shorter and thicker. When the muscles contract, they cause tiny hairs to stand straight up. As this happens, "goose pimples" appear on the skin.

Do You Know?

1. What is one way the body has of helping keep itself at about the same temperature?

2. What would your skin be like if you had no oil glands?

3. What can make you perspire more than usual?

4. What difficulties would you have if you had no sweat glands?

5. If you dipped a finger in water and then held it up in the air to dry, how would the finger feel as it dried? Why?

76

The Skin Is More Than a Cover

Your skin is an airtight, watertight covering. But it has other functions, too. It helps regulate temperature. It is a sense organ as well, because within it lie the many different kinds of nerve endings.

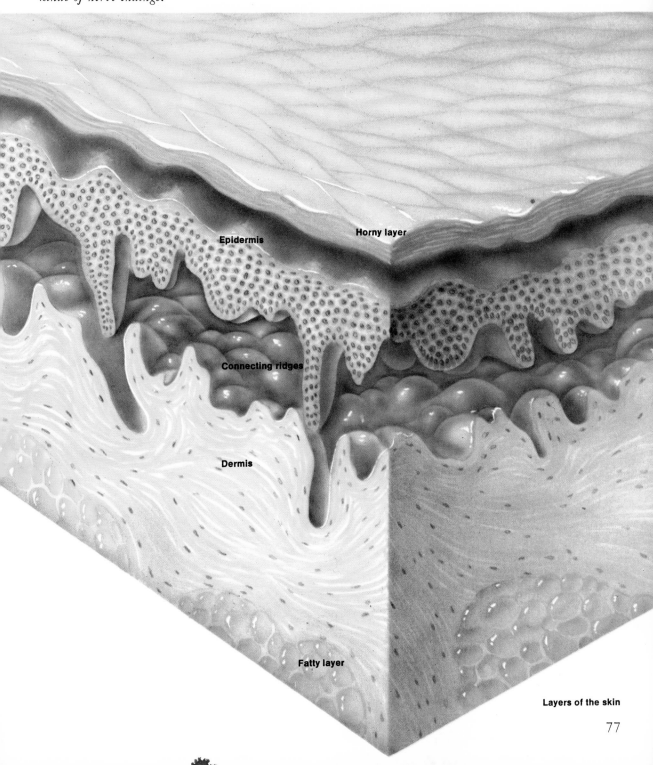

Epidermis

Horny layer

Connecting ridges

Dermis

Fatty layer

Layers of the skin

Here is a cross section of the many interesting things found in the dermis, or true skin.

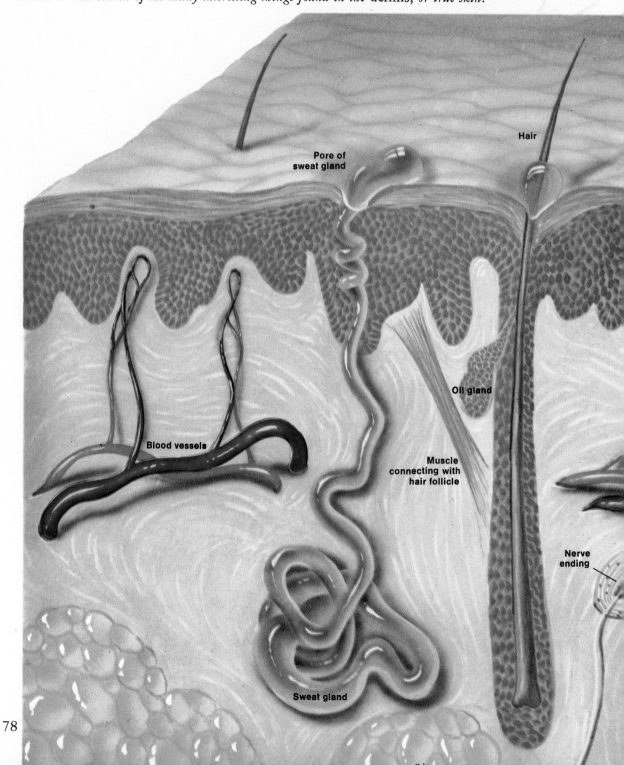

Pore of
sweat gland

Hair

Blood vessels

Oil gland

Muscle
connecting with
hair follicle

Nerve
ending

Sweat gland

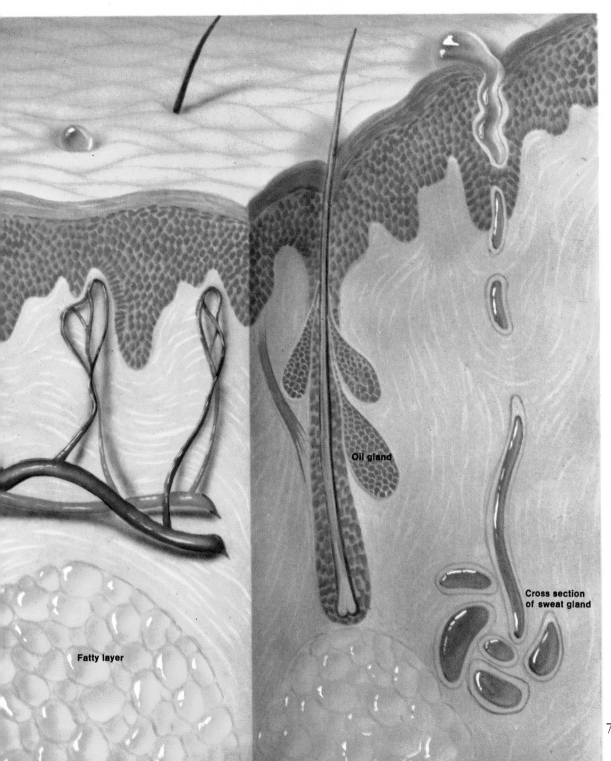

Oil gland

Cross section
of sweat gland

Fatty layer

Notice the many variations in skin tone. Notice, too, the different appearance of the skin among individuals of various ages.

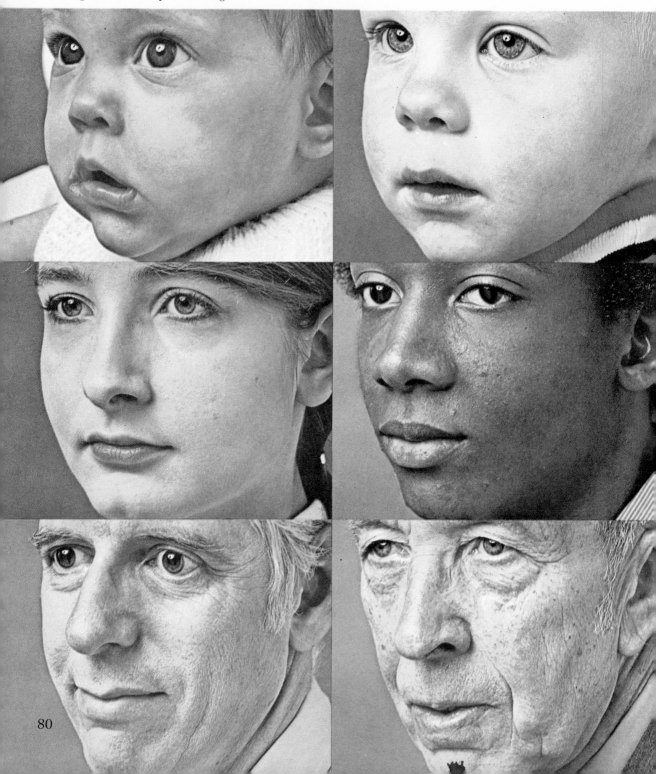

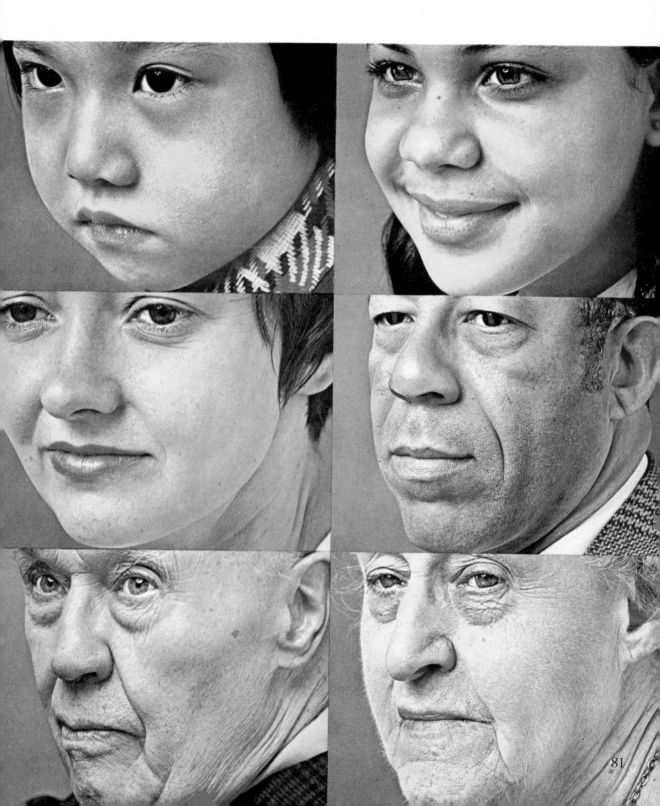

Below the dermis—and sometimes classed as a part of the dermis—is a layer of connective tissue. It is made up of threadlike parts with many spaces that are filled with fluid and with fat. This fat helps cushion you from bumps, and helps hold in body heat during cold weather. If a person is overweight, quite a bit of fat may be found in this layer. However, it is not healthy to have too much fat.

Ridges in the Skin

On page 77 you can see the connecting ridges that fasten the dermis and the epidermis together.

The ridges reach up from the dermis into the epidermis. If you look at the tips of your fingers, you can see a network of these ridges. With a magnifying glass, you can see them clearly.

If you press the tip of your finger on an ink pad and then on a clean piece of paper, you can see the design that these ridges make. This print of the ridges in your fingertip is called a *fingerprint*. No other person's fingerprints are exactly like yours. A fingerprint is thus a good means of identification.

Your fingerprints never change. If you should burn the skin of a finger, the same fingerprint will appear each time after the burn heals.

Each of your ten fingers shows a different design of ridges, or a different fingerprint. Usually the forefinger is used when a fingerprint is taken for identification purposes.

You can make a *footprint* in much the same way that you make a fingerprint. No one else has a footprint exactly like yours.

In some hospitals, footprints, instead of fingerprints, are taken of all the babies born there. Because a new baby's fingerprints are so small, it is easier to use a footprint for identification.

Here are some examples of different types of fingerprints.

How Does Your Skin Function?

You have learned some of the ways in which your skin helps you. What have you found out so far? Here are still other interesting things that your skin does.

The Skin and Body Temperature

The blood vessels in your skin help keep your body temperature normal, about 98.6° F. To understand how this is done, you have to keep in mind that heat is brought to your skin by the blood in the blood vessels. Your body is always making this heat, and some of the heat is always going from the blood into the air around the skin.

If you go out into the cold, the blood vessels in your skin contract. When this happens, not so much blood can enter the blood vessels of the skin. Then less warm blood from the body passes into these blood vessels. This means that there is less heat going out from the blood into the air, while more heat is kept in the body.

When your body gets very warm, the tiny blood vessels in the skin expand. More blood can then flow into these blood vessels in the skin, and more heat from the blood can pass from the body into the air. As this heat leaves by way of the skin, the body is cooled.

The Skin As a Storehouse

The fatty layer under the dermis is a storehouse, and a very roomy one at that. A boy or girl who weighs 100 pounds is carrying about 16 of those pounds in the fatty layer under the dermis — mostly as water and fat. These stored materials are returned to the blood as needed from time to time. The blood carries the materials to the different parts of the body that require them.

Do You Know?

Another function of the skin is to keep tissue fluid inside the body. Tissue fluid surrounds all the body cells. You would dry up and die if you had no skin to prevent the escape of body fluids.

The Skin Helps Remove Wastes

Not all the water you take in each day is used, or is stored, in your body. Water that is not used or stored is moved out of the body.

Some of the water, containing salts and a small amount of waste material, is moved out as sweat through the pores in your skin. You may lose as much as three to five glasses of water a day through perspiration if the weather is very warm or if you have been exercising hard.

Some water is moved out, too, through the large intestine, along with waste food. And a small amount of waste water is lost when you exhale, or breathe out. Most waste water is moved out, however, through the kidneys.

The Skin Helps Heal Cuts

Do you know what happens when you cut a finger? And do you know how the cut heals?

Blood runs out of a cut from the injured blood vessels in the skin. As this blood runs out, it washes away dirt and germs from the cut area.

Next the blood vessels in the skin contract, stopping the flow of blood. Before long, a *clot,* or thickened mass of blood, forms and fills the cut. This clot fastens itself to the two sides of the cut. Soon the blood clot starts to shrink. As it shrinks, it pulls the two sides of the cut closer together.

Later, threadlike connective-tissue cells enter the clot. These cells begin to build new tissue. Skin cells growing from each side of the cut join at the center of the cut. Sometimes a scar remains where the skin cells have joined.

The Skin Produces Vitamin D

When the invisible ultraviolet rays of the sun shine on the skin, they change a substance in the skin into vitamin D. This vitamin D is often called

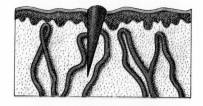

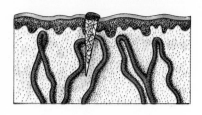

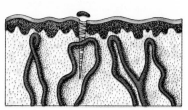

Use these drawings to help you tell the story of how a cut heals.

the *sunshine vitamin*. Of course, fewer of the sun's rays reach the skin when air pollution exists.

Vitamin D is needed to help build strong bones and teeth. Absence of vitamin D causes *rickets*. Today, vitamin D-fortified milk helps supply needed vitamin D for people all year round. In winter, babies and ailing children may be given cod-liver oil — which is rich in vitamin D — or they may be given vitamin-D pills.

Helping the Skin Do Its Work

Since your skin does such important work, it is a good idea for you to take care of it and keep it as healthy as you can.

Washing

Your face needs a thorough washing several times a day with warm, soapy water and at least once with a clean washcloth. Use your fingers or a clean washcloth to work the lather into your face. Rinse with warm water, followed by a second rinsing with cold water. Then pat the skin dry with a soft towel.

As you know, your hands should be washed before you eat and after you use the toilet. What are some other times when you should wash your hands?

If you have very dry skin, you may want to use lots of water and a small amount of soap.

Baths

It is a good idea to take baths often. Some people take a bath every day, and others take a bath several times a week. Just how often you take a bath depends partly on how much dirt you get on you during your work and play — and partly on what the temperature outdoors may be. In warm weather — when you are hot and sweaty — you may need to bathe more often than in cold weather.

What Do You Think?
1. Why do you think there are few cases of rickets among children in the United States today?
2. Why is rickets still a problem among children in some parts of the world today?

85

The best baths are the kind in which you use plenty of warm water and soap. Do you know why soap is needed? The soap helps remove the oil that is mixed with the dirt and bacteria on your skin; this can help prevent a skin infection. Then, if you rub yourself well with a towel after bathing, fresh oil will flow from the oil glands to keep your skin soft and smooth.

If your skin is dry, you may find that taking a bath every day with soap and water removes too much oil from your skin. In this case, take a few baths a week instead of a daily bath. Bath oil in the bath water also helps some people who have extremely dry or sensitive skin.

Baths can do more for you than clean your skin. When you are tired, a good warm bath can often make you feel relaxed and rested.

Showers

Many people prefer showers because a shower can be taken more quickly than a tub bath. A shower is fine as long as soap, a washcloth, and plenty of warm water are used.

"Stand-up" Baths

An efficient "stand-up" bath can be taken if no tub or shower is available. Using a washcloth, soap, and warm water, either in a washbowl or from a warm-water tap, wash each part of the body and dry with a towel. Campers, hunters, people on safaris, and many others use the stand-up bath.

Shampooing Your Hair

Your hair should usually be shampooed once or twice a week or at least once every two weeks.

Clean hair makes you more attractive, but there is another reason your hair should be washed often. A lot of dirt gets in your hair and not all of it can be brushed out. Usually by the end of a

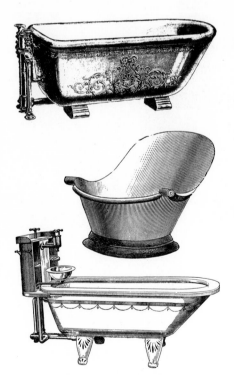

Three types of bathtubs that were used many years ago are shown here.

week or so, for health reasons, this dirt needs to be washed away.

Proper Clothes

By wearing proper clothes you can help your skin do its work of regulating body heat. Do you know how?

Your body is always making and losing heat. In warm weather you want to make it easy for the heat to leave your body through the tiny blood vessels in the skin. Thin clothes made of cotton, rayon, or other lightweight material let the heat pass easily into the outside air.

In cold weather you want to keep as much heat as you can from leaving the body. Clothes made of wool, of part wool, or of synthetic materials keep the heat from passing quickly into the outside air. These kinds of materials hold the warm air close to your skin.

In wet weather, you do not want the body to use up too much of its heat trying to dry out damp clothes and damp shoes. Sudden cooling of the skin in this way may cause the body to become chilled. That is why you should keep your clothes and shoes dry in rainy weather by wearing boots or rubbers and a raincoat whenever possible.

Avoiding Sunburn

Another way to take care of your skin is to avoid sunburn. Sunburn can be very painful, and a bad sunburn can be dangerous to your health.

When you are going to be out in the sunshine for long periods of time, be sure to have a hat to protect your head and wear clothes that cover your arms and legs. How can you protect your eyes?

Take just a little sun at a time, until your body gets used to it. Increase the amounts a little each day. That is the safe way to sunbathe.

Some Things to Remember
Don't forget that the "sky-shine" on a hazy day can give you a sunburn if you are not careful. Tanning lotions and sunburn-protection lotions cannot help you if you get too much sunshine at one time.

87

Health Questions Young People Often Ask

Here are some questions that pupils your age sometimes ask about the skin. Can you answer them?

1. What causes the skin to chap?
2. Why is the skin sometimes wrinkled?
3. What are calluses and corns?
4. What is a wart?
5. What is a mole?
6. What is a hangnail?
7. Why do some people bite their fingernails?
8. Why doesn't it hurt when your hair and nails are cut?
9. What causes naturally curly hair?
10. What are freckles?

Check your answers with the ones below and on pages 89 – 92. Then think of some questions about the skin that *you* would like to have answered. How might you find answers to your questions?

What Causes the Skin to Chap?

The oil glands in your skin send oil to the skin surface. This oil, together with perspiration, helps keep the skin smooth and moist.

In very cold weather, however, the oil may become thick on its way to the surface of the skin. Then less than the usual amount of oil reaches the skin surface. If this happens, your skin may become dry, rough, and perhaps even cracked. Then we say the skin is *chapped*.

If your skin becomes chapped, you can use creams or lotions with oil in them. The oil in the cream or lotion does the work that the oil from the oil glands in the skin usually does.

Why Is the Skin Sometimes Wrinkled?

Skin can be wrinkled for a number of reasons. A newborn baby's skin is wrinkled because his skin is too big for him. When his body fills out, the wrinkles disappear.

As people grow older, the oil glands do not make so much oil as they once did. Also, some of the fat under the dermis may be absorbed into the body. Less oil in the skin and less fat under it leave the skin somewhat loose and wrinkled.

The skin on your hands may be wrinkled for a short while if your hands have been soaking in water. You may have had wrinkled hands after washing dishes, for example. The wrinkles form because the water washes away much of the oil on your skin. When this oil is washed away, the outer layers of the skin soak up water. The water is not spread evenly through these layers, so that your skin becomes wrinkled from the little ridges that form in it. Later, more oil comes up to the outer layers of the skin; the extra water passes out of the skin, and the wrinkles smooth out.

What Are Calluses and Corns?

The outside part of your skin, or the epidermis, can get very tough and thick if there is a lot of rubbing or pressure on it. When the skin becomes very thick, the thick spot is called a *callus*. A callus prevents the inside parts of the skin from being hurt by rubbing. The callus will gradually go away when the rubbing or pressure is stopped.

Corns are small, cone-shaped areas, usually on the toes, in which the outer layer has thickened and grown into deeper skin layers. Corns are usually caused by ill-fitting shoes or hose, and they can be very painful.

What Is a Wart?

As you know, little ridges reach up from the dermis to the epidermis to fasten these layers together. (Look back at the picture on page 77.)

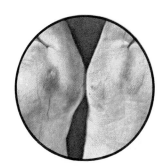

Skin calluses on feet

Sometimes several of these little ridges keep on growing until they form a small, hard lump on the skin. Such a lump is called a *wart*. Warts that grow on the soles of the feet are called *plantar warts*.

All warts are now thought to be virus infections, though they are not believed to be communicable to others. Generally, the warts are hard and dry. Sometimes, however, tiny blood vessels grow up into them.

Any treatment for warts should be given by a doctor.

What Is a Mole?

A *mole* is a brown or black area of the skin, sometimes flat, sometimes raised above the surface of the skin. Moles have pigment in them. Some have hairs growing out of them, while others do not. A mole should be let alone unless it is giving trouble by growing larger, bleeding, or becoming sore. If necessary, the mole should be treated by a doctor.

What Is a Hangnail?

The hardened skin around the base and sides of the nails is called the *cuticle*. There is very little oil in this part of the skin. Therefore, the cuticle cracks and gets rough edges very easily. If these rough edges are not cut off or softened, they gradually get longer and start tearing into the more sensitive skin. This causes a condition known as *hangnail*. Hangnails can become quite painful.

A simple way to prevent hangnails is to gently push back the softened cuticle from the nail with a towel every time you dry your hands. If the cuticle seems especially dry, rub a little oil or cream into it. This oil or cream will help keep the cuticle soft and smooth so that hangnails will not start.

It is a good idea, too, to know how to keep your nails in good condition. Use a nail file or an emery board to keep your fingernails shaped and rounded to the right length. Unlike fingernails, toenails should not be rounded but should be trimmed straight across so that you will not get "ingrown toenails." Ingrown toenails can become infected and should be treated by a doctor.

Why Do Some People Bite Their Fingernails?

Sometimes nail-biting results from a person's having upset or unhappy feelings — or from his worrying over a problem he does not know how to solve. Nail-biting usually stops after the person gets his feelings straightened out or his problem worked through. One way to handle upset feelings that may lead to biting the nails is by talking things over with your parents, your teacher, or with some other adult you like and trust.

Why Doesn't It Hurt When Your Hair and Nails Are Cut?

To understand why it does not hurt to cut your hair and nails, you have to know how hair and nails grow.

Your hair grows out of little pits in the dermis. The part of the hair that starts in each little pit is called the *root*. The hair root is alive and growing. It gets its food from the blood brought to it by the skin's blood vessels. If you pull a hair out by the root, you will feel a twinge of pain.

The cells in the hair roots grow from the bottom up, just as the skin cells do. As the cells in the hair roots grow, they push the old cells upward to form the part of the hair you see on the skin. As new cells are pushed upward, the old cells become dead cells. Because these dead cells have no special nerve endings for pain they can be cut without your feeling any pain.

Something to Do

Find out about the care of your fingernails. Is it easier for you to shape your nails with a file or emery board than it is with scissors?

91

Each time you brush your hair or comb it, you probably notice that a few hairs come out. This is normal. The hairs of the scalp may live about four or five years. The eyelashes live only six months or so. When an old hair falls out, a new one grows in its place. The hair is lost permanently only if the root of the hair is destroyed.

Your fingernails and toenails also grow from the bottom up. The nails grow out of live roots under the skin. As the nails grow out from their roots, the cells in them die and change into the horny sheet of material you can see. Because the cells in this material have no nerve endings to receive sensations of pain, there is no feeling at all in the fingernails and toenails. That is why it does not hurt when your nails are cut.

If your skin, hair, and nails look healthy, it is a good sign that you are eating enough of the kinds of foods you need each day. Lack of proper foods can cause your skin and hair to become dry and dull-looking and your nails to be brittle and ridged.

What Causes Naturally Curly Hair?

Your hair grows out of little pits in the skin. The shape of these little pits determines whether the hair is curly or straight. Round pits send out hairs that have a round or oval shape. Such hair is straight. Sometimes, though, the pits are oval and flattish in shape. The hair that comes out of these flat oval pits is usually curly.

What Are Freckles?

Freckles are tiny brown marks on the skin. They are caused when the pigment in the skin collects in little spots in the epidermis. Strong sunlight often causes freckles to form on the skin—usually on the face and arms—of some people.

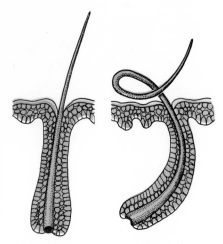

Left. *This cross section shows how a straight hair looks when growing.* Right. *In this cross section you can see how a curly hair looks when it is growing.*

Check Yourself

1. Look back at the questions on page 72. How would you answer them now?

2. Is the epidermis you have today the same that you had last year? Explain.

3. What keeps the skin from cracking?

4. Where does perspiration come from?

5. How are the epidermis and the dermis held together?

6. Why is there no pain when you have your hair cut?

7. What can make the skin wrinkle?

8. What are the advantages of the creases, or folds, in your skin?

9. How would you describe the parts of the epidermis? Of the dermis?

10. What is your explanation for these terms?

    a. albino   d. hangnail

    b. chapped skin   e. pigment

    c. fingerprint   f. pores

11. What is your explanation of why some people have naturally curly hair?

12. What helps keep the cells of the skin alive?

13. How does a cut heal itself?

14. What is the connection between the skin and vitamin D?

Things to Do

1. Here is a demonstration to try.

Put cold cream on the hands (to represent skin oil).

Sprinkle with cinnamon (to represent dirt).
Wash with plain water.

Dry hands with paper towel.

Repeat demonstration but this time wash with soapy water.

Compare the appearance of the paper towels used for drying hands.

2. Write a summary paragraph or so on one of these topics:

How the Skin Protects Us

Fingerprints

How Oil Glands Help the Skin

How Clothes Help the Skin Do Its Work

Special Research

1. Look up information about these topics: *Bunions, Pimples, Dandruff.*

2. Find out how doctors and dentists go about washing their hands to kill any bacteria that may be on them.

3. Make a report on how to avoid such injuries to the skin as splinters and small cuts. (In Unit 7 you will learn how to give first aid for these injuries.)

Use a ruler or a strip of paper to cover the answer column at the right. Read the first item and write the missing word or words on a piece of paper. Then move your ruler or paper strip down to uncover the answer and see if you are right. Go on in the same way with each of the other items. Do not write in this book.

The numbers by the answers show the pages in this book that give information about the subject. For the items you miss, go back and review this information.

1. Another name for the true skin is the _____.

dermis 74

2. The body's largest organ is the _____.

skin 72

3. Some of the glands that are found in the dermis are the _____ glands and the _____ glands.

oil, sweat 75 – 76

4. Another name for the coloring matter in the skin is _____.

pigment 74

5. Dead skin cells that are shed every day are found on the _____.

epidermis 73

6. A vitamin that the skin helps produce is vitamin _____.

D 84 – 85

7. Dirt is easily caught by the skin because the skin has oil on it as well as _____ in it.

folds (or creases) 73

8. The two main parts of the skin are the _____ and the _____.

epidermis dermis 72, 74

Health Test for Unit Three

Part I

Copy each number on a piece of paper. After the number, write the correct answer, *true* or *false*.

1. The skin is the smallest body organ.

2. The folds in the skin make it easy for the body to bend and stretch.

3. Perspiration comes out of tiny openings called pores.

4. The cells in the topmost layer of the epidermis are live skin cells.

5. The epidermis is known as the true skin.

6. Pigment is found in the epidermis.

7. There are many tiny blood vessels in the dermis.

8. The oil in the skin helps keep it from cracking.

9. Chapped skin is smooth and moist.

10. "Goose pimples" are caused by eating too much chocolate.

11. The skin helps keep harmful bacteria out of the body.

12. Only very old men and women have wrinkled skin.

13. Your fingerprint is just like that of every other person.

14. The skin is more or less waterproof because it has oil from the oil glands on it.

15. An albino usually has brown skin.

16. Your skin makes millions of new cells each day.

17. The skin is one organ that has no blood vessels in it.

18. As perspiration on the skin evaporates, the body becomes warmer.

19. Body fat helps cushion you from jars and bumps.

20. Your fingerprint never changes.

21. All the water you take in each day is stored in the skin.

22. A cut can heal itself.

23. A wart is another name for a freckle.

24. Woolen clothing can help keep heat from leaving the body.

25. A callus is usually the result of a poor daily diet.

Number of Answers   <u> 25 </u>
Number Right   <u>   </u>
Score (Number Right x 4)   <u>   </u>

Part II

Match the term in List A with its explanation in List B.

List A

1. albino
2. artery
3. callus
4. clot
5. dermis
6. epidermis
7. freckle
8. pattern of ridges on fingertip
9. pigment
10. pore

List B

a. thickened clump of blood
b. outer layers of skin
c. a small spot of collected pigment
d. person without normal coloring substances in the epidermis
e. true skin
f. a blood vessel that carries dissolved oxygen and food to body organs
g. opening on skin through which sweat comes out
h. coloring matter in epidermis
i. thickened area on skin caused by rubbing or pressure
j. fingerprint

Part III

On a piece of paper, copy each sentence below, filling in the blanks correctly. All blanks in a sentence must be filled correctly if a point is to be scored.

11. The part of the hair that starts in each little pit is called the _____.

12. The salty liquid that comes out through the pores is called _____.

13. To get your hands really clean you need warm water and _____.

14. The two main parts of the skin are the _____ and the _____.

15. The design made by the ridges on your fingertip is called your _____.

16. Perspiration helps _____ the body.

17. Every day your skin makes millions of new _____ and sheds millions of old ones.

18. Blood vessels and glands are found in the part of the skin called the _____.

19. Your skin is kept from cracking by the _____ from the _____ glands.

20. When you go out into the cold, the blood vessels in the skin _____.

Number of Answers _____20_____

Number Right _____

Score (Number Right x 5) _____

96

4 How Do Your Bones And Muscles Work?

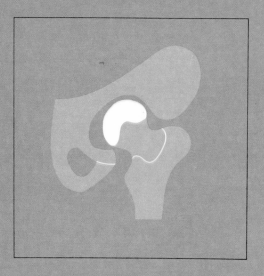

How much do you know about your bones? Do you know, for example, the answers to questions like these: About how many bones are there in your skeleton? What is the name of the only bone in your skull that can move? What are your "floating ribs"? What important substance is manufactured in some of your bones? And how do those skeletal muscles that cover bones work with the bones? You will learn about such things in this unit. You will come to understand, too, why the skeleton is sometimes called "wonderfully designed."

1. *Why could the skeleton be called "wonderfully designed"?*

2. *What is the special job of the skull? Of the backbone? Of the ribs?*

3. *How is the skull designed to do its important jobs? The backbone? The ribs?*

4. *How do small bones make the hands efficient?*

5. *How do your bones fit together and stay in place?*

6. *How can you help build skillful muscles?*

7. *Why do you need muscles and bones of different sizes and shapes?*

8. *What can help you have good posture?*

9. *What is a "bone bank"?*

10. *What are the sinuses?*

In What Way Is Your Skeleton "Wonderfully Designed"?

Something to Do

Look in the school or public library for books containing material about the skeleton. Some books of this kind are the following:
Goldsmith, Ilse. Anatomy for Children *(Sterling).*
Schuman, Benjamin N., M.D. The Human Skeleton *(Atheneum).*
White, Anne Terry, and Lietz, Gerald S., M.D. Built to Survive *(Garrard).*
Zim, Herbert S. Bones *(Morrow).*

You have a framework of bones from the top of your head down to your feet. This framework of bones is called the *skeleton,* and it gives the body its general shape. The skeleton also supports the body and protects many of the body organs.

There are more than 200 bones in the skeleton — little bones and big bones, flat bones and round ones, long bones and short ones. If you look at the picture on pages 104–105, you will get an idea of the many different sizes and shapes of bones in the skeleton. Each bone is the right size and shape to do its special work. For this reason the skeleton is sometimes described as being "wonderfully designed."

The Bones of the Skull

The bones of the head, or the *skull bones*, are designed to do their special work. How are they designed?

The skull bones include the *cranium*, or bones that enclose the brain, as well as the *bones of the face*. The cranium bones are flat bones which are held firmly together. Since one of the main jobs of the cranium is to protect the brain, the bones in this upper part of the skull are hard and thick.

One of the bones in the skull is a moving bone, the *jawbone*. If your jawbone could not move up and down and sideways, you could not talk or sing or chew.

The eye sockets in the skull form a safe "pocket" for the eyes.

The Backbone

Now let us see how the backbone, or *spine*, is designed to do its special work.

The backbone is fastened firmly to the skull at one end and to the hipbones at the other end. Thus the backbone, together with the strong back muscles, helps hold you erect.

The backbone lets you bend and twist because it is made up of many little bones, or *vertebrae*. There are pads of *cartilage*, an elasticlike material, between the vertebrae. These little pads act as shock absorbers. When you walk or run or jump, these pads cushion your bones and keep them from bumping together.

There are 24 vertebrae with cartilage pads between them. In addition, there are two other bones at the end of the spine; each one is made up of five vertebrae usually fused together. These two end-of-the-spine bones are called the *sacrum* and the *coccyx*. See the picture on page 108.

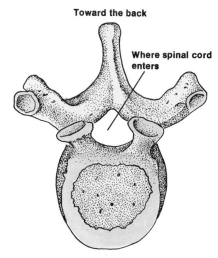

Toward the back

Where spinal cord enters

A single vertebra, one of the 33 bones of the spine, as seen from above

99

Each of the vertebrae in your backbone has a hole in it. The holes form a safe passageway for the main nerve cord, or *spinal cord*. The picture of a single vertebra is shown on page 99.

As you can see in the large pictures on pages 106 and 107, the *ribs*, along with the *breastbone* in front and the spinal column in back, form a kind of cage. This cage protects such vital organs as the heart and lungs. The ribs are also joined together in such a way that they can be raised and lowered during breathing. This action helps the chest cavity enlarge and contract as you breathe.

All the ribs, 12 pairs of them, are connected to the spine in back. Ten of these pairs curve around the body and are fastened to the breastbone in front. The top seven pairs of ribs are fastened to the breastbone with cartilage. The next three pairs are fastened by cartilage to the ribs above them. Although the last two pairs of ribs are attached to the backbone, they are free in front. They are attached neither to the ribs above them nor to the breastbone. For that reason, these two pairs are called "floating ribs."

The elasticlike cartilage on the ribs helps the chest get larger, or expand, so that the lungs can fill with air as you breathe in, or *inhale*.

Upward movement of the floating ribs also gives the lungs more space for inhaling.

The Hipbones

The hipbones, together with the sacrum and the coccyx of the spine, form a large bony cup, with a big opening in the bottom of the cup. This cup-shaped cavity formed by the hipbones and the end of the backbone is known as the *pelvis*. The pelvis helps support the upper part of the body and forms a protective ring around some of the organs of the

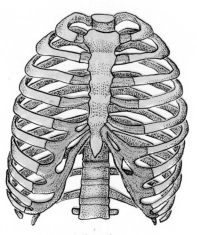

The rib cage

lower abdomen. The lowest and strongest parts of the hipbones are what you sit on—sometimes called "seat bones." Find the hipbones in the pictures on pages 106, 107, and 109.

The Leg Bones

In the long bones of the legs you can find another example of bones well designed to perform a particular job. These leg bones have to be strong since one of their main tasks is to help bear the weight of the body. The leg bones can do this work well because the bones are hollow and they are *porous*, or full of many tiny holes. And a hollow, porous column has been proved to be stronger than a solid column of the same size would be. What is more, if your long bones were solid, they would weigh so much that it would be difficult for you to move about. See the picture of the inside of the upper leg bone on page 110.

The long bones of the legs help the body make large motions. Where else in the body are some long bones that aid in making such motions? Use the pictures on pages 106 and 107 to find out.

The Foot Bones

The bones in each foot are set in arches. These foot arches give support to the body just like the arches that support a bridge.

The arches of the feet also bend and spring back each time you take a step. In this way you are not jarred as you move about. Your toes move and grip as you walk.

The Bones of the Hand

Just think of the many short, fast movements you can make with your hands. To help you make such movements, you have many short bones in your wrist, palm, and fingers—as you can see in the picture at the right.

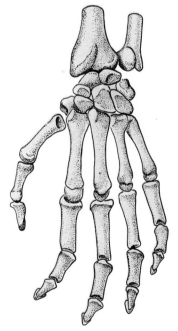

Your hand has many small bones and an opposable *thumb, that is the thumb is so designed that it faces the fingers. This is why you can pick up such varied things as a delicate thread or a round baseball.*

101

How Do Bones Fit Together and Stay in Place?

If you look again at the pictures on pages 106 and 107, you will notice places in the skeleton where one bone ends and another begins. These places where two bones come together and fit against one another are called *joints*.

Your Joints

Some joints in your body are known as *fixed joints*. As you would guess from their name, such joints will "give" but not move very much. Most of the joints in your skull, for example, are fixed joints. Other joints, such as those between the bones in your spine, move just a little. The partially movable joints in the spine give increased support to the body.

There are other joints in your body known as *movable joints*. Two kinds of movable joints are shown in the pictures at the left. What are they?

Ball-and-socket joints, such as those in the shoulders and hips, allow the widest range of movements — including back-and-forth and rotating movements. In the picture at the left, notice how the rounded end of one bone fits into the hollow socket of another bone.

Hinge joints, such as those in your knees, fingers, and toes, allow movement in only one direction. What would happen if your knee had a ball-and-socket joint instead of a hinge joint?

Movable joints have a substance around them which keeps them from becoming stiff. They are protected by a fluid that makes them moist and able to move smoothly. The joints in your body, like moving parts in machinery, need oiling to make the bones move easily against each other and keep them from getting stiff.

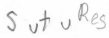

S u t u Res

Hip joint (ball-and-socket joint)

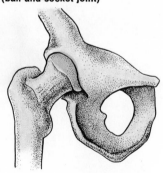

Knee joint (hinge joint)

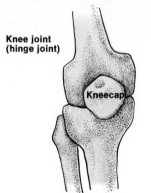

Kneecap

Where in the body are there other joints like these?

How Do Your Bones Look—Outside and Inside?

If you were asked to tell how bones look on the *outside*, you could probably describe them without any trouble. You would probably say that bones are smooth, whitish, and hard on the outside. Some of you might even mention the thin covering of the bones. It is in this covering that nerves and blood vessels are located. Some nerves and blood vessels go into the bones.

All the outer layers of your bones are made of hard material which is called *compact bone.*

There is another kind of bone, however, that you would see only if you looked *inside* the bones. This is *spongy bone,* and it gets its name because it is porous, that is, there are many little holes in it. These little holes make it look like a sponge. But spongy bone is not soft. It is made up of many crisscrossing bony tubes. This criss-crossing network gives strength without adding weight to the bones and helps the bones give the body the support it needs. In the picture on page 110, you can see some spongy bone on the inside of a long bone.

The Flat Bones

The flat bones in your body are put together somewhat like a sandwich. Flat bones, such as the rib bones, have two layers of compact bone outside, with spongy bone and a soft substance called *marrow* between them. Find some flat bones in the picture on pages 104–105.

The Long Bones

The long bones in your body are the heavy-duty bones, such as the arm and leg bones. In the long bones, the spongy part is found at the rounded ends. See the picture of the inside of long bone on page 110. *(Continued on page 111.)*

Something to Do

Thousands of years ago, people found that the bones of animals they hunted and killed were very useful. Find out some of the uses that were found for bones in long-ago times. One book that will help you is Bones *by Herbert S. Zim (Morrow).*

The Skeleton—a Masterpiece of Design

You can see here some of the many kinds of bones in the skeleton. What are some of the different sizes and shapes you see in the picture?

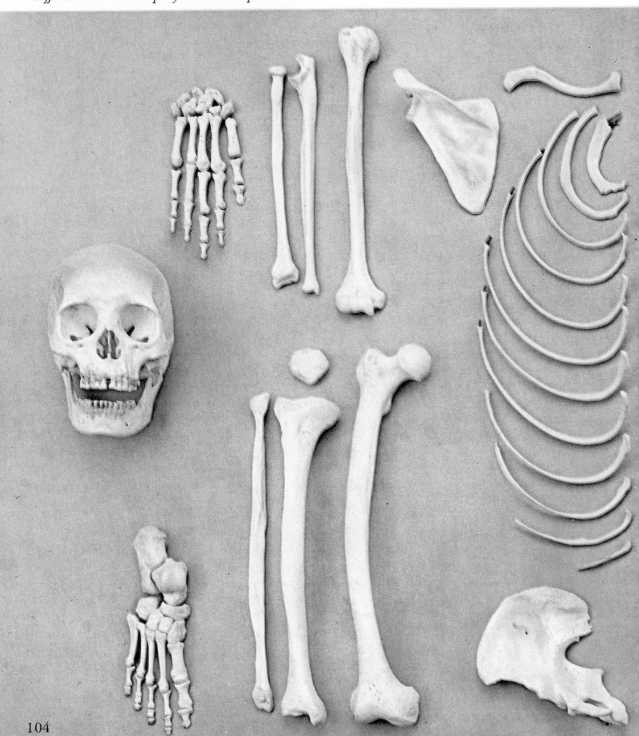

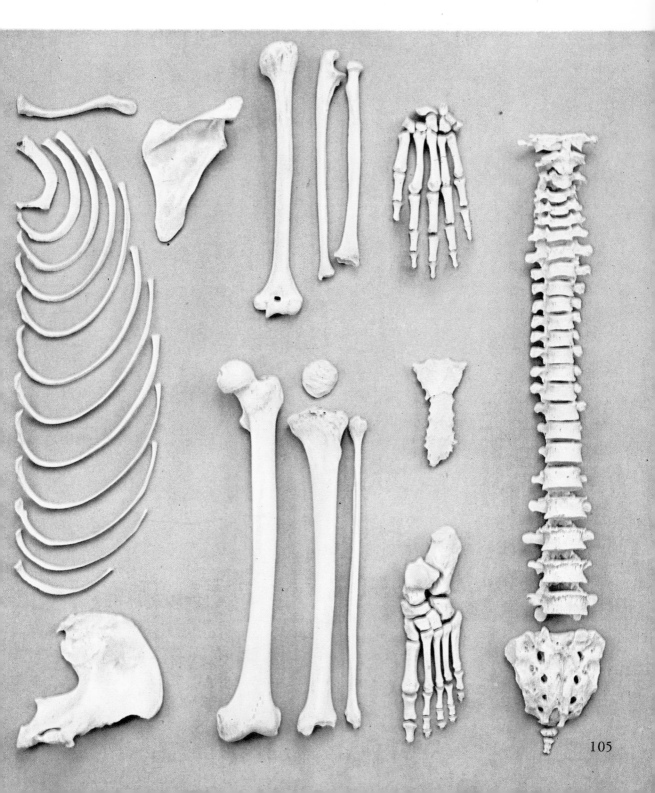

105

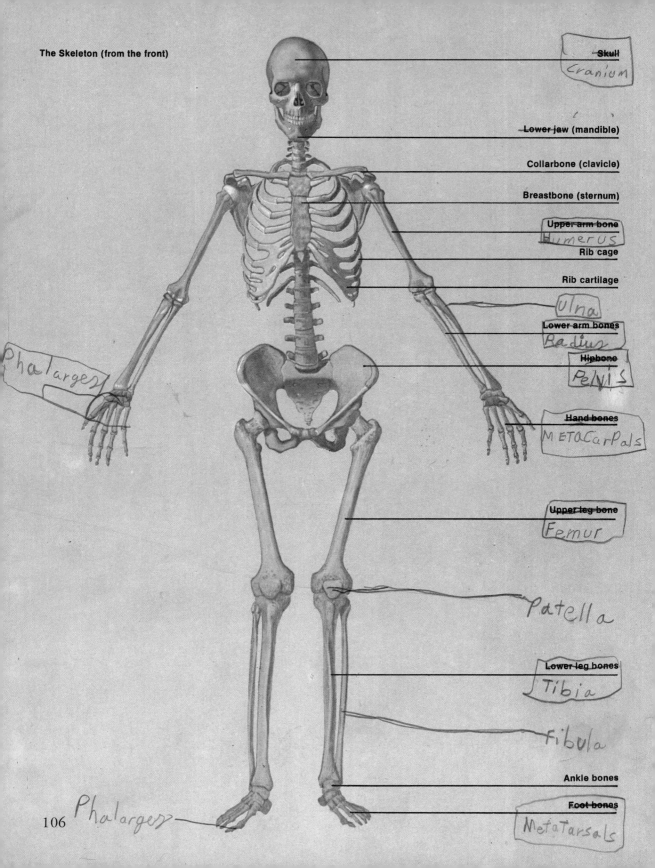

The Skeleton (from the front)

Skull
Cranium

Lower jaw (mandible)

Collarbone (clavicle)

Breastbone (sternum)

Upper arm bone
Humerus

Rib cage

Rib cartilage

Ulna

Lower arm bones
Radius

Hipbone
Pelvis

Phalanges

Hand bones
Metacarpals

Upper leg bone
Femur

Patella

Lower leg bones
Tibia

Fibula

Ankle bones

Foot bones
Metatarsals

Phalanges

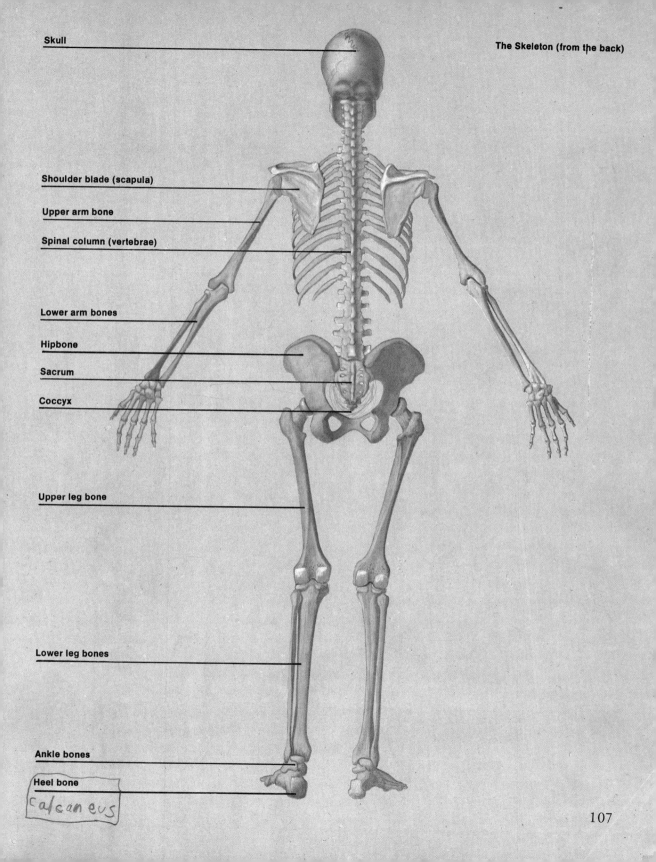

Skull

Shoulder blade (scapula)

Upper arm bone

Spinal column (vertebrae)

Lower arm bones

Hipbone

Sacrum

Coccyx

Upper leg bone

Lower leg bones

Ankle bones

Heel bone

calcaneus

The backbone, or spine, is made up of many small bones that permit movement of the spine. Each bone, or vertebra, is shaped somewhat like a spool, with projections sticking out from it. The bones are lined up end to end and held together by muscles and strong bands of tissue. Cartilage pads between the vertebrae help the body absorb shock.

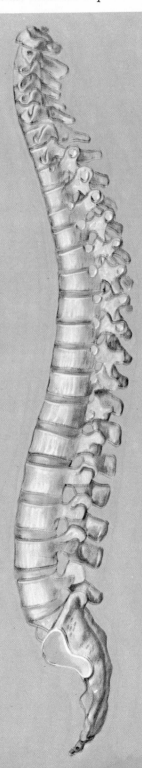

When you stand, your weight is supported by the bones of your legs down to your feet. But when you sit, the weight is carried by the arches of bones below the winglike parts of the hipbones, shown below. These open structures provide much good support for your body in a sitting position.

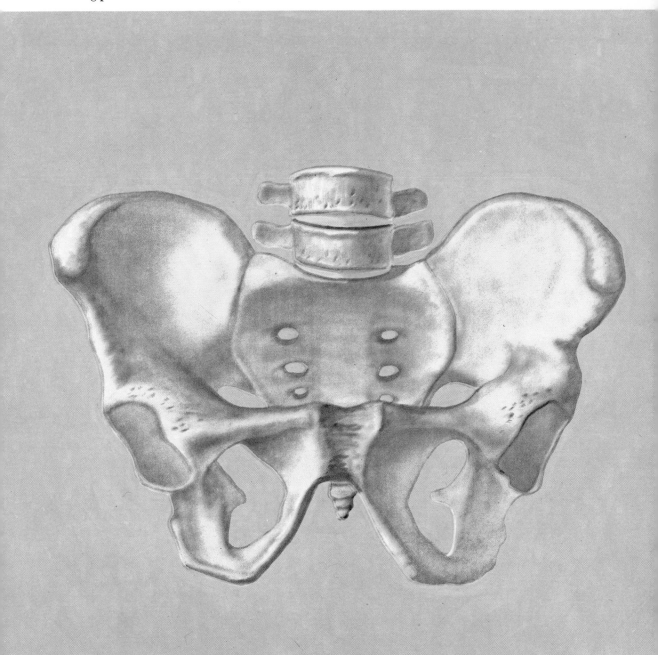

This cross-section view of a piece of long bone shows the end of the long bone and the hollow shaft where yellow marrow is located.

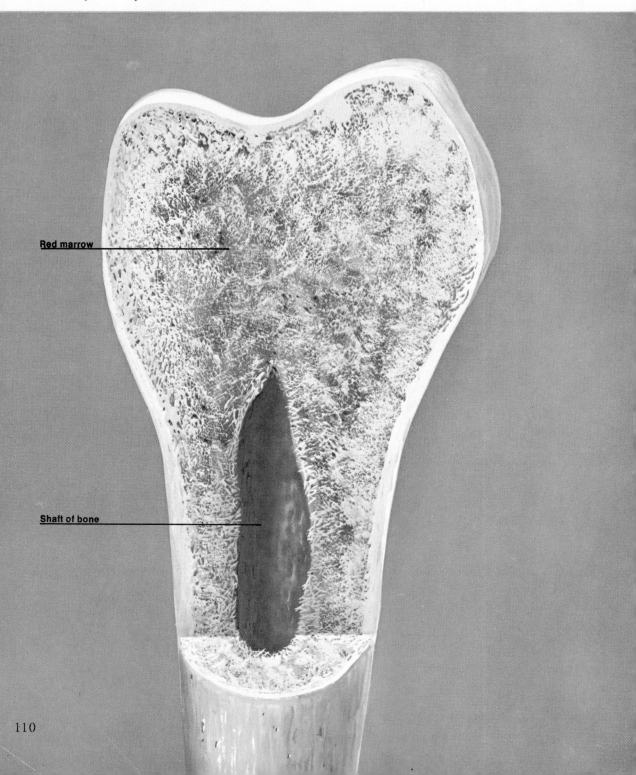

Red marrow

Shaft of bone

The hollow part in the long bones is filled with marrow. The marrow going up the middle of the bones is yellow and made up mostly of fat. The marrow in the ends of these bones is red.

The red marrow in bones such as the long bones is often called a "factory" or a "manufacturing plant." Do you know why? The red marrow makes red blood cells which are sent into the blood stream. They give the blood its red color.

These red blood cells float in the liquid part of the blood. Red blood cells are important because they pick up oxygen in the lungs and carry it to all parts of the body. The red blood cells also carry waste carbon dioxide back to the lungs.

The red blood cells manufactured in the marrow usually live for three or four months. Then the cells die and must be replaced by new ones. Each minute, millions of your red blood cells die and are replaced by millions of healthy new cells. The new red blood cells get into the blood stream by passing through the very thin walls of the capillaries present in bone and marrow.

If the marrow did not make new red blood cells to replace the dead ones, your blood would become watery. Then you would feel tired and ill because you would not be getting enough oxygen nor would carbon dioxide leave the body as it should.

The marrow in your bones also makes white blood cells. These white blood cells are needed to fight off disease germs that come into your body.

If you want to see the inside of some bones, crack open the bones from raw meat or chicken you have at home. Notice the spongy tissue, the red and yellow marrow, the hollow shafts, and the sandwich-like flat bones. Chicken legs, beef bones, spareribs, and ham bones are good ones to study.

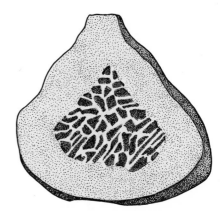

Cross section of the end of a long bone, showing the location of some red marrow

111

How Do Your Bones Grow?

When you were a baby, your bones were made mostly of elasticlike cartilage. There was very little calcium or other mineral matter in your bones.

As you grew older, however, your bones began to grow larger and stronger. Important minerals like calcium and phosphorus were taken from the digested food carried by the blood to help their growth. Most of the calcium and some of the phosphorus come into the body in the milk you drink.

During your growing years it is important for you to have a diet that includes not only milk but all the four main food groups. It takes food from each of these groups, eaten in the right amounts, to keep you healthy and strong. (On page 165 you can see the four kinds of foods needed to make up an adequate daily diet.)

If the bone cells are to build strong bones, for example, they must have plenty of vitamins C and D. Vitamin C is found in citrus fruits, berries, tomatoes, and leafy vegetables. Vitamin D comes from such foods as cod-liver oil, some fish, and egg yolks. Vitamin D is also made by a fat in the skin when the skin is exposed to the ultraviolet rays of the sun.

Minerals that are needed for bone-building, such as calcium and phosphorus, are found in fruits and vegetables, as well as in milk.

Growth in Thickness and Length

As you grow older your bones grow thicker. The outside cover of the bones puts down hard new bone cells to make the bones thicker and stronger.

Your bones also grow in length. To understand something of how this happens, look at the picture at the left and find the part called the *growth plate.*

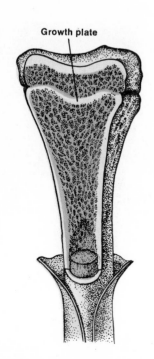

Growth plate

112

During your growing years, the ends of the long bones are fastened to the shafts by this growth plate, which is made of soft cartilage. Gradually hard new bone cells come up from the shaft. When they come up, they replace the soft cartilage and push the cartilage cells toward the ends of the long bones. As the cartilage pushes outward, your long bones grow. By the time you are eighteen to twenty years old or so, hard bone cells have replaced the cartilage in the growth plate. Then the bones cannot grow longer, and you can grow no taller.

However, if you do not eat enough of the right kinds of foods, the bone cells may be unable to replace the cartilage properly. For example, if there is not enough calcium in your bones, the cartilage will keep growing out toward the ends of the long bones. But hard new bone cells may not come from the shafts as they should, and the soft growth plate will grow wider and wider.

Wide cartilage plates in the long bones are not strong enough to support the body well. Then the bones are likely to bend out of shape.

Ligaments and Tendons

As you looked at the pictures of two kinds of movable joints on page 102, you may have wondered why the bones do not slip out of place. You do not have to worry, however, about your skeleton falling apart.

Your bones are kept in place by tough, stringy bands called *ligaments*. The ligaments reach from one bone to another and hold them together. You can see ligaments in the picture at the right.

There are other tough, stringy bands that fasten the bones to the muscles nearby. These bands are called *tendons*. You can see some tendons in the picture at the right.

bursa

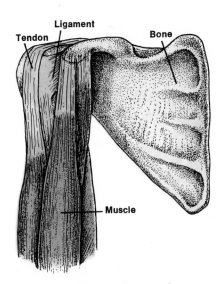

Bones, muscles, tendons, and ligaments work together to move the body. Here you see these various parts in the arm and shoulder.

What Do the Skeletal Muscles Do?

The muscles that cover the skeleton are called the skeletal muscles. What you may call the "flesh" on your body is really these more than 600 skeletal muscles, together with some fat. Flesh lies beneath the skin covering of the body. See the pictures on pages 118–123.

Without your skeletal muscles, you could not move at all. It is these muscles that allow movement of all the bones in your body.

The skeletal muscles not only help you move about, but they help hold your bones in place and so hold your body straight.

The skeletal muscles do other things, too. By squeezing the blood in the veins they help it return to the heart. And, by being in action so much of the time, these muscles help make a good part of the body's heat.

The skeletal muscles also round out the body and give it shape and symmetry.

The skeletal muscles, like the bones in the body, are of different sizes and shapes—flat, round, long, thin, diamond-shaped. And like the bones in your body, each muscle is the right size and shape to do its work well.

The muscles of the face, for example, are small and thin. They are the muscles that make possible the small but important movements which provide facial expressions, as well as movements involved in chewing and in closing the eyes.

Muscles of the Trunk

The *trunk* is the part of the body from the shoulders to the top of the legs. In the trunk of the body you see another example of muscles well designed to do their special jobs.

Something to Do

Note how the muscles of your face help you communicate feelings. Use your facial muscles to frown, to laugh, to wink, to show surprise, to express anger.

114

The front muscles of the trunk form a wall that protects the organs behind it. This is especially important since there is no bony structure there for protection of the delicate organs beneath—organs such as the stomach and liver. The large muscles of the back help hold your backbone straight.

Arm and Leg Muscles

You remember that the long bones in your body are in places like the legs and arms where big actions are needed. It is in these places, too, that you will find long, strong muscles.

Let us see, for example, how the long muscles in your arms are designed for their work of helping the arms bend and straighten out.

These muscles are fastened at one end to the shoulder bones and at the other end to the arm bones. The muscles pull to make your arm move. That is an interesting thing about muscles. They can *contract*, or become shorter and thicker. Then they can *relax*, or stretch out and become longer.

By feeling the large muscles in your upper arm when you bend your arm, you get an idea of the shape of these muscles. They have a thick middle part, but they become smaller toward each end where they form a tendon. The tendons fasten the ends of the muscles to bones.

To make a bone move, two muscles are needed. One muscle contracts and becomes shorter and thicker, while the other relaxes and extends or stretches out. The shortened muscle pulls one bone toward the other, as you can see in the picture.

To pull the bone back to its original position, the relaxed muscle contracts and becomes shorter and thicker. At the same time, the muscle which had been contracted before now relaxes and becomes longer as it stretches out.

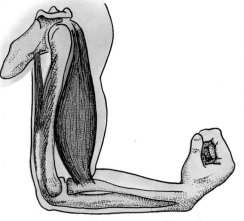

Notice how the upper arm (biceps) muscle changes shape as it contracts to help move the bone.

115

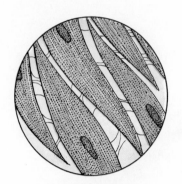

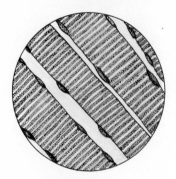

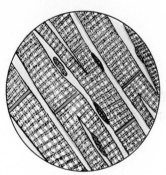

Top. *Involuntary (smooth) muscle fibers*
Middle. *Voluntary (striped) muscle fibers*
Bottom. *Heart (cardiac) muscle fibers*

What Are Voluntary and Involuntary Muscles?

The muscles that cover the skeleton, or *skeletal muscles*, work for you whenever you want them to. That is, whenever you want to walk or run, you can make your skeletal muscles move as you wish.

When you want to chew, swallow, turn your eyes, or talk, your muscles work on command to do these things, too. Your brain sends messages over the motor nerves to certain muscles in your body. Then these muscles do what the messages tell them to do. Muscles that you can make work whenever you want them to are called *voluntary muscles*.

There are other muscles that need no orders to start or stop; they work without any orders given consciously to them. These are *involuntary muscles.*

The involuntary muscles are found in the blood vessels and in such organs as the stomach, large and small intestines, and bladder. The heart muscle also works without any orders, although it acts in a slightly different way from your other involuntary muscles.

When you have upset feelings such as those of anger or fear, these feelings may keep the involuntary muscles from working properly. Then you may feel weak or sick or "tied in knots." Your voluntary muscles may be affected by strong feelings, too; when you are upset, these voluntary muscles may begin to twitch, causing you to tremble.

Every muscle is made up of thousands of thread-like fibers fastened together. When we talk about muscles, we really mean bundles of these little muscle fibers.

Striped Muscles

If you could use a microscope to look at the muscle fibers in your voluntary muscles, you would see

116

tiny light and dark markings, or stripes, across the fibers. Because of these markings, voluntary muscles are sometimes called *striped muscles*.

Smooth Muscles

If you could look through a microscope at the muscle fibers in most of your involuntary muscles, you would see that they look much smoother than the striped voluntary muscles. The involuntary muscles are sometimes called *smooth muscles*.

Muscle Fibers of the Heart

The muscle fibers in the heart, when seen under a microscope, look a little like the striped voluntary muscles. But they work like involuntary muscles. Muscle fibers in the heart have some qualities of both striped and smooth muscles but the heart muscle, or *cardiac muscle*, is quite different from either. It is a special set of involuntary muscles that keeps your heart contracting, or beating, regularly all by itself.

How You Can Build Strong Muscles

Muscles, like machinery, must be used regularly to keep them in their best working order. If the parts of a machine are not used for a long time, they have to be oiled and fixed up before they work well again. Your muscles, when not used for a long time, do not work very well either. They may become weak, and they may even get smaller.

Now you can see one good reason why you need lots of play and exercise, preferably outdoors, every day. What is *your* favorite form of exercise?

On page 124 you can see directions for two active games that you and your friends may enjoy playing. What are these games? How do you play each of them?

On page 125 you can see directions for some stunts that help build strong muscles.

Do You Know?

Strong muscles are not built in a few weeks or months. They are built by following year after year such healthful practices as exercising regularly, eating an adequate daily diet, and getting enough sleep and rest most of the time.

Muscles—the Body's Movers

Your framework of bones gives you a shape; your muscles fill out that shape. Muscles are the movers of your body. Every movable bone in your body has muscles to move it.

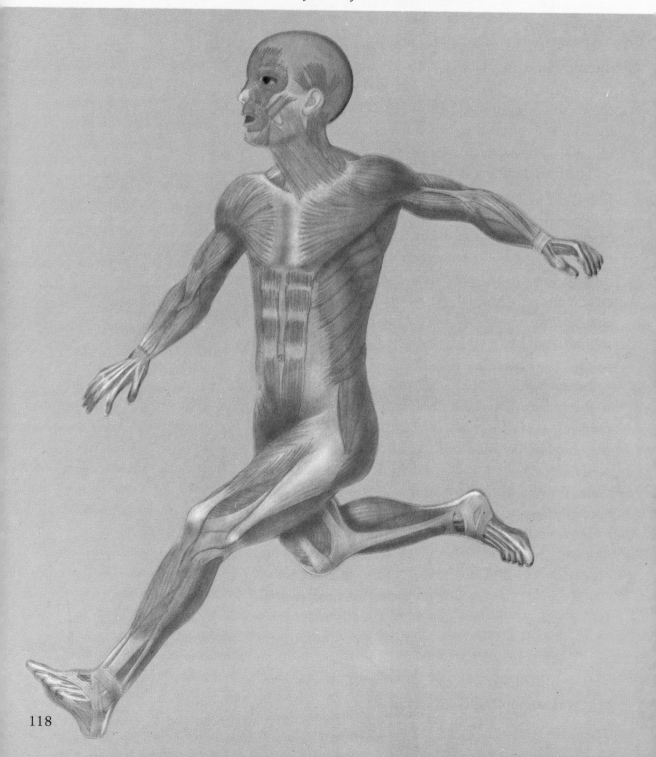

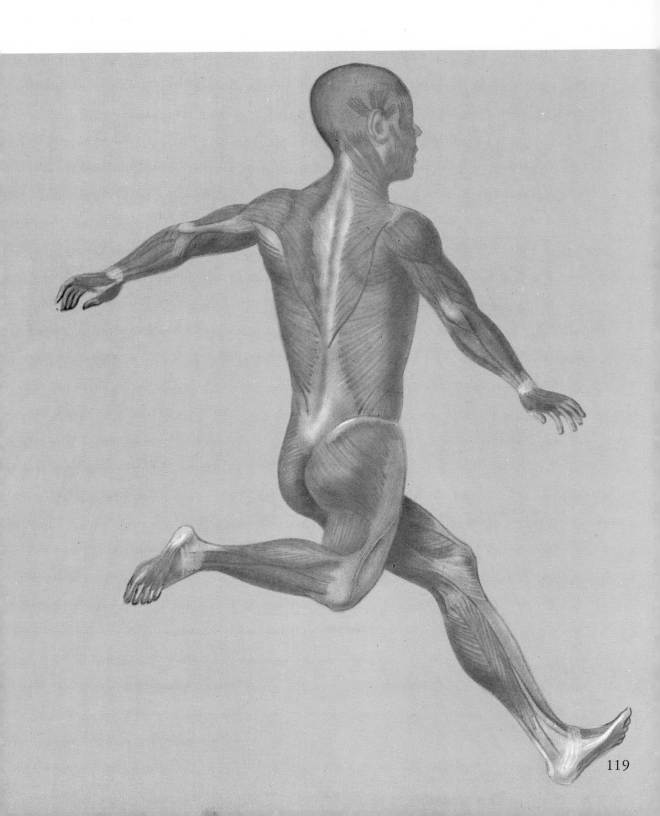

119

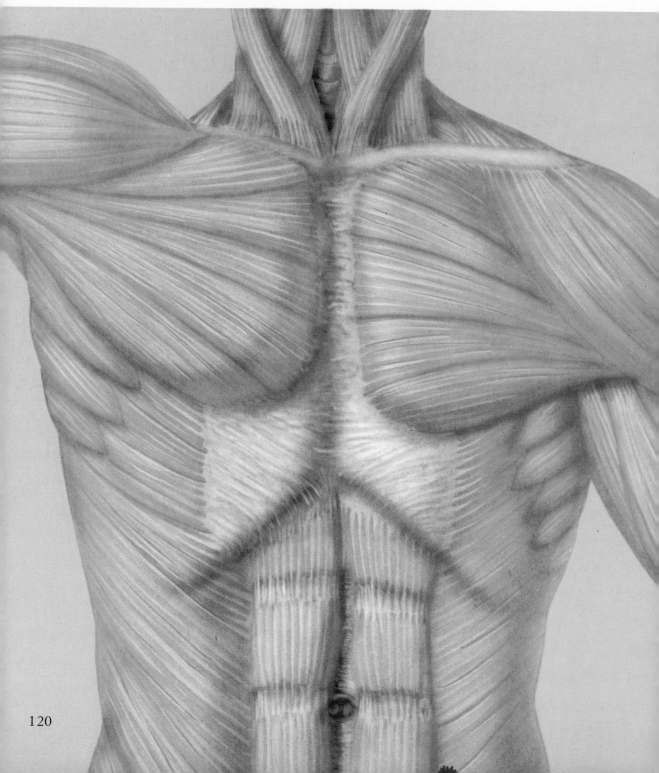

120

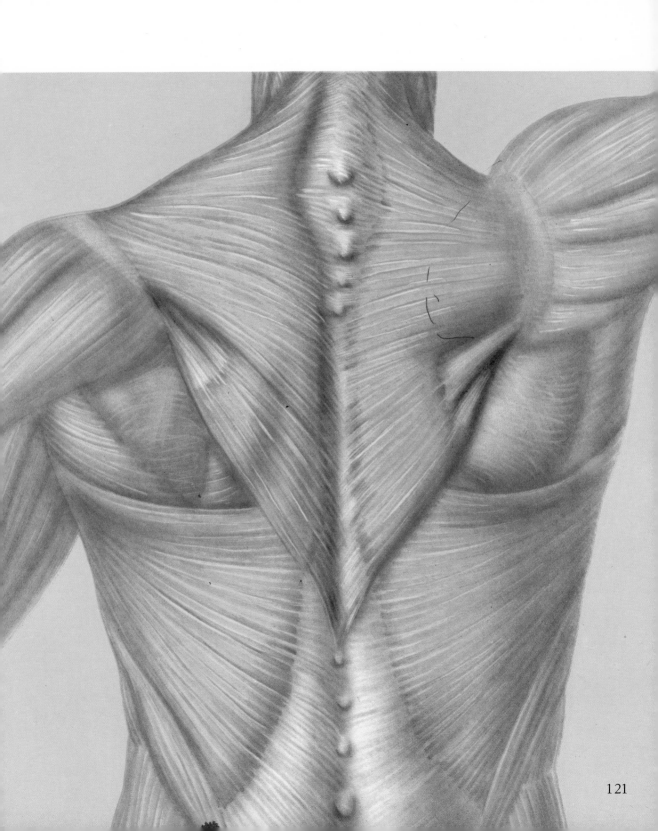

The muscles of the body are of many shapes. Some muscles overlap each other; some are twined in or around each other; some are squeezed in between other muscles and bones. All work together, though, to produce action.

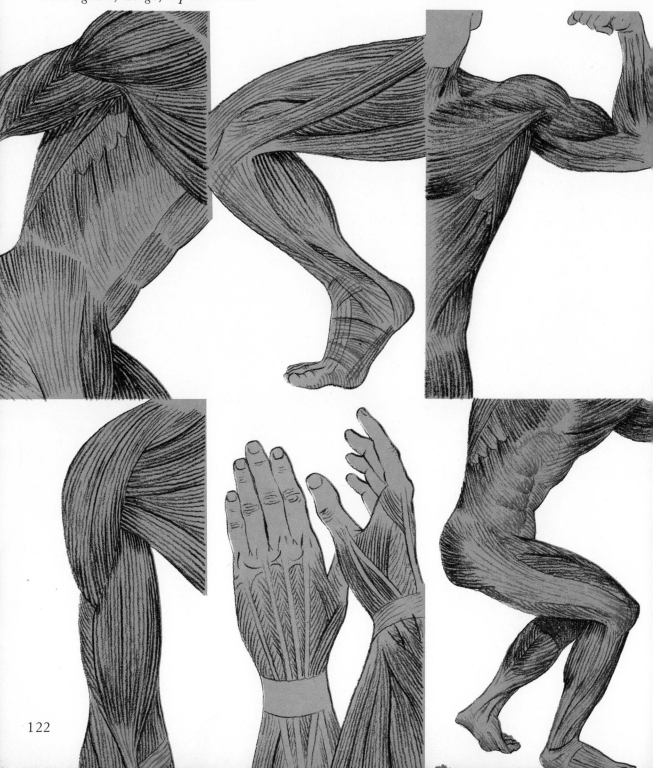

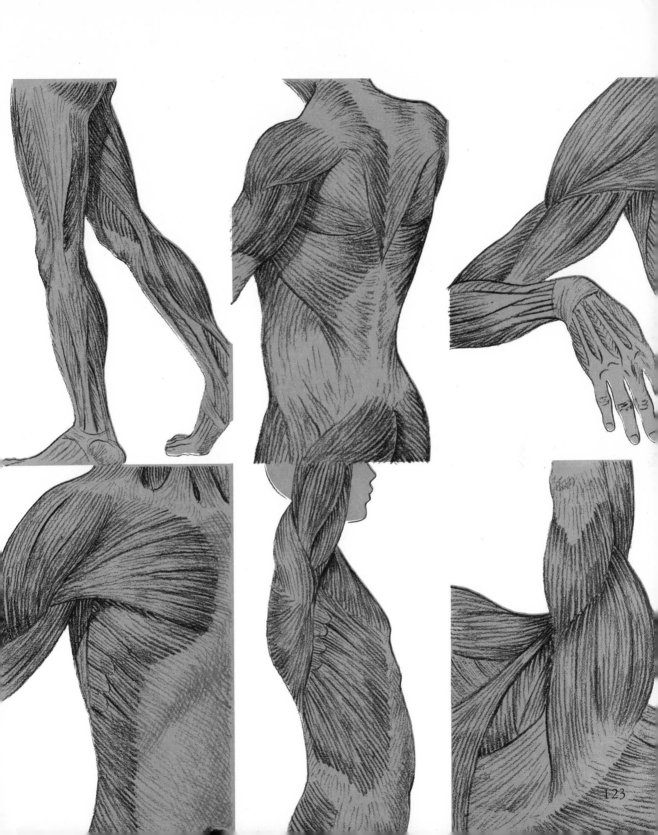

Some Active Games

Read the directions that are given for the two games below. Be ready to tell others how to play each of the games.

Run-Up-and-Kick-Back Relay

Equipment: 6 soccer balls or playground balls
Players: Even number, divided into four to six teams; line formation
Place: Playground, playroom, or gymnasium

The first player on each line runs with the ball to a goal line about 30 feet in front of the team. Each runner then turns, puts the ball on the goal line, and kicks it back to the team. The next player on each team receives the kicked ball, runs with it to the goal line, stands in front of the first player, and kicks the ball back to the third player on his team. The game continues until all players are lined up behind the goal line. The first team to be lined up behind the goal line wins.

Team Dodge Ball

Equipment: Volleyball or playground ball
Players: Class, divided into two teams
Place: Playground, playroom, or gymnasium

Members of one team form a circle approximately 20 feet in diameter. Members of the other team take positions inside the circle. The team members forming the circle try to hit with the ball as many running, dodging players of the opposing team as possible — in a time limit of two or three minutes. The hit must be below the waist.

(Instead of eliminating players hit, at the end of the specified time, ask all who have been hit once to raise their hands; those hit more than once should specify the number of times.) Continue the game with teams trading places. The team that has been hit the fewest times wins.

Something to Do

If you feel the need to relax—and cannot go outdoors or to the gym for active play—here are some relaxing exercises you can try:

Fill your lungs with air—as if you were blowing up a balloon. Breathe in, in, in, and in! Then slowly let the air out. Do it again.

Have someone in the group throw a paper handkerchief high in the air. The others laugh loudly until the handkerchief drops on the floor. Then all laughs must stop at once.

124

Some Good Stunts

Here are some stunts that many boys and girls your age enjoy doing. Be sure to keep in mind that there will be individual differences in the ability to do these stunts. Some of you may be able to perform the stunts easily; others of you may find them hard to do.

Dip

Kneel on the floor and place a well-crumpled piece of paper 12 inches in front of your knees. With your hands behind your back, bend and pick up the paper with your teeth.

Hand Wrestle

Two pupils face each other and grasp right hands — with each raising one foot behind him. At a signal, each tries to make the other touch either the free hand or foot to the floor.

Straight Leg Bend

Stand with your arms at your side and your heels together. Keeping your legs straight, try bending forward to touch the floor with your fingertips. If this is easy, try to place your hands flat on the floor and hold this position for five seconds.

Wicket Walk

Bend forward and grasp your ankles with your hands. Walk, keeping your legs straight.

Windmill

Stand with your feet apart and your arms raised high above your head. Bend forward, keeping your legs straight, and try to touch your left toe with your right hand. Return to starting position and bend forward again — this time touching your right toe with your left hand. If this is easy, try to touch your left heel with your right hand, then touch your right heel with your left hand.

Windmill

Can You Become More Skillful in Using Your Muscles?

Exercise can help you build strong muscles, and it can also help you become skillful in the use of your muscles. The more you use certain muscles, the more quickly and skillfully you are able to move. Your actions become better coördinated. And you waste less energy.

Do you remember when you first tried a new game such as softball or basketball? At first you may have found that you could not even hit the ball or make a basket. Not until you had practiced a lot could you hit the ball with a bat or make a basketball go into the basket. By much practicing, you made your muscles strong and able to move in a coordinated way.

Although lots of exercise can build strong muscles and can make you skillful in using them, you have to be careful not to exercise too much at one time. If you exercise strenuously for too long a time, your muscles become overtired.

When you are overtired, your muscles will not work so well as when you first started exercising. To make them work well again, you must stop and rest a little.

It is a good plan to "warm up" the muscles by light exercise before any *strenuous* exercise. Light exercise speeds up the work of the heart and lungs and gets them ready in a gradual way for strenuous exercise.

Have you noticed how basketball players always "warm up" by shooting baskets and by passing the ball from one player to another before the regular game begins? What additional examples of "warming up" exercise can you give?

Some Things to Think About

1. How does persistence help when you are learning to play a game such as baseball or basketball?

2. Why do people often become discouraged when they first try a new game or sport?

3. What are some good precautions about exercise to keep in mind?

4. What are some "warm-up" exercises you have seen high-school football or basketball players use? Why do they use these "warm-ups"?

126

What Do Food and Sleep Do for Muscles?

Food

Eating too little food — or not eating enough of the foods that build strong muscles and give you energy — can keep your muscles from working efficiently.

You will learn more about foods that make up a good daily diet in Unit 5. Foods from each of the four main food groups, shown on page 165, are needed to help you grow strong and well. No one of these foods is a "perfect" food. You need some foods from each group, all working together, to help the various body systems do their work.

Sleep

If you do not get enough sleep night after night, you may find that you cannot do things so well as usual the next day. Your muscles may be too tired to carry out the messages that come to them from the brain.

When you get plenty of sleep at night, you give your muscles a good chance to rest. Although sleep needs vary from one individual to another, most boys and girls your age need about ten hours of sleep each night.

A good way to check to see if you are getting enough sleep is to observe how you feel in the mornings. It is normal for some people to feel sleepy for a while after they first get up. The body does not always wake up completely at once. But when an early morning sleepiness does not go away within an hour or so, it is a good sign that a person probably needs more sleep.

How many hours of sleep did you get last night? Do you think it was enough? Be ready to explain your answer.

Some Things to Think About

1. Why do you think coaches encourage the players on their teams to get enough sleep?

2. What example can you think of when a lack of sleep kept you from performing as well as you should have the next day?

3. Can you think of a time when lack of sleep affected your ability to concentrate? Be ready to tell about it.

What Can You Do to Have Good Posture?

Before you think about how to improve your posture, you need to know just what posture *is*. Posture is the way you hold your body when you stand and sit and move about.

When you have good posture, your bones, muscles, and nervous system are working together properly to keep you "in balance." Your bones are in position to do the work they are designed to do. Your weight is spread properly over the parts of your body designed to support weight. You can sit or stand or move about without getting tired too soon. Good posture helps you feel comfortable and look attractive.

How can you maintain good posture or improve your posture if it needs improving? It helps, of course, to try to keep your body in balance when you sit and stand and walk. *But the most important thing you can do is to try to keep strong and well by following the guides for healthful living. Good posture goes along with good health.*

What are some of the guides for healthful living that you know about?

Perhaps getting enough of the right kinds of food comes to your mind first of all. That is certainly a factor in good posture. Getting enough sleep and exercise are important, too.

Shoes can affect your posture also. Can you explain or demonstrate how a person might walk if he is wearing shoes that do not fit right? On page 130 you will find some guides that will help you choose well-fitting shoes.

Learning to manage upset feelings can help your posture, too. How? You will learn more about feelings, or emotions, on pages 243–256.

Something to Think About
Some boys and girls were asked to suggest designs for changing the human body. Two of their suggestions were four hands and a swivel neck. What other suggestions could you make?

128

Health Questions Young People Often Ask

Perhaps after reading this unit on bones and muscles, you still have some questions you want answered.

Here are a few questions some boys and girls your age have wondered about. How would *you* answer each of these questions?

1. What are "flat feet"?
2. What is a "bone bank"?
3. What are the sinuses?
4. How can I buy shoes that fit?

After you have tried to answer each question, check your answers with the ones given below and on page 130. Be ready, too, to suggest some questions of your own about bones or muscles. How might you find the answers?

What Are "Flat Feet"?

There are different kinds of "flat feet." One kind is inherited. A person with this kind of foot difficulty is born with foot arches that are flat instead of curved. See the picture at the right. A person who is born with this foot structure usually adjusts to the condition and often has little or no trouble as a result.

There are other types of painful flat feet that sometimes develop long after birth. Flat feet of this kind may result from poor standing and walking habits. Then the muscles and ligaments that support the arches of the feet are weakened. In such cases, the feet may be forced into unnatural positions that are uncomfortable.

What Is a "Bone Bank"?

A "bone bank" is a deep-freeze storage place for human bones. These human bones may have come from the bodies of people who have died or from

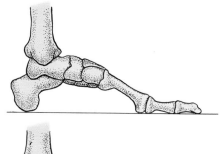

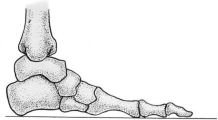

Top. *Side view of a foot with a normal curved arch*
Bottom. *Side view of a foot with a flat arch*

people who have lost various parts of the body in accidents. The "bone bank" can supply replacements for injured or diseased bones.

Increasingly, mechanical replacements are being used today. Thus knuckle joints that have been crippled by diseases like arthritis may be replaced by joints made of stainless steel, plastic, or some other substance. Metal hinges and specially made rods can sometimes be used to replace permanently injured joints of the knee, hip, or elbow.

What Are the Sinuses?

The sinuses are air cavities in the bones of the face. These hollow places open into the nose. The picture at the left will help you locate some of the main sinuses.

Usually the sinuses are healthy. They are lined with a membrane that is a continuation of the membrane of the nose. Sometimes when you have a cold the membrane that lines the sinuses swells and becomes infected. This condition is called "sinusitis," and it may need treatment by a doctor if it does not clear up in a few days.

How Can I Buy Shoes That Fit?

Here are a few guides that can help you in buying shoes:

1. When you are choosing new shoes, be sure to have both feet measured. Stand up while having feet measured, because your feet spread when they bear your full body weight.

2. If one foot is longer than the other, buy shoes that fit the longer foot.

3. Be sure the shoes fit snugly around the heel so that they do not slide up and down as you walk.

4. A space of about half an inch should be allowed between the tip of the longest toe and the tip of the shoe.

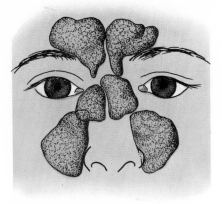

Here you can see some of the sinus cavities. Do you know that cigarette smoke, as well as a cold, may cause "sinusitis"? The cigarette smoke may sting and inflame the sinuses.

130

Check Yourself

1. Look back at the questions in the unit overview and at the top of page 98. How would you answer each question now?

2. Why are two muscles needed to make a bone move?

3. How would you describe each term?

a. ball-and-socket joints   e. hinge joints

b. cartilage   f. pelvis

c. cranium   g. spongy bone

d. fixed joints   h. vertebrae

4. What is the job of ligaments? Of tendons?

5. How would it affect you if your leg and arm bones were solid?

6. How do your bones grow stronger?

7. How do your bones grow in thickness and in length?

8. How would you describe these muscles?

a. involuntary muscles

b. heart muscle

c. voluntary muscles

9. How can you gain skill in using your muscles?

Things to Do

1. In which of the following activities are you using voluntary muscles?

writing   swimming

breathing   digesting food

2. Make an outline showing the important work that bones do. Here is a starter:

What Bones Do

I. Bones have many important functions

  A. Bones give the body support

  B.

3. Write a brief report on any of the following topics:

The Red Marrow in the Bones

The Wonderful Skeleton

How Feelings Affect Posture

How to Build Strong, Skillful Muscles

4. Ask a butcher for some bones. Make an exhibit of compact bone, spongy bone, marrow, flat bones, long bones, joints.

Self-Help Review

Use a ruler or a strip of paper to cover the answer column at the right. Read the first item and write the missing word or words on a piece of paper. Then move your ruler or paper strip down to uncover the answer and see if you are right. Go on in the same way with each of the other items. Do not write in this book.

The numbers by the answers show the pages in this book that give information about the subject. For the items you miss, go back and review this information.

1. Each bone in your skeleton is of the right _____ and _____ to do its special work.

size, shape 98

2. The bones of the skull that enclose the brain are known as the _____.

cranium 99

3. Between the bones of the spine are little pads of _____ that serve as shock absorbers.

cartilage 99

4. The rib cage protects the heart and the _____.

lungs 100

5. The red _____ found in the long bones of the body makes red blood _____.

marrow, cells 111

6. The strong bands that hold one bone to another are called _____.

ligaments 113

7. Tough, stringy bands that fasten muscles to nearby bones are called _____.

tendons 113

8. Muscles in the body that you do not start or stop are known as _____ muscles.

involuntary 116

Health Test for Unit Four

Part I

Copy each number on a piece of paper. After the number write the name of the thing that best answers the description.

1. Movable bone in the skull.
2. Protective cage of bones.
3. Tough, stringy bands that hold the bones together.
4. Tough, stringy bands that fasten muscles to bones.
5. Hard, outer layer of bone.
6. Soft yellow or red substance inside some bones.
7. Places where the ends of two bones fit together.
8. Muscles that work according to orders from the brain.
9. Muscles that work without orders from the brain.
10. Many little irregular-shaped bones of the spine.
11. Muscles that, with some fat, cover the skeleton.
12. All the bones of the head.
13. Cup-shaped cavity formed by hipbones and end of the backbone.
14. Body joints that do not move.
15. Joints that allow movement back and forth in only one direction.
16. Joints that allow movement in all directions.

Part II

Copy each number on a piece of paper. After the number write the letter that goes with the *best* answer choice.

17. In the skeleton there are
   a. some 1000 bones
   b. some 200 or so bones
   c. some 40 bones
18. Ribs are connected in back to the
   a. kidneys
   b. hipbones
   c. backbone
19. Movable joints are protected by a special fluid that
   a. keeps them moist and moving smoothly
   b. glues them together
   c. manufactures red blood cells
20. Involuntary muscles are found
   a. on the skeleton
   b. in the sacrum
   c. in the body organs

Number of Answers   20
Number Right   _____
Score (Number Right x 5)   _____

Part III

Copy each number on a piece of paper. After the number write the correct answer, *true* or *false*.

1. Bones are of different sizes and shapes.

2. Muscles are all the same size and shape.

3. Another term for the backbone is the spinal cord.

4. The jawbone is the one bone in the skull that cannot move.

5. Each of the vertebrae in the backbone has a hole in it.

6. All of the ribs in the rib cage are floating ribs.

7. Your skeleton would be more efficient if your arm bones and leg bones were completely solid.

8. The hand is made up of many short bones.

9. Your thumb makes it possible for you to become skillful in holding things and picking up things.

10. A hinge joint is found at the knee.

11. A ball-and-socket joint is found at the elbow.

12. Ligaments and tendons help keep the bones in place.

13. Spongy bone has many little holes in it.

14. Red marrow found in the long bones manufactures red blood cells.

15. The food you eat is important in helping build strong bones.

16. A growth plate is a kind of dish.

17. There are no muscles to be found in your face.

18. The trunk extends from the head to the toes.

19. Upset feelings can affect the way the muscles work.

20. Smooth muscles are found in such organs as the stomach.

Number of Answers	20
Number Right	———
Score (Number Right x 5)	———

5 How Does Your Body Digest Food?

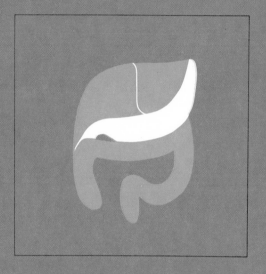

No doubt you have often wondered just what happens to the food you eat. What does the body do with it? How does this food help you? How do you choose the foods that can keep you strong, healthy, and looking your best?

You will find answers to these questions in this unit. You will discover, too, some fascinating stories of how people first began to learn the story of digestion.

Read to Find Out

1. *How have we learned about digestion?*

2. *What happens to food in the mouth? In the stomach? In the small intestine?*

3. *Why do you need teeth of different shapes?*

4. *How does the body get rid of wastes?*

5. *What important things does food do for the body?*

6. *How can you make sure you are getting enough of the right kinds of foods each day?*

How Have We Learned About Digestion?

One of the questions young people your age frequently ask is "What happens to the food we eat?"

Today, of course, you can find answers to that question in books like this one. But if you had been living about two hundred years ago, you could not have gone to books for correct information. At that time no one *knew* the answer for sure, although a few people had written books telling their ideas about the work of the stomach. Many of their ideas, as it turned out later, were wrong—but some were right!

Suppose you had been a scientist living in the mid-1700's, and you wanted to know about the work of the stomach in digesting food. There were no books then with full information. Nor were there medical tools such as X-ray machines to help you see inside the body. *How would you have gone about seeking in a scientific way the information you desired?*

Now that you have thought about the problems that faced a scientist some two hundred years ago,

Something to Do

Do you know exactly what is meant by the term digestion? *Check your ideas with the Glossary on page 271 of this book.*

136

you may be particularly interested to find how a few of these scientists went about seeking information. When you read about some of these people in the sections that follow, you will probably be fascinated by the experiments they tried. You will also learn some interesting facts about the part the stomach plays in the digestive process.

René de Réaumur and His Pet Kite

About 1750 or so, the seventy-year-old French scientist René de Réaumur was puzzling over the problem of what happens to food in the stomach. He knew that many wise people of his time thought food was digested simply by churning movements in the stomach. But he was not sure this was the whole truth.

Réaumur kept wishing he could study some food that had been in a stomach. Such a study, he thought, would indicate whether the food had just been crushed to pieces by the stomach's movements or *if something else had happened to it as well.*

One day an idea came to him as he watched his pet kite, a bird that resembles a hawk. The bird always vomited food it could not digest. So Réaumur decided to use the pet kite in some experiments.

In one experiment, Réaumur put small pieces of sponge into a tiny, round metal tube with holes in it. Then he let the bird swallow the tube.

The bird could not digest the metal tube and, before long, up it came. Réaumur took the sponges out of the metal tube and examined them carefully. He found that they weighed about five times more than when he had put them in the tube.

Next Réaumur squeezed out the liquid that the sponges had soaked up while in the bird's stomach. The juice was salty. When Réaumur dropped a bit

René de Réaumur

of it on blue *litmus paper*, the litmus paper turned red. This meant the juice had acid in it.

Réaumur repeated this experiment with the bird. Later he did a similar experiment with chickens and other animals. The results were the same.

Then he put some of the juice he got out of the animals' stomachs into jars in his laboratory. He found that if he dropped bits of meat and bone into these jars, the juice would soften the food and even dissolve some of it.

After a while, Réaumur gave a name to this stomach juice. He called it *gastric juice*, from the Greek word *gaster* which means stomach.

As a result of his experiments, Réaumur was able to point out that *the stomach does more than crush and churn food. It is also a "chemical factory" that makes an acid juice to help digest food.*

Lazaro Spallanzani and His Little Bags of Linen

In 1780, some years after Réaumur's experiments, an Italian scientist became interested in the same question: *What happens to food in the stomach?*

This scientist, named Lazaro Spallanzani, had read of Réaumur's work. He decided to try the same experiments, using birds and other animals as Réaumur had. This he did—and his results were the same as those of the French scientist. Spallanzani, too, found that acid juice from the stomachs of animals would soften and dissolve food.

He was still curious, however. He wondered if the *human* stomach worked in the same way that the stomachs of animals did. He decided that the best way to find out would be to experiment some more. So he experimented with his own stomach.

In one experiment he put into a tiny linen bag some food that he had chewed. After fastening a long string to the bag, he swallowed it. Later he

Some Things to Think About
1. What problem did Réaumur want to solve?
2. What was the experiment with his bird? Describe his purpose, materials, and steps in the experiment, as well as his conclusion.
3. Why did he repeat the experiment many times?
4. What other things did he do to learn more about the juice from the animals' stomachs?
5. What main conclusion did Réaumur draw from all his experiments?

138

pulled up the bag by the string. The bag was empty! The gastric juice in the stomach had dissolved the chewed food. And the dissolved food had then soaked out of the linen bag.

In another experiment Spallanzani used two linen bags. In one bag he put a piece of meat that he had first chewed well; in the other bag he put a piece of unchewed meat. Then he swallowed the two bags. Later he pulled them up and found that the bag with the chewed meat was empty. But the bag with the unchewed meat still had meat in it.

Spallanzani's experiments proved that Réaumur's ideas about the work of the stomach were correct. They applied to Man as well as animals. The stomach *is* a "chemical factory" that manufactures gastric juice which helps dissolve food.

Spallanzani added some new ideas, too. From his experiments it became clear that *chewing* is important in the digestion of food. The chewing of the food in the mouth, as well as the churning movements of the stomach, causes food to be broken into tiny pieces. These tiny pieces mix with the gastric juice more easily and make it possible for food to be dissolved in the stomach more quickly.

There was something else that Spallanzani *did not* know. He did not know that *saliva* in the mouth has the ability to break down, or change, some of the foods that are chewed. This was a discovery that was left for other scientists to reveal.

Dr. William Beaumont Watches a Stomach at Work

The next fascinating chapter in the discovery of what happens to food in the stomach took place between the years 1822 and 1833. This story centers around William Beaumont, a United States Army doctor. A strange accident let Beaumont see inside a man's stomach and watch it work.

Lazaro Spallanzani

The story of Beaumont and his experiments had its beginning in June of 1822 at an army post in northern Michigan. At that time Beaumont was called upon to care for a man named Alexis St. Martin.

This man had been traveling near the remote army post when he was accidentally shot. The bullet made a big hole in St. Martin's side, and it tore open part of his stomach. Although Beaumont did not think the victim could possibly live, he cleaned out the injured man's wound and nursed him with great care.

In time, St. Martin did get better, but the hole in his stomach never completely closed up. It stayed open, and a flap of loose skin came down over it. The doctor could lift up this flap and watch the stomach at work.

One day it occurred to Beaumont that he might use the opening in St. Martin's stomach for some studies on digestion. The doctor asked St. Martin to work for him and to let him try out some experiments. St. Martin coöperated, and later he traveled with the doctor to other army posts so the experiments could continue.

In the next ten years or so, Beaumont did more than a hundred experiments. In some experiments he put pieces of food, tied to a string, directly into St. Martin's stomach. Then he watched what happened. He also watched the stomach work after food had been chewed and swallowed naturally. He kept a careful record of everything he did and of everything that happened.

Beaumont learned that the stomach finished its work more quickly with some foods than with others. Foods like bread and potatoes were ready to leave the stomach within an hour or so. But

Do You Know?

Alcohol may damage the stomach of a person who is a frequent and heavy user of alcoholic drinks. One of Beaumont's experiments will help you understand why this is so. Read page 141 to find out about this experiment.

protein foods, like meat and eggs, stayed in the stomach for three or four hours or longer.

Another thing the doctor noted was the importance of the work of the teeth and the saliva in digestion. The food that St. Martin chewed thoroughly and swallowed was dissolved more quickly and easily than the food that was put directly into his stomach through the open flap. Food digested better when meals were eaten regularly and when the stomach had a chance to rest between meals.

Beaumont learned that when St. Martin was worried, angry, or unhappy, the gastric juice in his stomach did not flow so freely as it usually did. With less gastric juice, the stomach could not do its work so well. However, when the man was happy and calm, the gastric juice poured out freely to mix with the food. Then the stomach was able to do a good job of churning the food and mixing it with the gastric juice.

St. Martin's stomach worked better when he was fairly quiet than when he was exercising. If he sat quietly for a while after a meal, his stomach digested food more easily than if he cut wood.

Some other important things the doctor reported were that alcoholic drinks made the lining of the stomach red and sore-looking. Then again the stomach did not seem to work so well.

In watching the churning of food in the stomach, Beaumont discovered also that the stomach has two kinds of movements — crosswise and lengthwise ones.

Thus it happened that — even before the discovery of X rays — a curious-minded doctor in backwoods country was able to show what happens in the stomach. (On page 149, see an X-ray picture of the kind available to doctors today.)

William Beaumont

What Is the Complete Story of Digestion?

Experiments and studies to learn about the stomach did not stop with Beaumont. Others went on to learn still more about the work of the stomach and to add to the story of how food is digested.

X rays were discovered, for example, in 1895 and soon came into wide use. And in recent years such new tools as the electron microscope and the color camera have been developed. These tools have aided scientists who are still at work trying to understand even more fully the process of digestion.

Today a rather complete story of how food is digested can be told. You will find this story in the material that follows. As you read this material, refer to the pictures on pages 149 – 156.

Digestion Starts in the Mouth

Many things must happen to the food you eat before your body can make use of it.

The food must be broken down into tiny particles that can be carried throughout the body by the blood and that can enter the cells of your body. The process of breaking down food into a form that the body can use is called *digestion.*

Digestion starts as soon as you put some food into your mouth. Your teeth cut, tear, crush, and grind the food into small bits. As the food is chewed, the liquid *saliva* is poured onto it from three pairs of *salivary glands* that empty into the mouth. The thought of food — or the smell, sight, or taste of it — can start the flow of saliva.

Saliva moistens the food and makes it soft and easy to swallow. Saliva also helps digestion in another way. It contains chemicals that start changing the starch in such foods as bread and potatoes into one form of sugar. Starch will not dissolve in

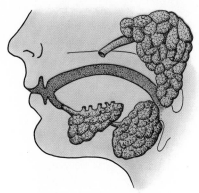

The three salivary glands on one side of the face. Ducts from these glands open into the mouth.

water, but sugar will; and since everything in food must be dissolved in liquid before it can be used by the body, the starch must be broken down during digestion.

You cannot taste food until it begins to dissolve. Thus saliva helps you taste the food you eat.

As the food is being chewed and moistened in your mouth, the tongue is at work, too. It forms the food into soft balls and then pushes them to the back of your mouth.

At the back of the mouth is the food tube, or *esophagus*, which leads to the stomach.

As the food starts down this tube, the roof of your mouth lifts back, covering the passage that leads to your nose. And a thin layer of cartilage, the *epiglottis*, covers the windpipe during swallowing. Thus food is prevented from "going down the wrong way."

Food that passes down the food tube does not just drop down. The food is pushed along by rings of muscles in the walls of the tube. This action is called *peristalsis*. Because of the action of these muscles that squeeze and push food along, it would be possible for you to swallow food even if you were standing on your head.

What Happens in the Stomach

Food that you have swallowed reaches the stomach in about five seconds. A glass of water can make the trip from mouth to stomach in even less time.

The stomach is rather small when it is empty. However, it is a bag made of muscle, and it stretches greatly when food comes into it.

When food enters the stomach, gastric juice pours out of many small glands in the stomach walls. This gastric juice contains chemicals that act on proteins and a few fats. The chemicals change

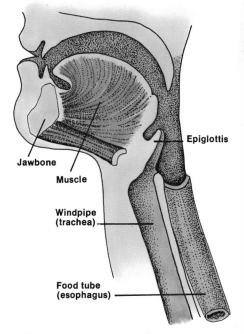

Which part shown here keeps food from going into the windpipe?

143

these foods into simpler forms that will dissolve more easily.

The saliva mixed with the food before it is swallowed also continues for a while to change the starches in the food into sugars. This is why thorough chewing of food to mix it well with saliva helps in the process of digestion.

Muscles then make the stomach walls twist and bend. These movements churn the food and mix it thoroughly with the gastric juice. Some of the food is dissolved by this strong gastric juice.

You may wonder why the strong digestive juice does not dissolve the walls of the stomach. It would do just that if it were not for a slippery substance called *mucus* which protects the stomach walls. This mucus also helps the food slide easily into the small intestine.

Some of the food eaten is ready to leave the stomach shortly after you have had a meal. It takes from two to five hours, however, for all the food that is eaten at a meal to move out of the stomach and into the small intestine. Foods high in fat remain longest in the stomach.

When food is ready to be moved through the muscle gateway from the stomach to the small intestine, it is in the form of a thick liquid called *chyme.* This thick liquid is squeezed out of the stomach by special muscles and sent into the small intestine a little at a time.

What Happens in the Small Intestine

The *small intestine*, or small bowel, is a coiled tube. If it were straightened out and measured, it would be found to be some 20 feet in length in a person your age. Of course, there is not room for the small intestine to be stretched at full length in your body. In spite of its great length, the small

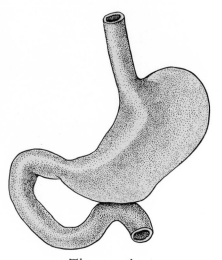

The stomach

intestine is not very big around; it gets its name, in fact, because of its narrow passage.

As the partly digested food moves into the small intestine, more digestive juices come from the walls of the small intestine itself. Other juices come from nearby organs and pour into the small intestine through little tubes, or *ducts*. These nearby organs are the *pancreas* and *liver*. (See the liver pictured on page 154.)

As a result of all these juices that pour over the partly digested food, digestion is completed in the small intestine. Most of the food by this time is dissolved by the various juices and is in a thin and watery form.

This dissolved part of the food is now ready for an amazing thing to happen to it. *It begins to pass out of the small intestine into the blood—not by going through any opening, but by passing through the walls of the small intestine itself.*

You may wonder just how this dissolved food can pass through the walls of the small intestine. The walls of the small intestine are lined with tiny fingerlike parts called *villi*. Each of the villi is about the size of a comma on this page.

The villi are right in the path of the digested food as it moves along—still pushed by the action of peristalsis. The now-watery dissolved food passes into the thin walls of the tiny blood capillaries in each of the villi.

Once the dissolved food enters the tiny capillaries and gets into the blood, the blood carries the food to all parts of the body.

This dissolved food is left by the blood wherever cells in your body are growing or need repairing —or wherever the different parts of the body need energy to help them do their work.

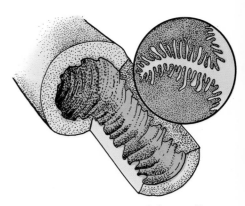

An inside view of the small intestine, showing villi

Some of the dissolved food is not needed at once by the body. So it is changed into forms that can be stored until needed. Some of the food is stored in the liver, some in the muscles, and some under the skin as fat.

What Happens in the Large Intestine

So far you have been learning about the part of the dissolved food that is watery enough to pass through the walls of the small intestine.

However, some of the food in the small intestine has not been broken down enough to pass through these walls. This material, which cannot be digested, is pushed by muscles of the small intestine into the *large intestine*, or the *large bowel*. (See the picture at the left.)

The large intestine is a wide tube—about an inch across. Although it is wider than the small intestine, it is not quite five feet long in a person your age.

When this material that your body has not been able to break down first enters the large intestine, it is a semiliquid mass. Gradually most of the water is drawn off through the walls of the large intestine into your blood stream.

The leftover material is made up of such things as fruit skins, seeds, outer parts of grain, and the stringlike parts of some vegetables. This undigested material, which also contains bacteria and some digestive juices, is called *roughage*. Almost everything that is useful to the body has been removed.

When your large intestine begins to fill up, this leftover material pushes against the walls of the intestine. This pushing action causes the muscles in the walls to begin working. These muscles squeeze the material along to an opening at the end of the large intestine. Then the leftover material, or

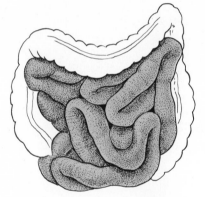

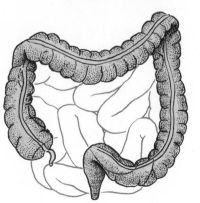

Top. *Small intestine*
Bottom. *Large intestine*

146

waste material, is ready to be pushed out of your body in a bowel movement. The time required for digestion—from the time food is eaten until the undigested leftovers are passed from the body—may be from 10 to 20 hours.

The waste material is moved out of your body through bowel movements at fairly regular time intervals.

It is not necessary for a person to have a bowel movement every day or at the same time every day in order to be healthy—although it is a good health practice to have regular habits in taking care of your body's needs.

Factors That Affect Digestion

If you follow the guides for healthful living, you can help your digestive system work in the way that is right for you.

There is something else that affects the way your digestive system works. And that is your feelings, or emotions.

When you read about Beaumont's unusual patient, you learned that when he was worried or angry or unhappy, his stomach did not work so well as it usually did. The gastric juice did not flow freely. But in some people just the opposite happens. When they are upset emotionally, the gastric juice pours out too freely in the stomach, and this speed-up affects other organs of digestion.

The same thing is true of the intestines. When a person is worried or unhappy, the intestines do not work so well either. In some people the action of the intestines is speeded up; in other people the action is likely to be slowed down. Because feelings can affect the digestion, it is a good idea to try to learn to manage them. (See the discussion of emotions on pages 243–256.)

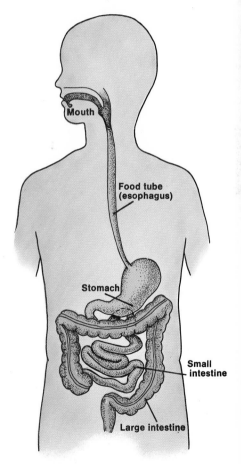

Some important parts of the digestive system

Getting Rid of Liquid Body Wastes

The large intestine gets rid of the solid wastes of digestion. But your body produces liquid waste materials it must get rid of, too.

Two organs that are concerned with getting rid of these liquid wastes are the *kidneys*. The kidneys are bean-shaped structures that are located high up in your back, under the lowest ribs. (See the pictures on pages 155 and 156.)

There is one kidney on the left side and another on the right side. Although you have two kidneys, you can live with just one, if necessary. The one kidney takes over the work formerly done by both.

Thousands of little filtering tubes in the kidneys take out of the blood excess water, cell wastes, and a few other materials the body cannot use. These substances come into the filtering tubes through the tiny blood capillaries. Other substances that are of value are in time reabsorbed into the blood.

One of the substances that is reabsorbed is water, which is essential for the body's transportation system. The remaining waste material — the material that is not reabsorbed in the kidneys — is known as *urine*. Urine flows through a small tube from each kidney into the *urinary bladder*. The bladder is a muscular bag in the lower abdomen.

Your bladder stores the urine and, like the large intestine, the bladder warns you when it is ready to be emptied. Then a special muscle at the lower end of the bladder relaxes long enough to allow the urine to leave the body during urination. From three to six glasses of waste water are passed off as urine each day. To help replenish the liquid, make a habit of drinking water at regular times, such as before breakfast and at playtime. Also whenever possible, drink water when you feel thirsty.

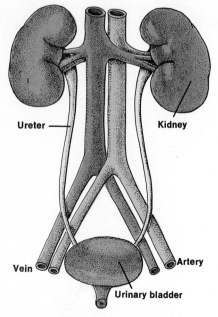

Some urinary organs

Ureter

Kidney

Vein

Artery

Urinary bladder

The Body Digests Food and Gets Rid of Wastes

Doctors today can study X-ray pictures to see how well the body's organs are working. This X-ray picture shows the stomach and small intestine of a ten-year-old patient. He drank a special chemical that made these organs show up on the X-ray film.

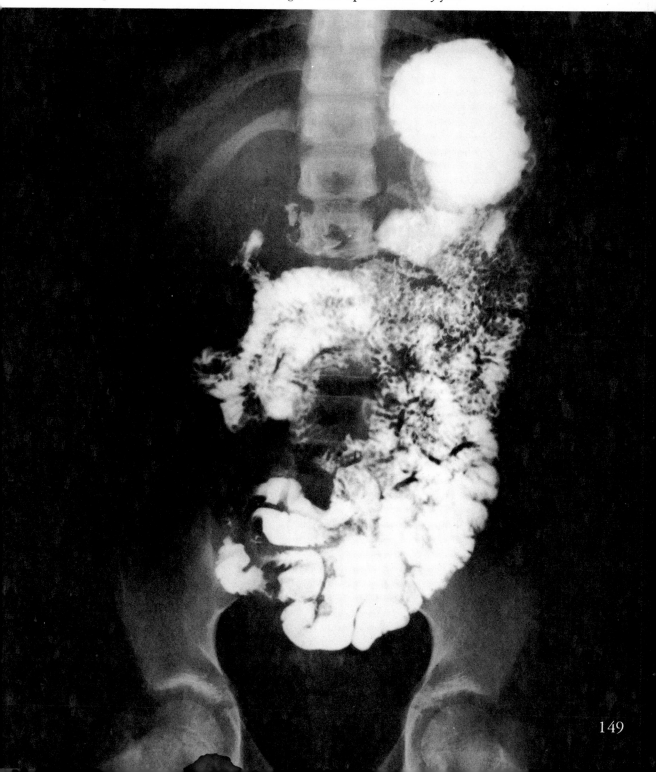

**How Food Is Digested:
A Diagram**

1. Teeth:
Crush and grind foods.
2. Salivary glands
pour juices
onto food.
Food
3. Esophagus:
All food
goes down
this tube.
Stomach
4. Food is churned
in the stomach
and acted upon
by certain
digestive juices.
Pancreas
5. Pancreas sends
digestive juices
to small intestine
to aid in digestion.
6. Liver makes bile
and sends it to
small intestine
to aid in digestion.
Liver
7. Gall bladder
stores extra bile.
10. Some sugars
are returned and stored
in the liver.

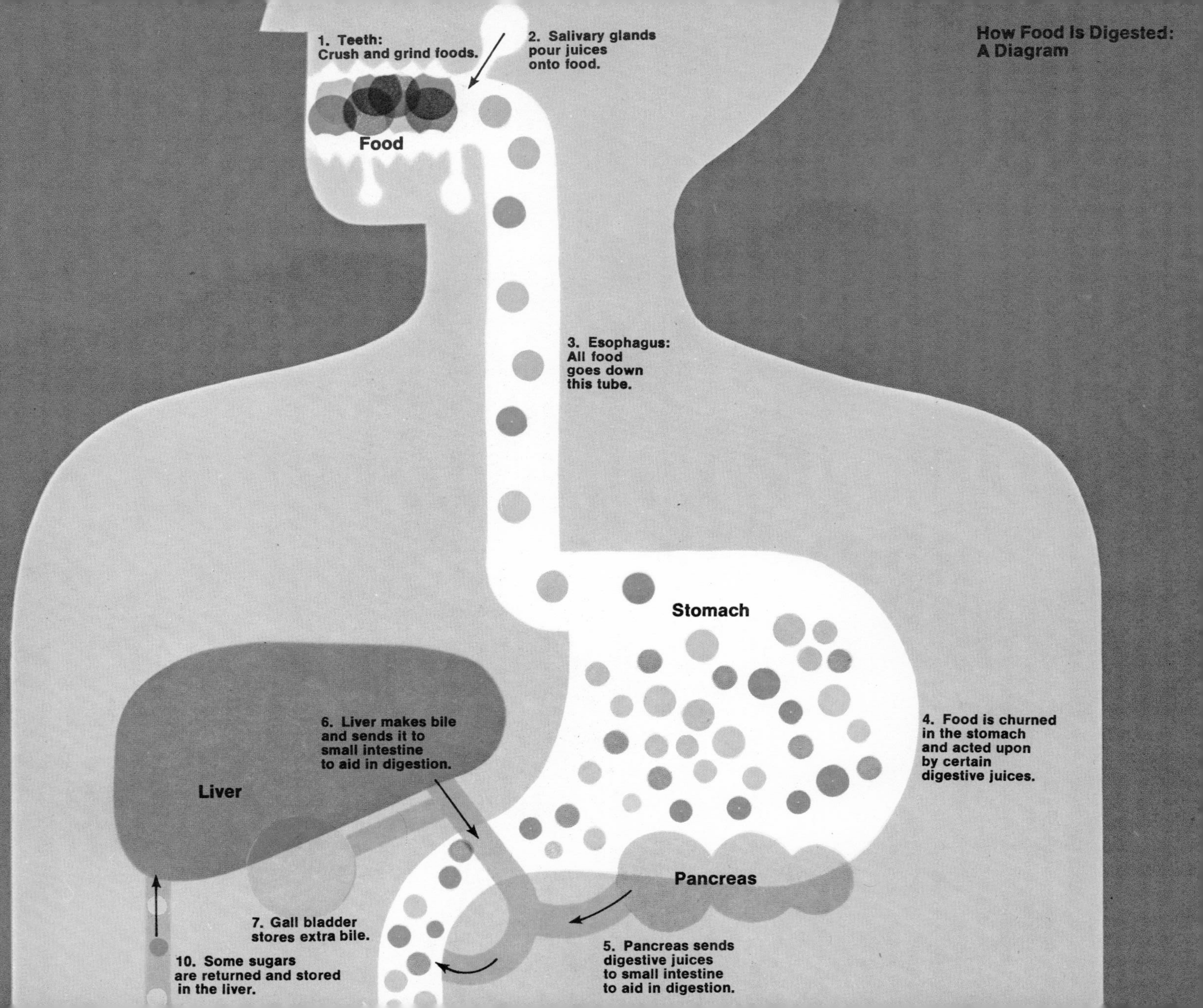

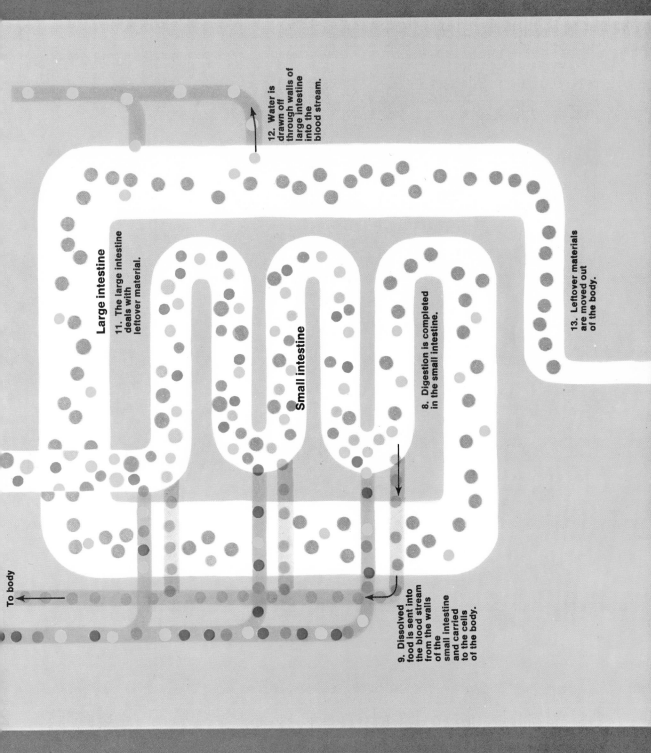

Large intestine

11. The large intestine deals with leftover material.

Small intestine

12. Water is drawn off through walls of large intestine into the blood stream.

13. Leftover materials are moved out of the body.

8. Digestion is completed in the small intestine.

9. Dissolved food is sent into the blood stream from the walls of the small intestine and carried to the cells of the body.

To body

After you have eaten a meal, it takes from four to six hours for the food to be ready to leave the stomach. Notice the changes in the shape of the stomach during digestion.

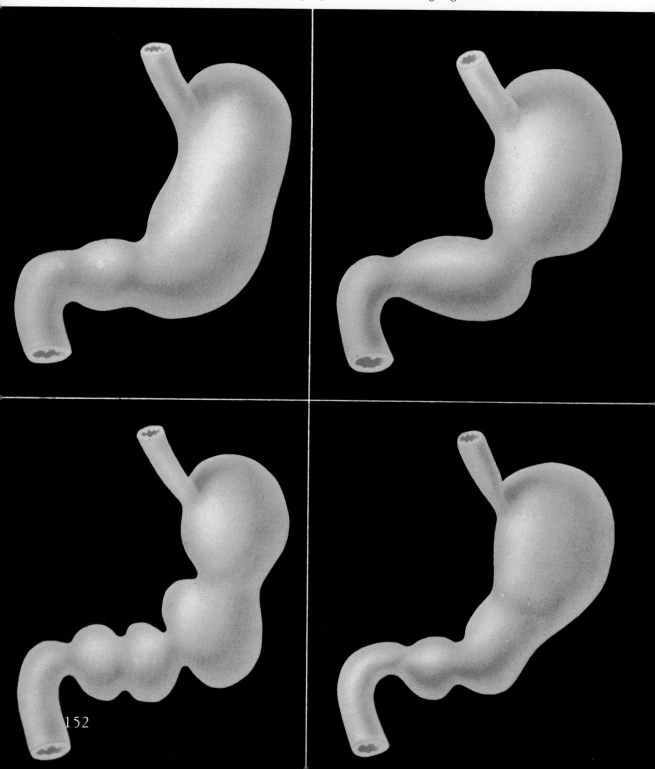

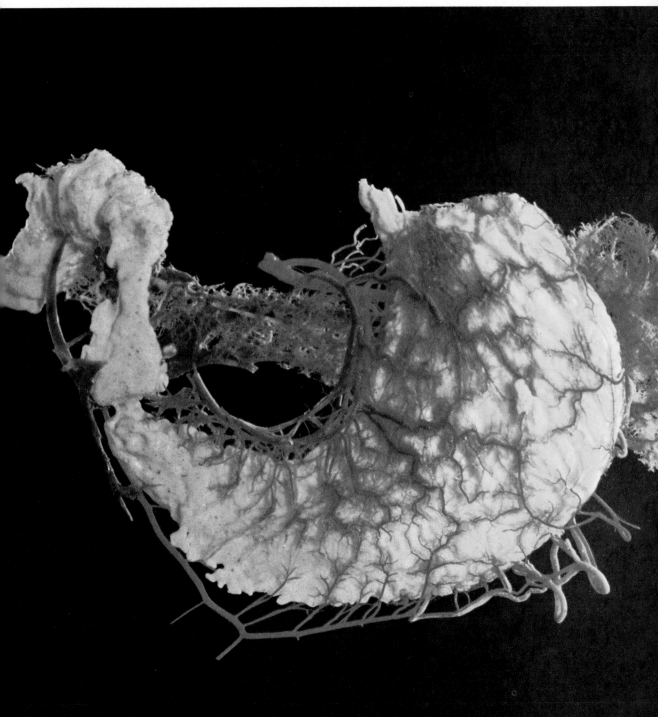

This model of the liver and gall bladder—shown from the back—was made in a health museum in Cologne, Germany. Bile made in the liver is stored in the gall bladder. Notice the network of blood vessels in the liver.

Another model from the health museum in Cologne, Germany, shows a single kidney and part of the tube that leads from it to the bladder. Notice the large artery that brings blood to the kidney and the large vein that returns the filtered blood to the circulation.

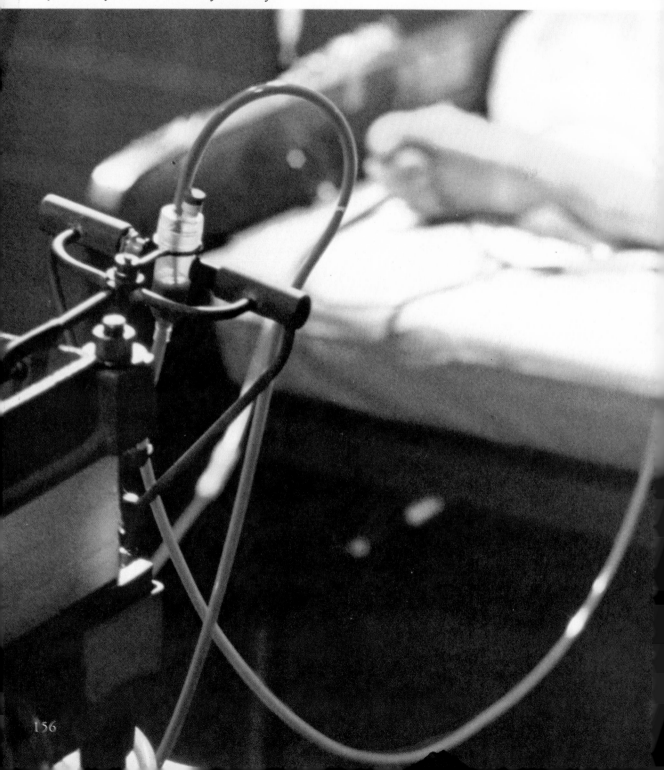

How Do Your Teeth Aid in Digestion?

You had some clues, in the stories of experiments done by early scientists, that the teeth aid in digestion. Spallanzani, for example, discovered that well-chewed food is more easily dissolved in the stomach than is unchewed or poorly chewed food.

Do you recall any of Beaumont's experiments that indicated the importance of the teeth in digestion? What did he find out?

There are demonstrations *you* can do, too, to show that the teeth help in digesting food by breaking it up into small pieces. For instance, one such demonstration is described on page 174 in column two. How do you carry it out?

Your Teeth and Their Jobs

Your teeth work together to cut, tear, crush, and grind food. To do their work, teeth of different shapes are needed.

The front teeth are called *incisors*. There are eight of these teeth, four in each jaw. They cut food. The incisors in the upper jaw come together with those in the lower jaw to do the job.

When the incisors have done their work, food is moved to the sides of the mouth. Here teeth called *cuspids* tear up the pieces into smaller bits. Cuspids get their name because each one has a cusp, or point, on the chewing surface. You have four cuspids — one on each side of your upper jaw and one on each side of your lower jaw.

Next to the cuspids in your first set of teeth are the primary or baby molars. Sometime when you are between nine and eleven years old, these teeth are shed. Teeth that are called *bicuspids* grow in to replace them. The bicuspids have two cusps, or points. The upper and lower bicuspids come

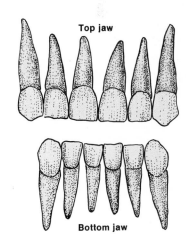

Top jaw

Bottom jaw

Eight incisors (four in the top jaw and four in the bottom) and four cuspids (two in the top jaw and two in the bottom) are shown in this diagram.

157

together to crush food into even smaller pieces. You will have eight of these bicuspids in your set of permanent teeth—two on each side of your upper and lower jaws.

Next the real work of chewing food is done with the teeth called *molars*. These molars are in the back of the mouth. Molars have broad tops with four or five cusps on them. Molars grind food into tiny bits.

When all your permanent teeth have come in, you will have twelve molars—three molars on each side of the upper jaw and three molars on each side of the lower jaw.

When you were six years old or so, your first permanent molars came in. Because of the time at which they come through, or *erupt*, these molars are known as *six-year molars*. The six-year molars are often called the most important teeth in the mouth. They must carry on the important job of chewing and grinding food during the years when your primary teeth are being replaced by your full set of permanent teeth. Your bite depends on the position of the first permanent molars.

Now look at the picture of the permanent teeth on page 161. Most of these teeth are in your mouth now. Which ones are they? Which teeth have yet to erupt in your mouth?

Taking Care of Your Teeth

You need every tooth in your jaw for the important work of cutting, tearing, crushing, and grinding food so that it can be more easily digested.

Because you need all your teeth, you should take care of them. No other teeth will grow in to take the place of your permanent teeth. To replace teeth that have been extracted can be expensive and sometimes unsatisfactory. (See the pictures on pages 160–162.)

Flossing removes plaque and bits of food from between the teeth especially near the gum line. It is important that you clean these areas daily with dental floss because decay and gum disease often start in these areas. These are places where your toothbrush cannot reach.
Hold the floss tightly (there should be no slack), and use a gentle sawing motion to insert the floss between your teeth. Never "snap" the floss into the gums! When the floss reaches the gum line curve it into a C-shape against one tooth and gently slide it into the space between the gum and the tooth until you feel resistance.

It may interest you to know that the most common health problem found among school-age youngsters is that of tooth decay.

Some communities add very small amounts of *fluorides* to the drinking water if it is not already present in the water. This practice is known as *fluoridation.* Fluoridation helps develop strong tooth enamel in children and thus reduces tooth decay.

Additional research is being done to find other substances to help reduce tooth decay. Some of these substances may eventually be added to foods such as bread and cereal. Some toothpastes also contain substances that help prevent tooth decay. Look at the tube of toothpaste you have at home. See if it has a statement on it from the American Dental Association. What does the statement say?

There is something else you should remember about tooth care and that is to be careful of the sweets you eat—sweets such as candy, cake, and soft drinks with sugar. Try not to let them stay on your teeth, for sweets left on the teeth even for short periods can cause tooth decay. To understand why this is so, you need to know some things about *dental plaque.*

Plaque is a sticky, colorless film of harmful bacteria that is always forming on the teeth. It is formed from the germs that normally live in the mouth and thus is found even in a healthy mouth.

Certain bacteria in the plaque change sugars in the mouth into acids. These acids begin the tooth-decay process that can cause cavities.

Plaque should be removed daily by careful brushing and flossing of the teeth. If you can, you should brush and floss your teeth after you eat. Be sure to clean your teeth thoroughly at least once a day. Also have regular dental checkups.

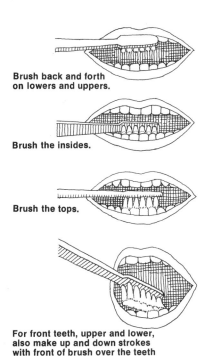

Brush back and forth on lowers and uppers.

Brush the insides.

Brush the tops.

For front teeth, upper and lower, also make up and down strokes with front of brush over the teeth and gum tissue.

Besides brushing the teeth, you should also use dental floss to remove the plaque between your teeth.

159

Your Teeth

Study the diagram below to get an idea of how the inside of a tooth looks. Find these layers: enamel, cementum, dentin, and pulp.

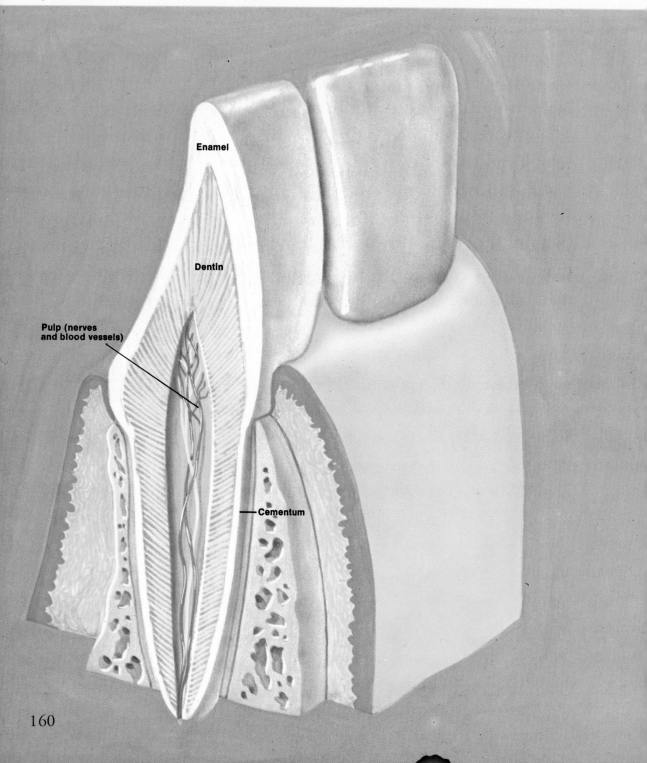

Enamel

Dentin

Pulp (nerves and blood vessels)

Cementum

160

Every tooth in your mouth has its work to do in the cutting and tearing and grinding of food. If even a few teeth are missing, the food will not be broken up properly. Your teeth also help give shape to your face and aid in clear speech.

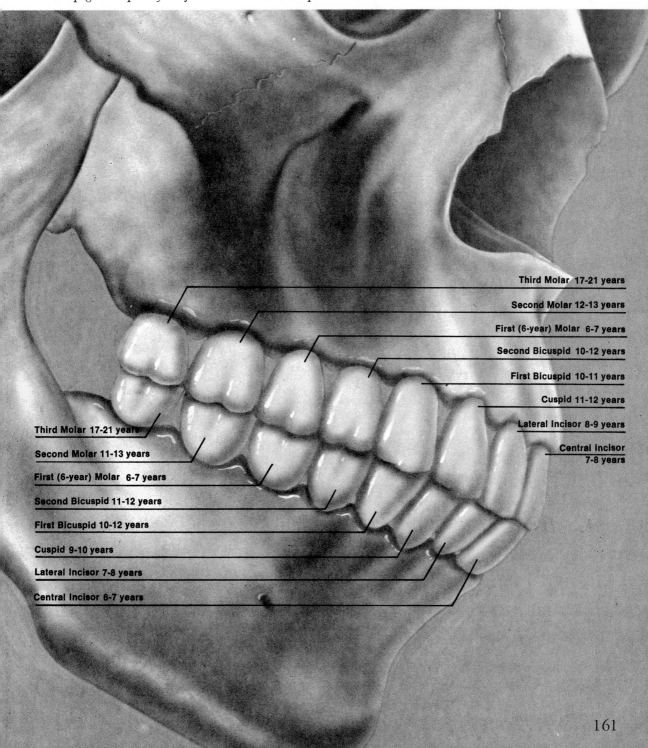

Third Molar 17-21 years

Second Molar 12-13 years

First (6-year) Molar 6-7 years

Second Bicuspid 10-12 years

First Bicuspid 10-11 years

Cuspid 11-12 years

Lateral Incisor 8-9 years

Central Incisor 7-8 years

Third Molar 17-21 years

Second Molar 11-13 years

First (6-year) Molar 6-7 years

Second Bicuspid 11-12 years

First Bicuspid 10-12 years

Cuspid 9-10 years

Lateral Incisor 7-8 years

Central Incisor 6-7 years

161

The four pictures here show decay in different kinds of teeth. All pictures are enlarged cross-section views.

Bicuspid: The start of decay

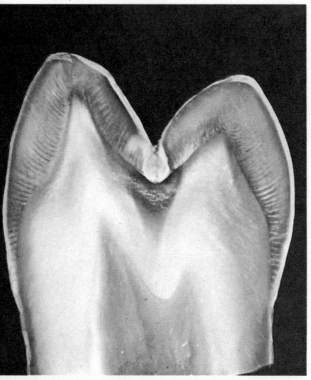

Bicuspid: A small cavity

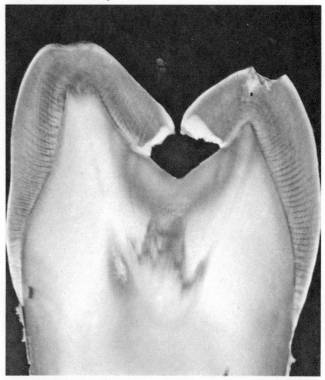

Incisor: Decay into pulp

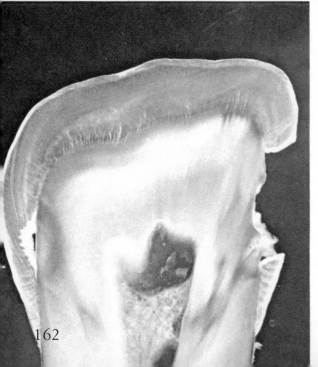

Molar: Decay into dentin

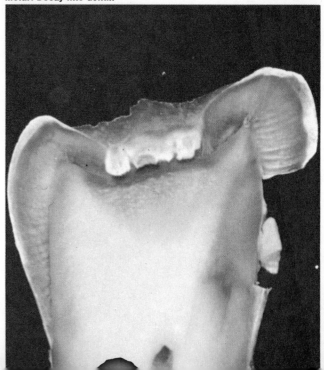

162

How Is Food Used by the Body?

You know now that digested food is carried by the blood to all parts of the body. But just how does the body use this food?

The digested food that passes from the small intestine into the blood stream has in it the materials the body needs for growth, energy, and repair of body tissues.

As the blood carries the digested food around the body, the different cells take out the materials they need to help them carry on their work.

Some of the digested food is used to make your body bigger and stronger. Some of the food is used to keep your body warm and to give it energy for work and play. Other food materials are used for important jobs of repair and upkeep of the body, and for keeping it healthy in every way.

Enough Food of the Right Kind

Although food can do all the important things you have just been reading about, it can do these things well *only* if enough food of the right kind is eaten. You may "eat like a horse" three times a day or more. But if your meals do not contain the proper amounts and variety of nourishing substances, you will not be well fed.

The food you eat must furnish all the nourishing substances, or *nutrients*, you need for growth, energy, and body repair and upkeep.

There are many different nutrients found in foods. But they can all be classed in these main groups: *proteins, vitamins, minerals, carbohydrates, fats,* and *water.*

To be well nourished, you need each day foods containing these nutrients in the right amounts. Although most foods do contain more than one

Something to Do

As you begin to think about nourishing foods, you might look for cookbooks prepared especially for young people your age. Such cookbooks may make you want to do some cooking at home. Look in the school or public library for such books as these:

Betty Crocker's Cook Book for Boys and Girls (*Simon*).

Brown, Helen E. and Philip S. Boys' Cook Book (*Doubleday*). *Advanced.*

McDonald, Barbara G. Casserole Cooking Fun (*Walck*).

163

nutrient, *no single food contains all the nutrients in the amounts you need.* And so from a variety of everyday foods you need to learn how to choose foods that together supply all the necessary nutrients and energy.

Some familiar foods, such as cookies, cake, soft drinks, and candies are not shown in the food guide. These foods are ones that can be included as "extras" — after you have eaten enough of the essential foods in the four basic food groups.

Foods such as vegetables, fruits, milk, eggs, meat, fish, cereals, and bread supply all the proteins, minerals, vitamins, fats, and carbohydrates that most people need.

Using a Daily Food Guide

There are daily food guides prepared by nutrition experts that can help you plan good daily meals. An easy-to-use guide is shown on page 165. It shows four groups of food you should try to include in your daily meals most of the time. It also shows you the number of servings needed from each food group. The four kinds of foods — along with such items as butter, margarine, other fats, oils, and sugars that are normally used in their preparation — will make your daily meals healthful.

What are the four food groups shown in the guide on page 165? How many servings from each group are recommended? A "serving" would vary in size from small for a young child to large (or seconds) for active adults or teen-agers.

By following this food guide, it is possible to have varied meals that include family favorites. It is not necessary to have foods from *each* group at every meal. It is important, though, to try to include at least the suggested servings sometime during the day — in regular meals or in snacks.

Some Things to Think About

1. What does food do for your body?

2. Can a person eat plenty of food and still not be well nourished? Explain.

3. What would be harmful about an all-milk diet or an all-vegetable diet day after day?

4. Do you think — after studying the daily food guide on page 165 — that you could write from memory the four main food groups and the suggested number of servings from each group? Try it.

164

Food for Fitness — A Daily Food Guide[1]

[1]Adapted from Leaflet No. 424, U.S. Department of Agriculture.

Vegetable-Fruit Group
Four or more servings. Include —
A citrus fruit or other fruit or vegetable important for vitamin C
A dark-green or deep-yellow vegetable for vitamin A — at least every other day
Other vegetables and fruits, including potatoes

Milk Group
Some milk for everyone
Children under 9: 2 to 3 cups
Children 9 – 12: 3 or more cups
Teen-agers: 4 or more cups
Adults: 2 or more cups

Meat Group
Two or more servings
Beef, veal, pork, lamb, poultry, fish, eggs
As alternates — dry beans, dry peas, nuts, peanuts, peanut butter

Bread-Cereal Group
Four or more servings
Whole-grain, enriched, or restored

Plus other foods as needed to complete meals and to provide additional food energy and other food values.

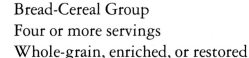

Thinking About Your Daily Diet

Now think of the foods you ate at each meal yesterday. On a separate sheet of paper marked as shown below, write what you ate at each meal, the number of servings, and what you had for snacks.

For breakfast:

For lunch or noon meal:

For supper or evening meal:

For snacks:

Next check your diet for yesterday with the food guide shown on page 165. Then on your paper, tally the number of servings you had from each group. For instance, if you had five servings of food from the Vegetable-Fruit Group, your tally would look like this:

Vegetable-Fruit Group   𝍩𝍩

After all your marks are tallied, you can see at a glance if you had enough food from each of the four food groups.

Last of all, ask yourself these questions, "Did I eat enough food from each food group? If not, what foods should I have added to make the diet complete?" Remember that your food record is your own and is to be kept private.

Keep in mind, as you think about your diet, that snacks can be an important means of helping you get enough of the foods you need. When snacks consist of foods like apples, carrot sticks, peanut-butter sandwiches, milk, and hamburgers, they can help make your diet more nourishing.

You will find it worth while not only to check your daily diet from time to time but also to see if you can plan some properly nourishing meals for a day.

Something to Do

Make some food models by cutting out magazine pictures and mounting them on cardboard. Use these models to assemble sample daily menus that meet the requirements of the daily food guide shown on page 165.

166

Try, for example, to plan some menus for your family for a whole day; include menus for breakfast, lunch, supper, and snacks. Use foods that you know you are likely to find at your house or that are easy and inexpensive to get. Then check to see if your menus include enough servings from each group.

Here is one boy's menus for a day. Check to see if he had enough foods of the right kind.

Breakfast: 1 dish corn flakes, 1 cup milk, 1 orange, 1 jelly sandwich

Lunch: 1 serving pork short ribs, 1 serving cabbage slaw, 1 slice corn bread, 1 cup buttermilk

Supper: 2 pancakes, syrup and margarine; 1 cup buttermilk; 1 peach

Snacks: 1 peanut butter sandwich

Mealtime Food Preparation on Your Own

One way you can help out at home is to try your hand at preparing some easy-to-make but nutritious foods. Casseroles—or one-dish meals—are easy to make and good to eat. The casserole recipes on page 168 are inexpensive and use foods that are easy to obtain. A lettuce or cabbage salad goes well with them.

Below and on page 168 are some recipes you may want to try. Copy the ones that interest you and take them home. See if your mother will let you prepare some of them from time to time.

Filled Celery Sticks

Clean and stuff celery sticks with a soft yellow cheese. Or try other fillings such as cream cheese, liver sausage, or peanut butter.

Carrot Sticks

Dip carrot sticks in cream cheese that has been softened with a little milk.

Something to Do

Here is another menu to check. Note that you cannot judge a day's menus until all *the meals and snacks are checked.*

Breakfast
1 serving stewed apricots
3 slices bread and butter
2 slices bacon
1 glass milk

Lunch
1 peanut butter and jelly sandwich
2 carrot sticks
1 apple
1 glass milk
1 chocolate cupcake

Snack
1 root beer
2 oatmeal cookies

Supper
2 servings cheese-sausage pizza
1 serving tossed green salad
1 glass milk
1 serving canned pears

Snack
1 glass frozen orange juice

Apple Crisp

3 medium-sized apples
3/4 cup quick-cooking rolled oats
3/4 cup brown sugar
1/2 cup flour
1/2 cup butter or margarine

Peel apples and remove cores. Slice apples in thin slices and put in lightly greased round pie pan. In a bowl, mix oats, sugar, and flour. Add butter or margarine and stir until you have a crumbly mixture. Put mixture on apples. Bake for 35 minutes in a 350° oven. Serves 6.

Tuna-Potato Chip Casserole

1 can of cream of mushroom soup
1/3 cup milk
7-ounce can of tuna
1 cup crushed potato chips
1 cup cooked or canned peas

Empty the can of soup into a casserole dish. Add milk and drained tuna and stir well. Stir in 3/4 cup of crushed potato chips and the peas. Sprinkle the remaining potato chips over top. Bake 25 minutes in a 350° oven. Serves 4.

Meat-Potato-Tomato Casserole

6 medium white potatoes
1 or 1 1/2 pounds of ground beef
1 large onion, cut into small pieces, if desired
1 large can or 2 small cans of stewed tomatoes

Peel potatoes and cut into *very thin* slices. In a casserole dish put a layer of potatoes and a layer of ground beef. Sprinkle with salt and pepper. Add onion pieces as a layer, too, if desired. Continue with these layers until all the ingredients are used. Pour 1 large can or 2 small cans of tomatoes over the mixture. Bake 50 minutes in a 350° oven. Serves 6.

Something to Try

Here is an easy-to-make and tasty milk drink you can try for a snack. Add 1¼ tablespoons of molasses and a dash of salt to a cup of cold milk. Shake it well.

Health Questions Young People Often Ask

Here are some questions young people your age sometimes ask about food. Can you answer the questions?

1. What is a food allergy?
2. Is it true you can "cook out" the vitamins and minerals in foods?
3. Are frozen and canned foods as healthful as fresh foods?
4. Are white eggs better than brown eggs?
5. What are the effects of alcohol on the body?
6. What is being done about the problem of hunger in the world?

Check your answers with the ones below and on pages 170–173. Then think of some questions about food or about digestion that you would like to have answered.

How might you find answers to your questions?

What Is a Food Allergy?

If a doctor finds that a person gets a stomach ache or a skin rash from a certain food, the doctor diagnoses the condition as a *food allergy.*

Sometimes headaches, hay fever, and asthma are signs also that a food allergy exists.

Common foods that may cause allergies are egg whites, wheat, pork, milk, nuts, seafood, and strawberries. Only persons who are sensitive to such foods have an allergic reaction when they eat them. A person is not born with an allergy. However, the tendency to develop the most common kinds of allergies may be inherited.

Is It True You Can "Cook Out" the Vitamins and Minerals In Foods?

Yes, it is true. Vitamins and minerals can be lost in the cooking of foods such as vegetables.

Do You Know?

Are there other kinds of allergies besides food allergies? Look on page 269 of the Glossary and see what you can find under the entry allergy.

Some suggestions for proper cooking of vegetables — to retain the vitamins and minerals — are these:

Avoid soaking vegetables in water before cooking them.

Keep fresh vegetables covered and in the refrigerator or other cool place until you are ready to prepare them.

Cook vegetables in boiling water, using no more water than needed.

Cook quickly; stop cooking when vegetables are tender.

Follow the directions on the package when you are cooking frozen vegetables.

Are Frozen and Canned Foods As Healthful As Fresh Foods?

Yes, because the nourishing values of foods are only slightly decreased by modern food processing methods.

Canned and frozen foods can be even more nutritious than fresh foods that have been improperly stored or cooked.

Are White Eggs Better Than Brown Eggs?

The nutritional value is the same in brown eggs as in white ones. The color of the egg depends upon the kind of hen that lays it. For example, Plymouth Rocks lay brown eggs while White Leghorns lay white eggs.

While the color of the shell is not important, the condition of the shell is. If it is cracked or broken, do not use the egg. Such an egg can contain disease-producing germs.

What Are the Effects of Alcohol on the Body?

When alcohol is taken into the body, it goes almost at once through the walls of the stomach and small intestine and begins to enter the blood stream. It does not need to be digested the way other foods

Do You Know?

The alcohol in whiskey, gin, rum, beer, and wines is ethyl alcohol. Ethyl alcohol is a drug. Misuse of alcohol is thought to be the most serious drug problem in the United States. On page 171 you will learn some serious effects that misuse of alcohol can have on health and on safety.

170

do; it is absorbed into the blood stream without any change. Within two minutes after alcohol is drunk, some of it enters the blood stream. The alcohol is then carried to all parts of the body, including the brain.

When alcohol reaches the brain, it has its greatest effect. Alcohol is a *depressant;* that is, it slows down the way the body works. Even small amounts affect the way the brain works. Then a person will be unable to reason or make judgments as well as he or she normally does.

Continued drinking makes a person unable to walk steadily, to talk clearly, or to see properly.

A person who drinks alcoholic drinks heavily day after day may lose his or her appetite and fail to have an adequate diet. He or she may become ill because the body is not properly nourished.

Habitual use of alcoholic drinks may lead to a loss in strength of the muscles and to less skillful use of them.

Because alcohol affects body functioning, airline pilots are forbidden to drink 24 hours before flying.

Then, too, liquor can lead to accidents. It is estimated that more than half of all traffic accidents involve motorists or pedestrians affected by excessive amounts of alcoholic drinks such as beer, whiskey, gin, or rum.

What Is Being Done About the Problem of Hunger in the World?

As you know from magazines and newspapers you read, and the TV programs you see, there are people all over the world who do not get enough to eat. And there are people in our own country, too, who suffer from hunger or poor nutrition.

What causes the problem of hunger? There are many reasons. In some cases, families do not have enough money to buy the food they need. In some

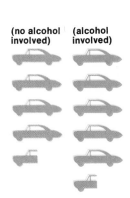

Traffic accidents

parts of the world, it is not possible as yet to produce enough foods of the right kinds for all the people. Or there may be famines due to dry periods and floods that destroy the crops during certain years.

What is more, the number of people in the world is growing. For example, it is estimated that the number of people on the earth will grow from four billion in 1975 to seven billion by the year 2000. To feed these seven billion people it will be necessary to greatly increase the world's present food supply.

To meet the challenge of hunger that exists in the world today and that could become more serious in the future, scientists are working hard to improve methods of farming, to seek new sources of food, and to develop new kinds of foods.

For one thing, new ways are being discovered to increase food crops. For instance, newer types of seeds are being developed that can enable farmers in Asia to grow two or three rice crops a year instead of one crop a year.

In some parts of the world, people have little variety in their food. Often they have a diet that lacks important nutrients such as proteins. To help add variety, soft drinks and candy bars have been developed that are tasty and rich in proteins. Also a tasteless, odorless fish flour has been made. This flour can be added to sauces, cakes, bread, and other foods. When it is used, nutrition is improved. And occurrence of the disease *kwashiorkor*, caused by lack of protein, is decreased.

In South Africa, a dry corn cereal enriched with soybean flour, peanuts, fish meal, and dried skim milk has been developed. It is called ProNutro and has been successful in improving nutrition.

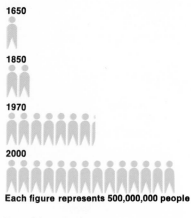

1650

1850

1970

2000

Each figure represents 500,000,000 people

In this picture you can see how world population has increased since 1650. Notice that the population is expected to almost double between 1970 and the year 2000.

172

Much study has been made, too, of where to find new sources of food. Today, for example, attention is being given to using seaweed to enrich such basic foods as flour. It is even thought that someday huge farms will exist on the bottom of the oceans where sea plants can be grown for use as food and where "fish farms" can flourish.

Scientists are also learning how to take materials such as soybeans and make them into tasty, flavorful foods that resemble meat. For example, they have made chickenlike, beeflike, and hamlike dishes from soy products. (See the pictures below.) After they are cooked, you would have a hard time tasting the difference between the real thing and the dishes made from soybeans.

Below you can see soybeans and some protein-rich foods made from soybeans. These foods can be used as alternates for meat. When these foods are prepared according to directions, they can be used as sandwich fillings, stews, casseroles, creamed dishes, and patties.

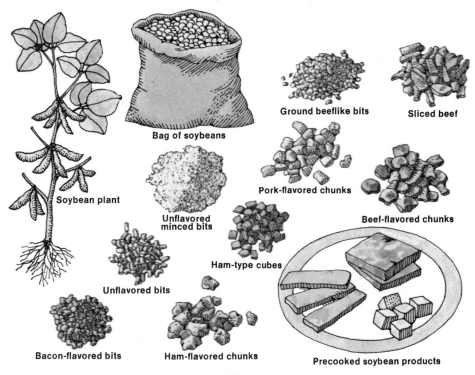

Soybean plant

Bag of soybeans

Ground beeflike bits

Sliced beef

Unflavored minced bits

Pork-flavored chunks

Beef-flavored chunks

Ham-type cubes

Unflavored bits

Bacon-flavored bits

Ham-flavored chunks

Precooked soybean products

Check Yourself

1. Look back at the questions on page 136. How would you answer them now?

2. How would you describe the appearance and work of each of the following organs?

   a. stomach   c. kidneys

   b. small intestine   d. bladder

3. What are some functions of these things?

   a. saliva   c. mucus

   b. gastric juice   d. peristalsis

4. What part do the following play in the digestion of food?

   a. pancreas

   b. liver

   c. gall bladder

5. How does digested food get to all parts of the body?

6. What is an artificial kidney?

7. Most people have two kidneys. What would happen to a person if one of the kidneys stopped working?

8. How would you describe each of these teeth?

   a. incisors   c. bicuspids

   b. cuspids   d. molars

9. What are some things you can do to help yourself have healthy teeth? What are some things a community can do?

Things to Do

1. A demonstration to show how teeth aid in digestion by breaking up food is this one:

Put a whole lump of sugar in one glass of water.

In another glass of water put a lump of sugar that has been crushed into small pieces.

Stir each glass.

Wait to see in which glass the sugar dissolves more quickly.

2. There are tests you can do to see if a food has fat or has starch (a carbohydrate) in it.

To find out if a food has fat in it, press some of the food against a piece of paper. If the food leaves a greasy spot, the food has fat in it. Try this with foods such as butter, margarine, a shelled nut, an apple, an orange, a piece of cheese.

To find out if a food has starch in it, put a little iodine on a bit of the food. If the food turns purple or black, it has starch in it. Try this test on foods like bread, potato, lettuce, boiled rice, apple.

Use a ruler or a strip of paper to cover the answer column at the right. Read the first item and write the missing word or words on a piece of paper. Then move your ruler or paper strip down to uncover the answer and see if you are right. Go on in the same way with each of the other items. Do not write in this book.

The numbers by the answers show the pages in this book that give information about the subject. For the items you miss, go back and review this information.

1. The six main kinds of nutrients needed by the body are proteins, fats, carbohydrates, _____, _____, and _____.

vitamins, water, minerals 163

2. The teeth that grind food into tiny bits are called _____.

molars 158

3. Digestion of food starts in the _____.

mouth 142

4. Food goes from the mouth to the stomach through a tube called the _____.

esophagus 143

5. The stomach helps digest foods by its churning movements and by the _____ juice it produces.

gastric 144

6. Digestion of food is completed in the small _____.

intestine 145

7. Digested food passes through the walls of the small intestine into the _____.

blood 145

8. Solid waste material the body does not digest passes out through the large _____.

intestine 146–147

9. The four main food groups in a commonly used food guide are meat, milk, bread-cereal, and _____-_____.

vegetable-fruit 165

Health Test for Unit Five

Copy each number on a piece of paper. After the number write the correct answer, *true* or *false*.

1. Your body gets energy from the food you eat.

2. The only function of saliva is to moisten food.

3. Another name for the food tube is the epiglottis.

4. Most of the time the food you eat goes down the windpipe.

5. The stomach is always the same size.

6. Your small intestine is about 20 feet long.

7. Your large intestine is about 40 feet long.

8. The pancreas and liver send digestive juices into the small intestine to help digest food.

9. Digestion is completed in the large intestine.

10. Once dissolved food gets into the blood stream, it is carried to cells in all parts of the body.

11. The cells of the body need and use the dissolved food carried to them by the blood.

12. The walls of the small intestine are lined with tiny fingerlike parts called villi.

13. Food that is not needed at once can be stored in the body.

14. Your emotions can affect the way your digestive system works.

15. You have only one kidney.

16. The urinary bladder is a storage place for food.

17. You can live with just one kidney.

18. Digestion of food starts in a person's stomach.

19. The front teeth are called the molars.

20. Chewed food is easier to digest than food that is improperly chewed or not chewed at all.

21. There are 32 permanent teeth.

22. Sweet foods clinging to the teeth can help cause tooth decay.

23. Food is needed to repair the body.

24. Milk contains all the nutrients you need daily in the right amounts.

25. Another name for a food allergy is a "chemical factory."

Number of Answers   __25__
Number Right   _____
Score (Number Right x 4)   _____

176

6 How Do the Heart and Lungs Work?

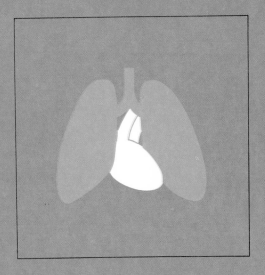

Your heart and lungs work so
automatically that you may not have
given very much thought to them. In
this unit you will have a chance to
learn some interesting details about
the structure of these organs and
about how they function.

1. *What did these scientists of many years ago discover about the circulatory system: William Harvey? Marcello Malpighi?*

2. *What are three important parts of the circulatory system?*

3. *How big is the heart?*

4. *What does the inside of the heart look like?*

5. *What happens when the heart beats?*

6. *What does the doctor hear when he listens to your heart with a stethoscope?*

7. *What is blood made of?*

8. *What are some important parts of the respiratory system?*

9. *What happens when you breathe?*

10. *Why is the nose sometimes called the body's "air conditioner"?*

11. *Why are the lungs often called "cleaning plants"? What can reduce their air-cleaning functions?*

12. *What life-giving exchange takes place in the lungs?*

Something to Do

Look in your school or public library for books like these that give added information about blood circulation:

Riedman, Sarah R. Your Blood and You: The Story of Circulation *(Abelard-Schuman). Advanced.*

Schneider, Leo. Lifeline: The Story of Your Circulatory System *(Harcourt). Advanced.*

Showers, Paul. A Drop of Blood *(Crowell). Easy.*

White, Anne T., and Lietz, Gerald S. Secrets of the Heart and Blood *(Garrard).*

Zim, Herbert S. Your Heart and How It Works *(Morrow).*

How Was Blood Circulation Discovered?

Suppose that you are a doctor living 300 years or so ago. You want to know what happens to the blood in the body, but there are no books to tell you and no laboratory equipment to aid you. How do you think *you* would go about finding the answer to your question?

Dr. William Harvey's Discovery

Now that you have thought about how a doctor of long ago might find out what happens to blood

178

in the body, you may be especially interested to learn about the work of a famous physician, William Harvey. Dr. Harvey carried out his studies in England in the early 1600's.

In the years before Harvey's time, people did not know the true story of how blood circulates in the body. Even the doctors of long ago were convinced that blood flows through the body only once.

Many of these early doctors thought that food was changed into blood in the liver, was sent to the heart to be warmed, and then disappeared into the body tissues. New blood, they believed, was made in the body every day or so.

Dr. Harvey began to question these ideas about blood in the body. He studied 40 different kinds of animals to see what happened to the blood in their bodies. He carefully observed the human heart and blood vessels, too, as he performed operations on people.

At last, in 1628, Dr. Harvey made known his conclusions: *The same blood is pumped around and around the body; and valves in the blood vessels keep the blood flowing in one direction.* He stated, correctly, that the heart pumps the blood into the arteries, that from the arteries the blood goes into the veins, and that these veins bring the blood back to the heart. Harvey did not know *how* the blood got from the arteries into the veins, but he knew that somehow or other it did get from one set of blood vessels to the other.

The reason Dr. Harvey could not tell exactly how the blood entered the veins from the arteries was that he had no microscope. When he operated on people, he could see the arteries and the veins; but he could not see the tiny connecting tubes now

William Harvey

179

known as *capillaries*. These capillaries are so small that they cannot be seen by the eye alone.

Dr. Marcello Malpighi's Work

In 1661, four years after Dr. Harvey's death, an Italian doctor discovered how blood gets from the arteries to the veins. This doctor's name was Marcello Malpighi.

Dr. Malpighi had heard of Dr. Harvey's ideas about the circulation of the blood. He had also heard of a wonderful new invention called the microscope. He wondered if this microscope could help him see how blood gets from one set of blood vessels to the other.

The microscope had been invented about 1590. Whether it was invented by a Dutch spectacle-maker named Janssen or the Italian scientist Galileo, no one seems to know for sure. But Galileo was the first man to describe its use in detail. The magnifying power of the microscope Galileo described was very small compared to modern microscopes. But it opened the way for scientists to study extremely small things.

Malpighi thought this remarkable invention might help answer the question that had puzzled Dr. William Harvey and other scientists. He decided to send for a microscope.

When the microscope finally arrived, Malpighi began his experiment. He put a drop of water in the artery of a frog's lung. Then he waited. Soon he saw the watery spot appear in a vein. Quickly he focused his microscope on the area. Then he saw the tiny, tiny blood vessels that we now call capillaries.

With the aid of the microscope, Malpighi had discovered that the arteries and the veins are connected by these tiny capillaries. Malpighi had completed the proof of the circulation of the blood.

Marcello Malpighi

What Is the Circulatory System?

In the years that have passed since Malpighi's time, much more has been learned about the *circulatory system*. This system is made up of the heart, the blood, and the blood vessels.

The Heart

The part of your circulatory system that you probably know most about is the heart. Your heart is located in the front part of your chest.

The heart lies in a slanting position, with the small tip end pointing downward and toward the left of the body. If you put your hand on your chest, a little to the left of the center of your body, you can feel your heart beating.

Your heart, which is about the size of your closed fist, constantly beats and rests — day and night. With each beat it sends blood through your blood vessels to all parts of your body.

In boys and girls your age, the heart normally beats approximately 90 times a minute. A baby's heart beats about 140 times a minute. A grown person's heart beats about 70 to 80 times a minute. The heartbeat is not the same in all persons, of course, nor is it the same in any one person at all times. The heart beats faster, for example, when a person exercises, or when he is excited, angry, or worried.

Your heart is made of involuntary muscle, though the heart muscle does not act exactly like other involuntary muscles you have read about. Heart muscle is a special kind of muscle that works naturally, all by itself.

One certain part of the heart has the special job of timing so that the two upper chambers beat together, then the two lower chambers.

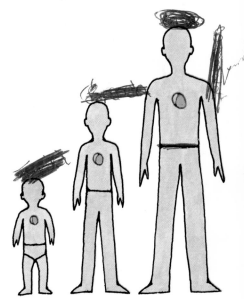

How many times does a baby's heart beat in a minute? A ten-year-old's? An adult's?

181

A covering protects the heart from rubbing against the lungs and the walls of the chest.

Inside the Heart

The heart is made up of two pumps. These two pumps are placed side by side, and they work at the same time. Each pump has an upper part or chamber called the *auricle* and a lower part called the *ventricle*. A wall of muscle goes down the middle of the heart and separates the pumps.

Each pump has a special job to do. The job of the pump on the right side of the heart is to pump blood containing wastes such as the gas carbon dioxide to the lungs. Here the blood gives up the carbon dioxide and other wastes and takes on a fresh supply of oxygen. The job of the pump on the left side of the heart is to send out oxygen-rich blood to all parts of the body.

The right auricle receives the blood after it has traveled to all parts of the body. Large veins, called the *venae cavae*, bring this blood back from the body to the right auricle. The blood is then sent down through a valve that opens into the right ventricle.

The right ventricle pumps the waste-filled blood through the *pulmonary artery*, a branch of which goes to each lung. *The pulmonary arteries are the only arteries in the body that carry blood filled with wastes such as carbon dioxide.* All other arteries carry oxygen-rich blood.

The left auricle receives oxygen-rich blood from the lungs. The veins that bring fresh blood back from both lungs to the left auricle are called the *pulmonary veins. The pulmonary veins are the only veins in the body that carry oxygen-rich blood.* All other veins carry "used" blood.

From the left auricle the oxygen-rich blood is pumped through a valve into the left ventricle.

Something to Do

Prepare a special report on the effects on the heart of alcohol and other drugs and of tobacco. Use the reference books Drugs and You *by Arnold Madison (Messner) and* About You and Smoking *by Norman Houser (Scott, Foresman).*

182

The left ventricle pumps this blood to the rest of the body through the main artery, called the *aorta*. The aorta branches off into many smaller arteries that extend throughout the body.

The left side of the heart is slightly larger than the right side because it must do the hard work of pumping blood out to the entire body. A larger amount of muscle is needed to do this job.

Now look at the picture on pages 188–189. See if you can trace the blood through the heart in this picture. The big venae cavae, which lead to the right auricle, are the best starting point.

From there go on to the right ventricle, and to the pulmonary artery that goes to the two lungs (not shown). Then find the pulmonary veins that come back from the two lungs to the left auricle. Trace the route to the left ventricle from which the blood flows to all parts of the body, starting off through the aorta.

The blood that is pumped through the body returns to the right auricle to begin the complete circuit once again.

There are valves between each auricle and ventricle—and between each ventricle and the artery leading from it. These valves work like one-way doors.

The heart valves open to let some blood pass through, then they snap shut. The valves make sure that blood flows in one direction only.

The two sides of the heart send the blood on different routes, as you have learned. The right side sends waste-laden blood—which is a dark, bluish-red color—to the lungs to get a fresh supply of oxygen. The left side receives the fresh blood supply—now a bright red color—and sends it to all parts of the body.

Although the two sides of the heart have special jobs, the timing of their action is the same. They fill at the same time, pump at the same time, and relax at the same time. Therefore you can feel only *one beat* instead of two.

Your heart beats away, day and night, pumping, pumping, pumping, your whole life long.

What Happens When the Heart Beats

There is a demonstration you can do that will help you understand just what happens when the heart beats.

Make a small hole in a hollow rubber ball. Fill the ball with water through the hole. When you squeeze the ball, you will notice how some water comes out in a spurt each time you squeeze. After each spurt, when you relax your grip, the ball comes back to its round shape again.

Something like this happens when your heart beats. The heart's muscle fibers contract and squeeze blood out of the heart. Each time this happens, the heartbeat can be heard.

Following each beat of the heart there is a short pause while the heart muscle relaxes and springs back into shape. During this pause, the heart rests and refills with blood.

To make room for each spurt of blood as it is pumped away from the heart into the arteries, the elastic walls of the arteries stretch. Then, as the heart rests, the stretched arteries spring back to their original size. As the stretched arteries spring back, the blood is pushed farther along. In this way, the blood is kept moving continuously onward.

This stretching of the arteries that takes place after each heartbeat is called the *pulse*. You can feel this pulse at places where a large artery is fairly

Something to Do

Try this to get an idea of the heart's strength. Open and close your fist about ninety times a minute. Keep in mind that you are squeezing nothing but air. Yet your hand will soon become tired and perhaps begin to ache. Then think about your heart beating at this speed (and sometimes faster with exercise or strong emotions) minute after minute, day after day.

184

close to your skin; for example, in front of your ear, at your neck, at your wrist.

A healthy heart is a strong organ. Hard work or play normally will not hurt it.

Checking the Heart at Work

A doctor can tell a great deal about how your heart is working when you go to him or her for a health checkup.

When examining you, the doctor tries to feel the tip end of your heart as it beats against the wall of your chest. He or she also thumps on the chest over the heart. By feeling and thumping, the doctor gets a good idea of the size and shape of your heart.

To help find out if your heart is beating evenly and if the valves are closing tightly, the stethoscope is used. The doctor puts a contact piece, or listening device, on your chest. Hollow tubes lead from this device to ear pieces. Sound waves from the heartbeats are directed by the stethoscope right into the doctor's ears.

The doctor hears *two* sounds each time your heart beats. The first is made when the blood enters the ventricles and the valves close behind it. This first noise is a low "lub" sound. The second sound is a high, short "dup" sound. This sound is made when the blood is squeezed out of the heart, and the second set of valves snap shut. "Lub-dup. Lub-dup." Those are the sounds the doctor hears when he or she listens to your heart with a stethoscope.

If one of the valves does not close tightly, there may be a rushing or blowing sound called a *murmur*. Instead of "lub-dup," the doctor hears "lub-shhh." There are other causes of heart murmurs, too, and many of these variations in heart sounds are quite unimportant.

Something to Do

Look in the encyclopedia or other reference books to find the story of how the French doctor René Laënnec invented the stethoscope over a hundred years ago.

185

Where Does the Blood Go?

Do you remember the last time you cut your finger or your foot? You know that blood flowed out of the cut. Of course, blood would flow out no matter where you cut yourself because there is blood in the network of blood vessels that stretches all over your body. The blood is there because the heart has pumped it there.

You may be interested to know in more detail just how the blood vessels extend to all parts of the body. The picture at the left and the one on page 192 will help you understand this.

As you look at these pictures, you will see many blood tubes, or blood vessels, that carry the blood from the heart, through the body, and then back to the heart. The pictures cannot show all these vessels but suggest the great number of them.

Notice on page 192 that the aorta branches off into some smaller arteries, and these in turn branch off into still smaller ones. The smallest blood vessels branch off into the tiny hairlike tubes called capillaries.

Capillaries actually are fifty times thinner than the thinnest hair. On page 193 you can see how these tiny capillaries appear when seen under a microscope. Find them at the junction of the arteries and the veins.

When the blood from the arteries enters the hairlike capillaries, an important thing happens. *Oxygen from the blood is drawn through the thin capillary walls into the surrounding cells of the body. And from these cells, carbon dioxide and other cell wastes enter the thin-walled capillaries. The wastes are produced by the cells of various tissues as they do their particular work in the body.* (Continued on page 193.)

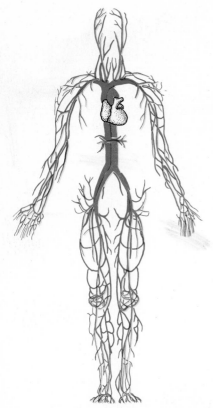

Blood vessels in the body

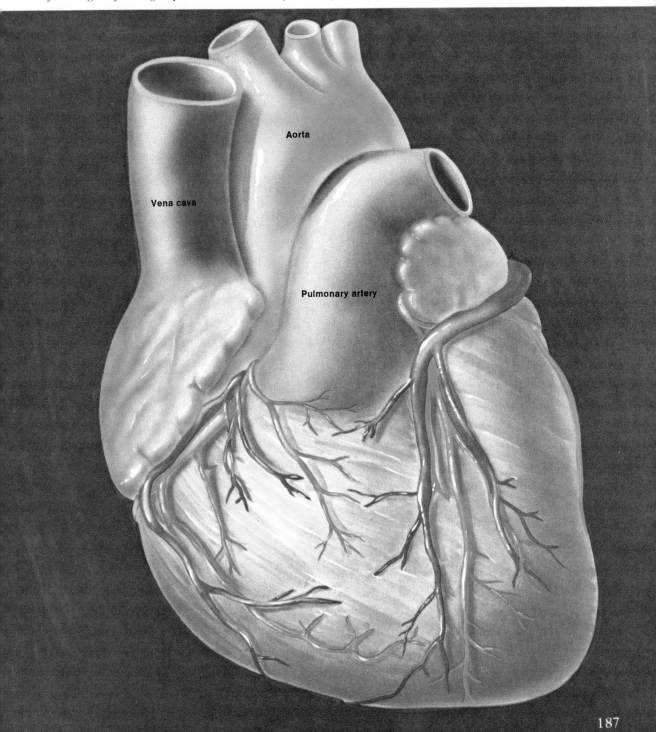

The route that blood takes through the heart

Blood enters the right auricle from the venae cavae.

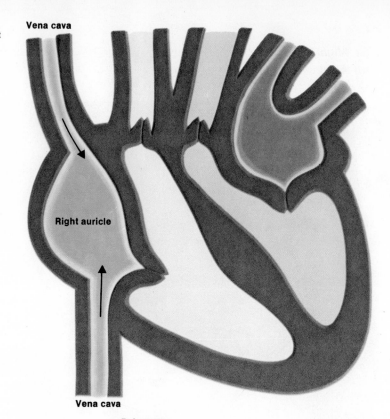

Vena cava

Right auricle

Vena cava

Blood goes from the right auricle to the right ventricle and on to the lungs through the pulmonary artery. It returns from the lungs through the pulmonary veins to the left auricle, then goes to the left ventricle.

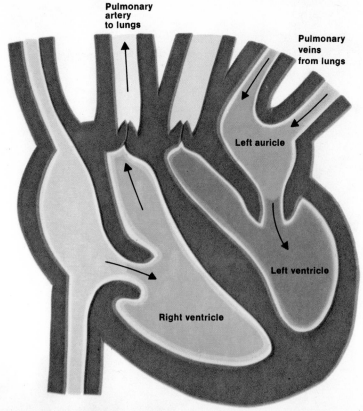

Pulmonary artery to lungs

Pulmonary veins from lungs

Left auricle

Left ventricle

Right ventricle

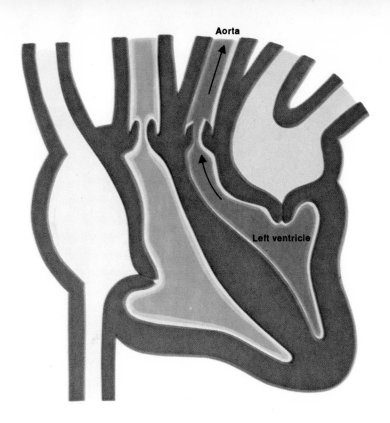

From the left ventricle the blood passes into the aorta to be pumped throughout the body.

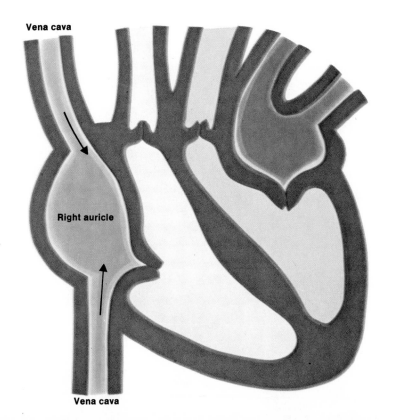

The blood that has been pumped throughout the body returns to the right auricle to begin its round trip once more.

The pictures on pages 190 and 191 are photographs of models from a health museum in Cologne, Germany. Which picture shows the heart's network of blood vessels? Which picture gives you a front view of the outside of the heart?

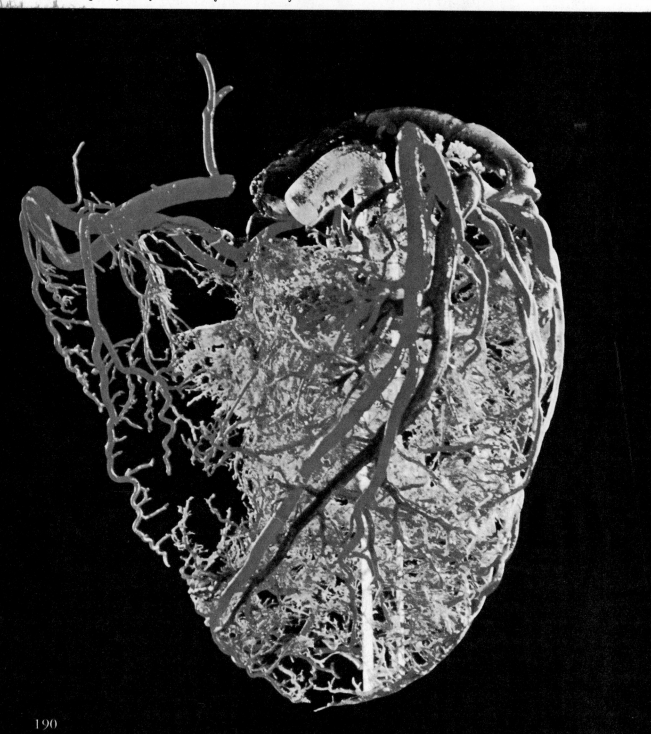

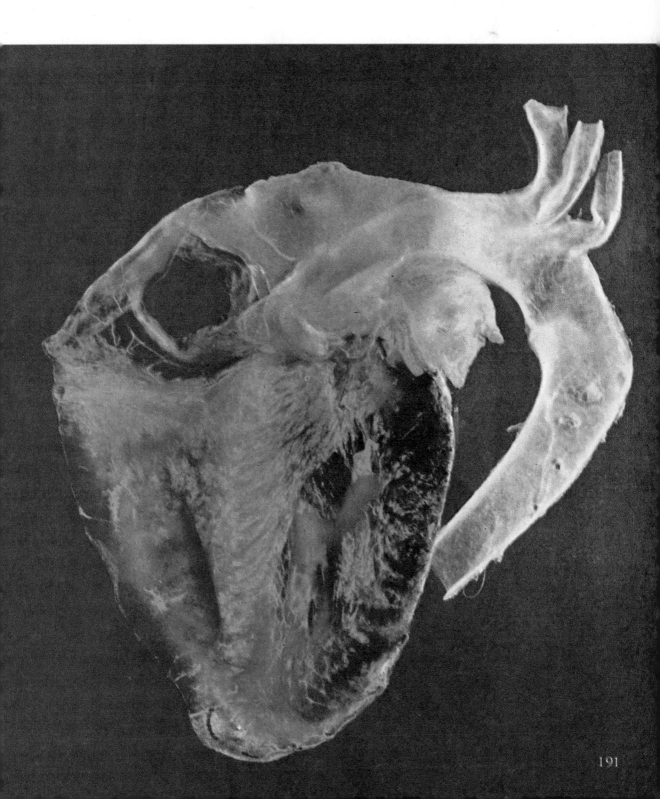

191

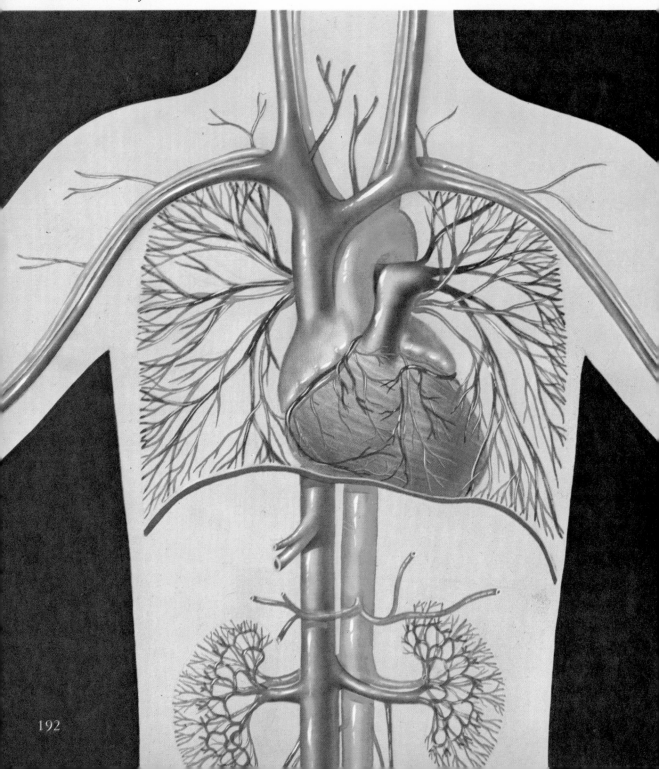

This diagram shows the network of blood vessels in some important organs: the lungs, heart, and kidneys.

Waste-filled blood flows into very tiny veins. These branch off into larger and larger veins. Finally, the two large veins, the venae cavae, carry the blood back to the right side of the heart. The upper vena cava brings blood from the head and arms. The lower vena cava brings blood from the trunk and legs.

If you look closely at your wrist, you will see some little blue lines. These are some of the veins that carry the blood back to your heart. The arteries are deeper in your body than the veins; that is why you cannot see the arteries.

Look back at the picture on page 186. This picture does not show all the blood vessels, but.it gives you an idea how they extend to all parts of the body. As you look at the picture, review the process of blood circulation in the text below.

The blood pumped by the heart through the aorta and its branching arteries contains oxygen —all except the pulmonary artery, which leads from the right ventricle and branches off to each lung. The blood in all but the pulmonary artery is bright red in color. But when the different cells of your body have used up what they need from the blood and have discharged their wastes, the blood is not fresh any more and its bright red color changes. The blood that goes back in the veins to the right auricle of the heart is a darker color.

The darker blood will make a special trip from the right ventricle through the pulmonary artery to the lungs to be purified. Then it will go back to the left side of the heart through the pulmonary veins. The blood makes its round trip from the heart through the body, to the right side of the heart, to the lungs, and back to the left side of the heart in less than *one minute*.

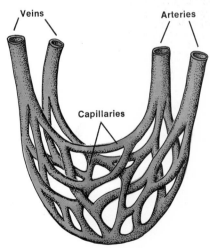

Capillaries that connect arteries and veins are shown here greatly enlarged.

What Is Blood Made Of?

If you were to examine a drop of blood under a powerful microscope, you would see millions of tiny *red blood cells* floating in a liquid. These red blood cells are shaped something like tiny saucers hollowed out on both sides. You would also see other tiny, odd-shaped specks. Some of these specks are *white blood cells*; others are *platelets*.

The red blood cells are made in the marrow of your long bones and they give the blood its red color. These red blood cells are so small that 50,000 of them could fit on a pinhead.

Inside each red blood cell is a substance called *hemoglobin*. This hemoglobin carries the oxygen which is "dropped off" by the red blood cells as needed by the body tissues.

The white blood cells are somewhat larger than the red blood cells, but there are not nearly so many white cells as red cells. Most of the white cells are made in bone marrow.

The white blood cells are sometimes called the body's "soldiers." They increase in number when the body is fighting disease germs. Certain of these white blood cells slip out of the blood vessels and hurry to the place where the germs are. They kill the germs by surrounding them and "eating" them up. Some white cells also form a wall around the germs. In this way many of the germs can be kept from spreading through the body.

White cells can be found in the *pus* of a sore or boil.

The platelets in your blood are helpful when you have an injury such as a cut. For when a blood vessel has been cut, the platelets come to the surface of the cut and begin to crumble. As they crumble, a

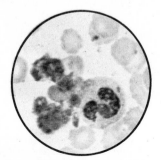

A drop of blood under a microscope

194

special chemical is released from each platelet. This chemical is a substance that causes the blood to thicken, or *clot*. The clot stops up the opening in the blood vessel that has been cut, and blood can no longer flow through it to the skin surface.

The liquid part of your blood is called *plasma*. Plasma is made up mostly of water. However, it does contain other important substances. Plasma has in it, among other things, the digested food that is being carried to all parts of the body. It also contains antibodies, which are substances that the body manufactures to help protect itself from certain disease germs.

Blood plasma, as well as products made from it, has a number of valuable medical uses.

To get the plasma, blood is first taken from the veins of a healthy person at a hospital or a blood bank. Then a machine is used to separate the plasma from other parts of the blood.

Plasma can be stored in the form of a liquid at room temperature — or it can be made into a dry powder. In powder form, the plasma can be stored easily and therefore can be kept for long periods of time.

When plasma is in powder form, sterile water can be added to turn it into a liquid again. Liquid plasma is used in many emergency situations, such as when a person is in shock after an injury.

Fresh, frozen plasma — specially prepared — is used to treat certain bleeding conditions.

Whole blood, which can be stored for a limited time under refrigeration or by freezing, is used in some cases for transfusions. It is also used to treat certain kinds of illnesses for which other forms of blood cannot be substituted.

Something to Do

1. Look in the Glossary for additional information about these topics: antibodies, plasma, transfusion, shock.

2. Find out what advantages plasma *has over* whole blood *in emergency transfusions.*

195

What Is the Respiratory System?

To keep alive, you must have oxygen, which is found in the air. When you breathe in, your *respiratory system*, or breathing system, allows oxygen to enter the body through the nose or mouth and to be drawn into the lungs. In the lungs, oxygen is picked up by the blood and carried to all the body cells. When you breathe out, carbon dioxide and other wastes are sent out of your body.

Let's find out more about the different parts of your respiratory system — your *nose*; your *windpipe*, or *trachea*; your *bronchial tubes*; and your *lungs*.

How Your Nose Helps

When you were very young, you may have thought that your nose did all the work of breathing. You may also have thought that all the air going into your body had to go through your nose. Now, of course, you know that air can also go in through your mouth. However, you should try to breathe through your nose most of the time. There is a good reason for doing this.

When you take in air through your nose, instead of through your mouth, the air is in better condition for use in the lungs. For one thing, the air is filtered by the many tiny hairs in your nose. These hairs catch some of the larger particles of dirt, dust, and germs you breathe in.

Also, the sticky fluid called *mucus* in the lining of your nose moistens the air passing through the nose. The mucus also helps trap some of the dust, dirt, and germs. Much of what is caught in the mucus is expelled when you blow your nose, or it is carried to your throat.

From your throat this material is swallowed, or it is coughed up, which prevents it for the most

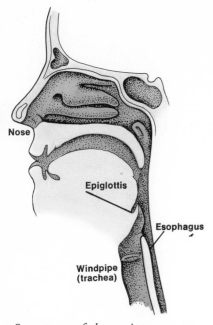

Some parts of the respiratory system

196

part from going into your lungs. However, if the air you breathe is very, very dirty, or *polluted*, neither the hairs in the nose nor the mucus can prevent all the dirt from reaching your lungs. That is why the problem of dirty air, or *air pollution*, is a serious one and one that must be solved more successfully in the future than it has been in the past.

As the air you breathe in passes over the folds of the nose, it is warmed somewhat. The warm air helps keep the body from being chilled.

Because the nose helps clean the air you breathe by filtering out impurities and by moistening it, this organ is sometimes called the body's "air conditioner."

How the Air Gets to the Lungs

After the air comes into your body through your nose or mouth, it goes down a tube called the wind-pipe, or *trachea*. In the upper part of the windpipe is the voice box, or *larynx*.

The windpipe extends down into your neck, and then it divides into two large branches called the *bronchial tubes*. One bronchial tube goes to each of the lungs. See the picture at the right.

In the picture on page 196 you can see the nose, the windpipe, and the epiglottis. The *epiglottis* is the thin piece of cartilage or flexible gate that covers the entrance to the windpipe when you swallow food. This happens automatically. It prevents food from going into the windpipe and choking you.

How You Breathe

Inside each lung the bronchial tube keeps branching into smaller and smaller tubes. Every one of these tiny tubes ends in little balloonlike air pockets, or sacs. There are many thousands of these tiny air sacs in the spongelike lung tissue.

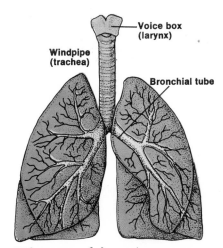

What parts of the respiratory system do you see here?

When the air sacs are filled with air, they get bigger — just as balloons get bigger when they are filled with air.

To understand how you breathe, or how air is drawn into and sent out of the lungs, you have to know something about the structure of the chest. Study the pictures on pages 202 – 203 as you read the following material.

Your chest is somewhat like a cage with walls and a floor that can move. The chest walls are made up of the ribs and the muscles between them. The floor is made up of a big tentlike muscle called the *diaphragm*.

Both the chest walls and the diaphragm move in rhythmic fashion during breathing. When you breathe in, or *inhale*, this is what happens. The muscles between your ribs lift the ribs upward and outward away from the lungs. And the diaphragm moves down. This makes the chest size bigger and causes air to be sucked into the lungs through the windpipe.

Then when you breathe out, or *exhale*, the muscles between the ribs move the ribs downward and inward — and the diaphragm moves up. The chest size becomes smaller, and the muscles of the chest draw together to make the lungs smaller, too. As the lungs become smaller, air is forced out of them.

This act of breathing is largely automatic. You can hold your breath — but only for a minute or so. Your nervous system sees to it that you go on breathing day and night without your having to direct the movements of breathing or even think about them.

Do you know about how many times you breathe in a minute? Time yourself and see. How many times did you breathe a minute?

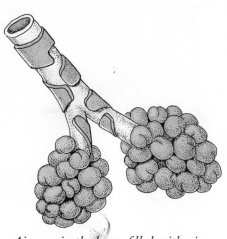

Air sacs in the lung, filled with air (greatly enlarged)

198

What Happens in the Lungs

Around each little balloonlike pocket, or air sac, in the lungs is a network of the tiniest of the blood vessels, the capillaries.

When the air comes into the lungs, oxygen from the air is drawn through the thin walls of the air sacs into the blood in these capillaries. At the same time, wastes such as the gas carbon dioxide pass from the blood into the air sacs and are breathed out.

Thus, you see that an important, life-giving exchange takes place in the lungs. The air that goes into the lungs gives up its oxygen and takes on wastes such as carbon dioxide to be breathed out. And the "used" blood that is pumped into the lungs from the right side of the heart gives up carbon dioxide and other wastes in exchange for oxygen.

In the picture on pages 188–189, you were able to trace the path your blood takes in getting a fresh supply of oxygen from the lungs and in returning to the left side of the heart to be pumped to all parts of the body. You can see why the lungs, which keep the blood fresh, are sometimes called the blood's "cleaning plant."

When You Need More Air

You breathe faster when you run, jump, or walk very fast. Such strenuous exercise makes you breathe much faster than usual for a very good reason. You need to supply additional oxygen that your blood can take to your muscle cells to create energy quickly.

You also need to get rid of carbon dioxide and other wastes produced by the contracting action of the muscle cells. The speed-up in breathing helps the body do this efficiently. *(Continued on page 205.)*

	Heartbeats per minute	Breaths per minute
Mouse 600		163
Cat 120		26
Humans 70-80		12
Elephant 35		10

What are the heartbeats and breaths per minute for a man, a mouse, a cat, and an elephant?

199

Your Lungs

The lungs are larger than you may think. They reach from the neck down almost to the middle of your trunk. In the millions of balloonlike air sacs of the lungs an important exchange takes place. What is that exchange?

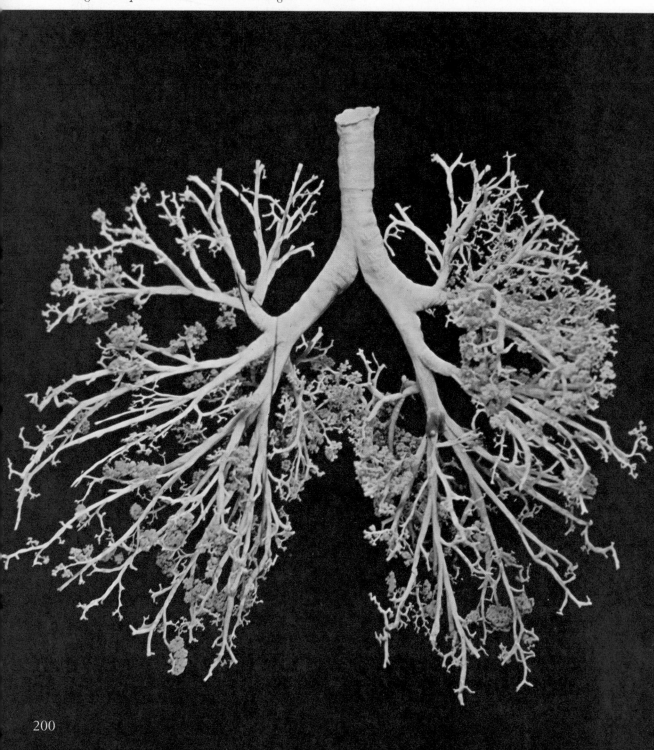

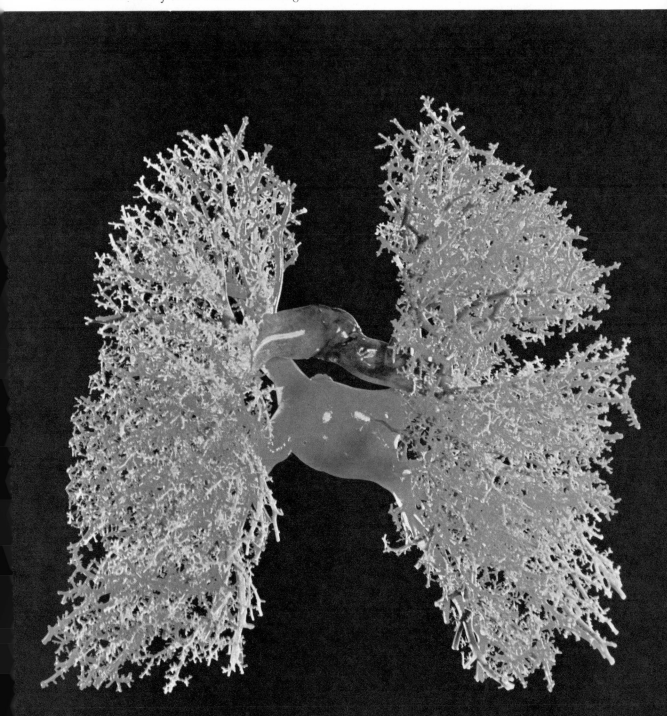

Here you can see how the lungs and diaphragm look when air has been drawn into the lungs. Compare the shape of these lungs with the ones on page 203—when air has been exhaled. What changes have taken place in the shape and position of the diaphragm in the exhaling picture?

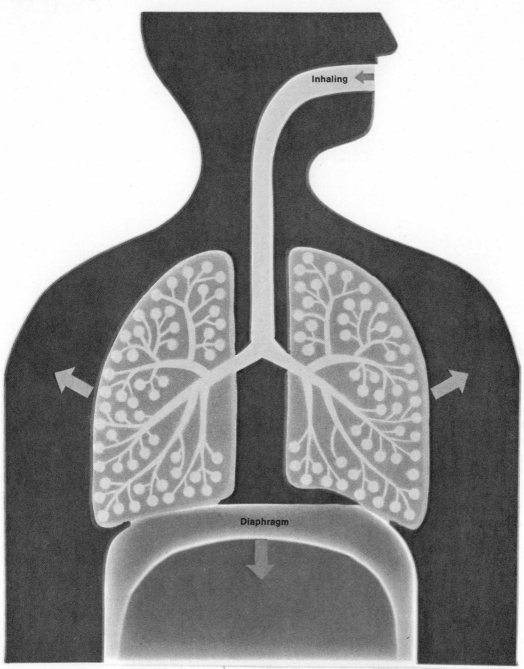

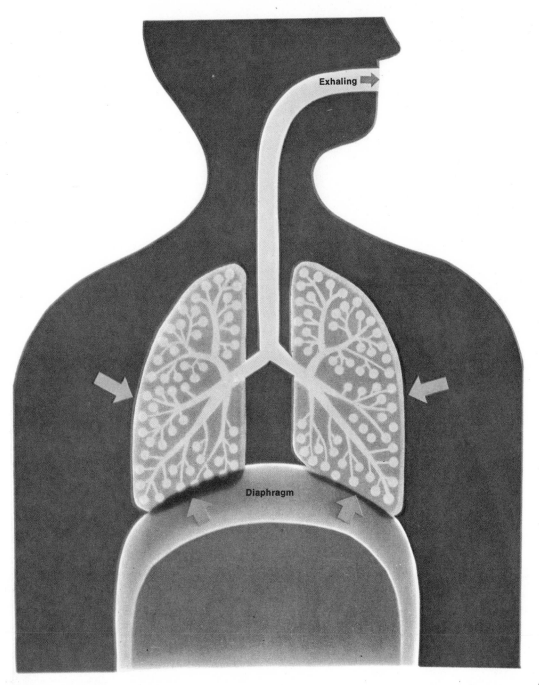

Exhaling

Diaphragm

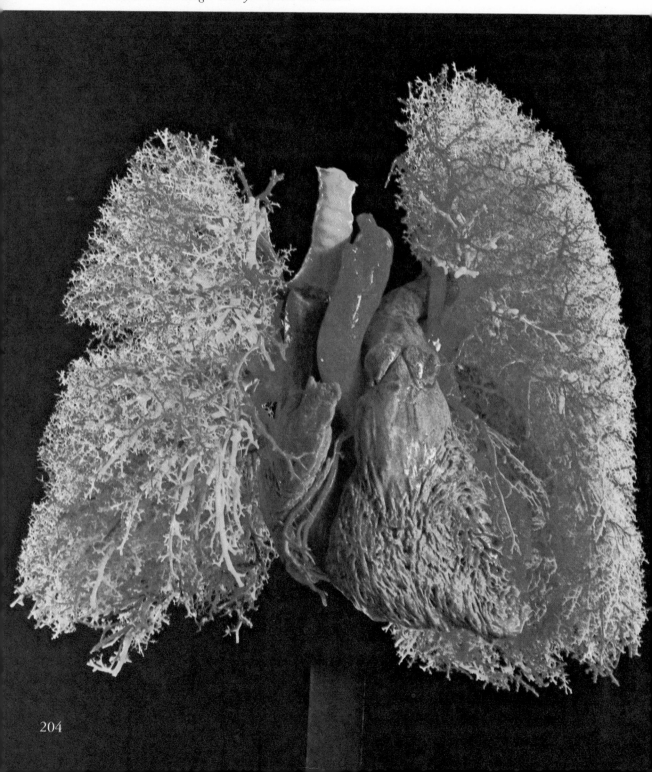

This model—from a health museum in Cologne, Germany—shows the position of the heart in relation to the lungs. Can you locate the heart?

Your feelings, too, sometimes cause you to breathe faster. Have you noticed what happens when you are seeing an exciting part of a movie or a television program — or when you are reading an exciting book? Or you may remember what happened when you got a sudden scare, such as having a traffic light change when you were in the middle of a busy street. At times like these, you may have found yourself breathing much faster than usual, perhaps even in gasps, in order to quickly take in additional air.

You also need more air when you talk or sing. Actually you would be completely "speechless" — you could not make any noise at all — if you did not take in air or if your voice box did not function properly.

Inside your voice box are two straight, elastic-like bands called *vocal cords*. When you are not speaking or singing, these vocal cords are relaxed against the sides of the voice box.

When you are talking or singing, tiny muscles bring the vocal cords closer together into the pathway of the air coming up the windpipe from the lungs. The air makes the vocal cords vibrate. And when the vocal cords vibrate, or move back and forth very fast, sounds are produced.

Your vocal cords are very much like the strings on a violin. When the violin strings move, or vibrate, they make sounds. In the same way, air coming against your vocal cords causes them to vibrate and make sounds too.

It takes a great deal of air to make the clear sounds that are required for talking and singing. So, of course, you need more air when you are talking and singing than when you are just sitting quietly, without making a sound.

Something to Try

To produce the sounds of speech, the sound waves sent out by the vibrating vocal cords are changed in different ways by the tongue, nose, lips, and teeth.
Pronounce the letters of the alphabet while you are looking in a mirror. Notice what happens to your tongue, lips, and teeth as you say each letter.

Below are some questions young people your age often ask as they are learning about the work of the heart and lungs. How would *you* answer these questions?

1. About how much blood is in the body?

2. How much blood can you lose and still stay alive?

3. What is meant by blood types?

4. Why is it hard to breathe when you have a cold?

5. How does air pollution affect your lungs?

6. How does smoking affect the lungs?

7. How can you take care of your heart and lungs?

8. Why is there difficulty with heart transplants?

After you have tried to answer each question, check your answers with the ones below and on pages 207 – 211.

About How Much Blood Is in the Body?

In the body of a boy or girl weighing about 100 pounds, there are about $7\frac{1}{2}$ pints of blood.

How Much Blood Can You Lose and Still Stay Alive?

A strong, healthy person can stand the sudden loss of as much as a third of the total amount of blood in the body. Sometimes in cases of great loss of blood, people's lives may be saved by blood transfusions. In transfusions, blood given by one person is put into the veins of another. In the United States, about five and one half million pints of blood are given in transfusions in one year.

Plasma may sometimes be used, as you learned earlier. Or whole blood may be taken from a donor's veins and stored under refrigeration in a blood bank. When whole blood is used for a trans-

Do You Know?

If the blood vessels in the human body were stretched out in a straight line, they would reach three or four times around the earth at the equator.

Capillaries are so small that ten of them could lie side by side on the width of one of the hairs of your head, with room to spare.

fusion, it is matched to the blood type or blood group of the person who receives it.

What Is Meant by Blood Types?

There are four main blood types, or blood groups, A, B, AB, and O, named according to certain substances the blood contains. These four main blood groups are found among all people everywhere. When a transfusion of whole blood is given, it is necessary to match the blood type of the donor with that of the receiver. Otherwise the patient's life might be endangered.

Why Is It Hard to Breathe When You Have a Cold?

When you have a cold, a large amount of the sticky substance called mucus forms in the nose. And the lining of the nose may become swollen. Then the nose gets "stopped up" because there is little room for air to pass through, and breathing becomes difficult.

How Does Air Pollution Affect Your Lungs?

Dirty air, or polluted air, is caused mainly by the gases given off by motor vehicles. It is also caused by the burning of oil, coal, and gases in factories, in power plants, in homes, and in apartments. Such burning results in gases and particles of dirt that pollute the air.

Air made dirty in these ways is dangerous. For example, it can contribute to such respiratory diseases as bronchitis, emphysema, and lung cancer—especially in older people.

Sometimes the pollution in the air is invisible. But whether it can be seen or not, polluted air breathed in year after year can cause much damage to the lungs.

How Does Smoking Affect the Lungs?

As you know, there are air tubes in your lungs that branch out into smaller and smaller passages.

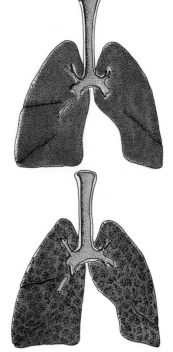

Top. *Inside of lungs of a person who has lived most of his life where the air is clean*
Bottom. *Inside of lungs of a person who has lived where the air is heavily polluted. Eventually his lungs will work less efficiently than they should.*

The walls of these passages are made of individual cells that are packed closely together. Some of these cells have hairlike parts called *cilia*. The cilia move back and forth, and normally they sweep particles of dust and smoke upward from the lungs into the back of the mouth to be breathed out. But when a cigarette is smoked, microscopic particles of tar are carried into the lungs with the smoke. These particles, together with the hot smoke, slow down the brushing motion of the cilia. Then the cilia are less able to do their work of "sweeping out" and keeping the lungs clean. Eventually the tar in tobacco collects in the lungs.

Substances in cigarette smoke not only affect the lungs, they also irritate the nose, throat, and heart. Some of these substances speed up the heartbeat and raise the blood pressure. *If these things happen day after day, year after year, what will be the effect upon your body and your health?*

To help you answer that question, doctors and research scientists have studied large groups of smokers and nonsmokers. Their research points to an alarming increase in deaths from lung cancer among cigarette smokers. Such a sharp increase in the number of deaths from a single disease has started scientists searching for additional facts on the relationship between smoking and lung cancer.

Here are some of the facts known already: For a given age group of people, lung cancer today causes nearly ten times as many deaths as it did 30 years ago when there was not such a high percentage of people smoking cigarettes. At the same time, there are fewer deaths from all other causes.

Studies conducted among smokers and nonsmokers have shown that those who have never smoked at all have the lowest death rate from lung

Something to Do

Look in your school or classroom library for the paperback called About You and Smoking *by Norman W. Houser (Scott, Foresman). Find out more about how the respiratory and circulatory systems are affected by smoking.*

cancer. But from there on, the more cigarettes a person smokes, the higher is the death rate from lung cancer.

Scientists continue to study the relationship between cancer and cigarette smoking, and their new findings are published regularly. These findings indicate beyond any doubt that the chances of getting lung cancer increase if a person smokes cigarettes.

Why do many, but not all, cigarette smokers get lung cancer? Doctors do not yet know the answer. They do know a number of things, however, about lung cancer and about what causes it, and you should know these facts.

The organs in your body—heart, lungs, stomach, liver, and so on—are made up of many cells working together. In the top diagram at the right you can see how a group of normal cells in a lung would appear. In the bottom diagram you can see the uncontrolled growth of cancer cells. This growth interferes with the lung's work. Since your lungs have no nerves to tell you when something is wrong, lung cancer may start and grow for a long time without being detected.

In some cases of lung cancer, the diseased part of a lung, or often an entire lung, is cut out. In other cases, lung cancer is treated by radiation. But whether surgery or radiation or both are used, the patient is very sick and requires long and costly care. Even with this care, the patient may die.

Cigarette smoking can cause another serious disease—emphysema. In emphysema the lungs become inefficient in supplying oxygen to, and removing carbon dioxide from, the blood.

Emphysema begins with the breaking down of the air sacs in the lungs. Two or three air sacs may

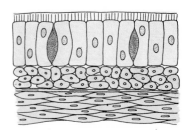

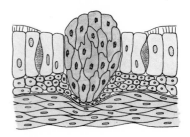

Lining of lung
Top. *Normal cells*
Bottom. *Cancer cells shown in brown*

209

become one large irregular one. The air tubes may lose their elasticity. Then stale air, laden with carbon dioxide, is trapped in the lungs and fresh air, with oxygen, cannot get in. When that happens, the whole body suffers from a lack of oxygen.

There is no cure for emphysema but if it is detected in the early stages, some help can be given to check its progress.

Bronchitis may also result from smoking. The linings of the bronchial tubes may become inflamed by the irritating smoke; then more mucus is produced to cleanse them. This mucus finally clogs the air passages, and the smoker has to cough a lot to get rid of it. This condition can become long lasting and serious.

Now that you know some effects that smoking has on the body and the relationship between cigarette smoking and lung cancer, emphysema, and bronchitis, ask yourself this question: Is smoking a habit I want to form?

How Can You Take Care of Your Heart and Lungs?

Your heart is a wonderful organ and a very strong one. It can go on working efficiently year after year. *You can help take care of your heart by getting enough sleep and rest.* Get plenty of sleep each night. Do you know why? When you sleep, your heart makes fewer beats each minute and gets a longer rest between beats. You need about 10 or 11 hours of sleep most nights.

It is a good idea not to let yourself gain too much weight — now or later. If you get too fat, you give your heart extra work pumping blood over larger areas of your body.

Cigarette smoking, too, can overwork the heart. Smoking causes the arteries to contract, then the heart must work harder to pump blood.

Something to Do

Find out about the smoking machine used by research scientists to trap the substances found in tobacco smoke. Look, for example, in the paperback About You and Smoking *mentioned in the margin on page 208.*

You can help your lungs by getting plenty of exercise. Do you know why? Exercise makes you breathe deeply and helps make the lungs more efficient.

Why Is There Difficulty with Heart Transplants?

Before a doctor can make a heart transplant, he must have a healthy heart to take the place of an ailing one. Thus a healthy heart must be removed from the body of someone who has just died. This heart must be transplanted almost immediately to the person with the faulty heart.

What is more, a doctor must keep the patient alive while the heart is being replaced. This is done by connecting the patient's blood vessels to a machine called the heart-lung machine. The machine does the work of the heart and lungs while the operation is being performed.

Often the body of the person who has received a new heart will, sooner or later, reject or try to get rid of this heart. This is because the human body makes an effort to fight off foreign materials. The body rejects a transplanted heart by producing special white blood cells which attack the transplant and destroy it.

Drugs have been found that can help keep the body from rejecting the new heart. However, these drugs at times work so well that they keep the body from fighting off disease germs, too. But research goes on so that this difficulty may eventually be overcome and the body will not reject a new heart.

To help prevent rejection, the doctor tries to match the new heart to the make-up of blood, muscles, and body chemicals of the patient.

In the future, surgeons may develop techniques for transplanting artificial hearts made of substances such as plastic or Dacron. These materials do not seem to be so readily rejected by the body.

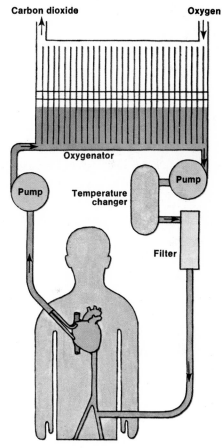

This diagram shows how the human heart is by-passed when the heart-lung machine is in use. From two tubes inserted in the large veins (venae cavae), a patient's blood is pumped into the artificial heart-lung. The machine takes out carbon dioxide and adds oxygen, much as if the blood had passed through the patient's lungs. The oxygenated blood is cooled, filtered, and carried back to the body through a tube inserted into a main artery.

211

Check Yourself

1. Look back at the questions on page 178. How would you answer them now?

2. About how fast does the heart beat in a boy or girl your age? What can make the heartbeat speed up?

3. What have you learned about these parts of the circulatory system?

a. aorta	e. heart valves
b. arteries	f. veins
c. auricles	g. venae cavae
d. capillaries	h. ventricles

4. What have you learned about these parts of the respiratory system?

a. nose   b. lungs   c. bronchial tubes

5. Why must the blood in each side of the heart be kept separate from the other side? How is this done?

6. What is the life-giving exchange that takes place in the lungs?

7. What must happen before your voice box can produce sounds?

8. What can you do to help take care of your heart and lungs?

9. How might the problem of heart transplants someday be solved?

10. What have you learned about cigarette smoking and health?

Things to Do

1. To examine a heart, try to obtain a beef heart from the local butcher. Cut it in half and examine it carefully to see if you can find the auricles, ventricles, valves, muscle wall dividing the two sides of the heart, and blood vessels.

2. Watch the newspapers for articles about the effect of cigarette smoking on health. Bring in clippings that can be put in a class scrapbook or on the bulletin board.

3. Try to find the following books in your library. Volunteers might report on them.

Chester, Michael. *Let's Go to Stop Air Pollution* (Putnam).

Kavaler, Lucy. *Dangerous Air* (John Day).

Pringle, Laurence. *The Only Earth We Have* (Macmillan).

Shuttlesworth, Dorothy E. *Clean Air — Sparkling Water* (Doubleday).

Special Research

Find out if air pollution is a problem in your community and, if so, what your community is doing about it.

Use a ruler or a strip of paper to cover the answer column at the right. Read the first item and write the missing word or words on a piece of paper. Then move your ruler or paper strip down to uncover the answer and see if you are right. Go on in the same way with each of the other items. Do not write in this book.

The numbers by the answers show the pages in this book that give information about the subject. For the items you miss, go back and review this information.

1. On the outside of the heart is a covering that helps _____ it.

protect 182

2. There are three kinds of blood vessels in the body: the _____, the veins, and the _____.

arteries
capillaries 186

3. The cells that give the blood its color are the _____ blood cells; these blood cells contain a substance called _____ which carries _____.

red, hemoglobin,
oxygen 194

4. The upper parts or chambers of the heart are called _____; the lower parts are called _____.

auricles
ventricles 182

5. The liquid part of the blood is called _____.

plasma 195

6. Blood cells that fight off germs are called _____ blood cells.

white 194

7. In the lungs the blood gives off the waste gas _____ _____ and takes on fresh _____.

carbon dioxide
oxygen 182

8. The two branches of the windpipe are called _____ tubes.

bronchial 197

9. The floor of the chest is a large muscle known as the _____.

diaphragm 198

10. Sounds are produced when air makes the vocal cords _____.

vibrate 205

Part I

On a piece of paper, copy each sentence below, filling in the blanks correctly. All blanks in a sentence must be filled correctly if a point is to be scored.

1. To prevent the backflow of blood in the heart, there are structures called _____.

2. Capillaries are tiny blood vessels that connect the _____ and _____.

3. The _____ side of the heart is slightly larger than the _____ side.

4. At the end of each tiny tube in the lungs is an air _____.

5. Air pollution can slow down the work of hairlike parts called _____ in the walls of breathing passages.

Part II

Copy each number on a piece of paper. After the number write the correct answer, *true* or *false*.

6. Your heartbeat slows down when you exercise strenuously.

7. Breathing is a voluntary action.

8. Capillaries are large blood vessels.

9. The lungs supply oxygen to the body.

10. Upset feelings can speed up your heartbeat and breathing.

11. The vocal cords are located in the lungs.

12. Both sides of the heart pump together.

13. The blood in the veins of your hand is a brighter color than the blood in the arteries of your hand.

14. Your heartbeat is an involuntary action.

15. Your heartbeat speeds up when you are asleep.

16. Epiglottis is another name for the windpipe.

17. Blood platelets cause bleeding to stop.

18. There are more than two blood types, or blood groups.

19. The same blood circulates over and over in the body.

20. You have 30 pints of blood in you.

21. The air you breathe out is full of fresh oxygen.

22. The normal heart is not damaged by hard work or hard play.

23. Red blood cells carry oxygen.

24. Young people your age need ten or more hours of sleep most nights.

25. The hairs in your nose have a useful purpose.

Number of Answers	25
Number Right	_____
Score (Number Right x 4)	_____

7 Do You Know How to Keep Your Body Safe?

If you want to keep strong and well, you have to know important guides for *safe* as well as *healthful* living. This unit will help you learn some of these guides. It will suggest, too, some ways of looking ahead to prevent certain kinds of accidents. You will consider various first-aid procedures as well.

1. What would you do if you were in a high-rise apartment and a fire broke out?

2. If there should ever be a fire in your house at night, what would you do?

3. What might cause fires at home? How can such fires be prevented?

4. What safety guides should a bicycle driver know? What checks should be made to see whether a bicycle is really safe to use?

5. What are some ways to prevent falls?

6. What is meant by "first aid"?

7. What is correct first aid for a small cut? A splinter? A broken bone?

What Would You Do About a Fire at Home?

Suppose you live in a high-rise apartment, such as the one pictured on page 218. You are awakened in the middle of the night by cries of "Fire!" What should you and your family do?

What would you do if you lived in a house and heard a similar warning of "Fire!" Or what would you do if you smelled smoke?

What is just as dangerous to your life as flames from a fire?

How might you help avoid home fires?

After you have talked over these questions, read the following sections through page 219 to compare your ideas with the ones given there.

Learn How to Escape Fire's Greatest Dangers

It is important to know that by far the greatest number of people who are killed in fires are

Something to Do

Be ready to tell or write about a fire you have seen or read about, what caused it, and how it might have been prevented.

216

suffocated by deadly gases and smoke before the flames ever reach them.

The gases given off by burning objects are lighter than air. For this reason, the gases rise through stairways, elevator shafts, laundry chutes, heating vents, and the like, and they quickly fill the upper floors. That is why you need to know the best ways of escape in case of a fire, especially a fire at night.

A Fire in a High-Rise Apartment

If you and your family live in a high-rise apartment and find that your building is on fire, crawl to the exit door with a towel or handkerchief or some other piece of cloth over your nose and mouth. Staying near the floor will help keep you out of dangerous gases that tend to rise to the higher part of the room; the cloth will help keep smoke and gases from getting into your lungs.

When you reach an exit door, test the door. If the door is warm, *leave it closed*. If it is cool, carefully open it a crack, bracing yourself against it as you do. A blast of hot air could rush in and suffocate you and others. If no smoke or hot air comes in, it is safe to open the door.

If the hall outside the exit door is not full of smoke or flames, crawl down the hall to the nearest fire-escape stairs. Be sure to close the door when you leave the apartment, but leave the door unlocked. Also be sure to close the door of the stairwell or of the fire-escape stairs as you go out. Keep your nose and mouth covered at all times.

If there is no convenient way to get out of the burning building, stuff towels, clothing, or bedding — dampened if possible — around the apartment exit door or doors to keep out smoke. Open a window and stay near it until firemen come to your

Something to Do

Someone from your class might write to the National Safety Council, 425 North Michigan Avenue, Chicago, Illinois 60611, and order copies of these data sheets on safety:

Bathroom Hazards, Bicycles, Cigarette Fire Hazards, Electrical Equipment, Flammability of Wearing Apparel, *and* Flammable Liquids in the Home.

rescue. Or stand on a balcony if there is one. Why do you think this is a good idea?

A Fire in a House

If you discover a fire in your house, alert your family at once. Then everyone should leave the house, even if the fire seems small. Once a fire is started, it grows with frightening speed. The fire department can be called from a neighbor's home.

It is best to have an adult call the fire department, but if you ever have to do it, follow this procedure: Dial the fire department or the operator. Give your name and address. Then briefly tell what has happened — whether the house is on fire, the furnace has exploded, or what. Do not hang up until you are sure the message has been correctly understood. Know where the nearest fire-alarm box is. Learn how to use it properly.

Suppose there is a fire in your high-rise apartment building. The door to the outer hall is cool. You open the door a crack. No smoke rushes in. What would you do next?

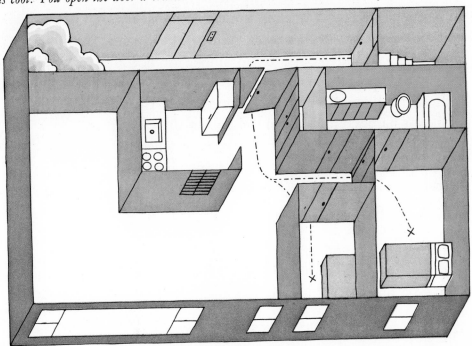

Once you are out of a burning house, do not go back into it for any reason whatever.

If fire and smoke have spread through the house before you have a chance to leave a room by the stairs or hall, you will need another means of escape. Keep the door or doors closed. If possible, leave by a window and wait for the fire department on a porch roof or garage deck. Or stay by an open window, keeping your nose and mouth covered, until you are rescued.

Some common causes of fires at home are cigarettes, electric heaters, cleaning fluids such as naphtha and benzine, and frayed electric cords. How do you think each of these things can lead to a fire?

How might clothing be a cause of fires?

What might cause fires around holidays such as Christmas and Halloween?

What would you do? Suppose you wake up and smell smoke in your house. Your closed bedroom door is hot. What other means of escape could you use?

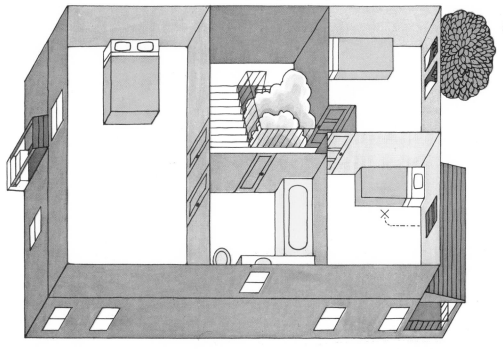

Could You Pass a Bicycle-Safety Test?

Suppose that your community or your school is setting aside time for some bicycle-safety tests. What kinds of tests do you think you would have to take? What questions do you think you might have to answer? To find out, look at some typical tests given in the sections that follow. Study, too, the Bicycle Test of Mechanical Condition in the picture on pages 224 – 225.

Check Yourself on Some Typical Bicycle-Safety Tests

Performance Tests[1]

A. Drive slowly through a test lane 60 feet long and 3 feet wide. Tires should not touch the lines on either side. This test will check your ability to balance.

B. Drive at an average riding speed toward a white STOP line 100 feet ahead. Apply your brakes when you reach the STOP line. *If your bike goes more than 10 feet beyond the STOP line, your brakes need to be fixed.* (And you fail this part of the test!)

C. Drive through an obstacle lane. The driver starts from a position back of the first obstacle so that he gets his balance before he reaches the first obstacle. He passes to the right of the first obstacle and weaves in and out among the rest. When the last obstacle has been passed, the driver returns over the same route. (See the obstacle lane at left.)

Standards for success on the obstacle test:

1. Touching neither foot to the ground.

2. Having neither tire touch an obstacle.

3. Passing first to the right and then to the left of the obstacles.

Bicycle obstacle lane. Eight obstacle blocks made of wood or rubber, one-half inch thick and two inches square, are placed five feet apart on a straight line. What must the driver do in this line?

---

[1]Adapted from *Skill Tests for Pedal Pushers*, National Safety Council, 425 N. Michigan Avenue, Chicago, Illinois 60611.

4. Not using the brake excessively.

5. Not sliding the rear wheel on stopping.

6. Using not more than an average amount of energy to control the bicycle.

D. Give the proper hand signals for turning and stopping. (If you need to brush up on this test, study the pictures at the right.)

Bicycle-Safety Knowledge Test

(Note: This will be an oral test. To help you prepare for a test of this kind, examples of correct answers for the two questions are given below.)

1. What are at least *six* common safety violations of bicycle drivers?

2. What twelve items can you suggest for a Bicycle-Safety Code, including some good rules for safe bicycle driving?

Examples of Correct Answers for Question 1 and Question 2: (What other answers can you add?)

1. *Common safety violations:*

Driving too fast

Driving against traffic instead of with it

Failure to use hand signals when turning

Stunt driving

Hitching rides on moving vehicles

Zigzagging in traffic

Driving in the middle of the street

Driving two or three abreast

Failing to stop at intersections

2. *Items for a Bicycle-Safety Code:*

(Be ready to give a reason for each one.)

Drive with vehicle traffic and keep well to the right side of the street.

Drive single file.

Carry packages in a basket or saddlebag.

Use both hands to steer, except when signaling.

Walk the bicycle across busy intersections.

Hand signals
Top. *Left turn*
Middle. *Right turn*
Bottom. *Stop*

Bring the bicycle to a stop and look in all directions before driving from a driveway, yard, or alley into a street.

Use your light at night—and wear something light-colored.

Do not drive so fast you cannot control your bicycle properly.

If driving on sidewalks is permitted, watch for pedestrians. Signal (with bell or horn) when approaching them.

Use a reflector and light-reflecting tape on back and front fenders—red for rear; white or yellow for front and sides.

Do not drive on icy pavements or during snow and heavy rains. Also be careful of wet leaves, sand, and gravel. They can cause you to lose control.

Do not make a habit of slamming on the brakes suddenly.

"Hi-Riser" Bicycle Quiz

Question: What special features does a "hi-riser" bicycle have?

Answer: The moderate hi-riser has "butterfly" handlebars; a "banana" saddle; a long seat post; and an oversized, treadless rear tire. Its compact size makes this bicycle easy to handle. If the driver is careful, this bicycle can be operated safely. Extreme hi-risers are now banned by law.

Question: What possible dangers are there in use of the hi-riser bike?

Answer: Because it is lightweight, drivers are sometimes tempted to do jumps, "wheeling," and other stunts on it, causing a large number of accidents in its use.

Question: Can handlebars be any height?

Answer: In some states, it is illegal to have handlebars above the shoulder level.

Something to Do
Plan a talk that you could give to younger children about safety precautions with "hi-riser" bicycles.

How Can Falls Be Prevented?

Many accidents occur when boys and girls your age fall from bicycles. But a very large number of the falls among students your age result from bumping into objects and people — rather than from falling from one level to another. What might cause these "bumping" accidents?

Look at the pictures on pages 226–227. What could be done to "fall-proof" the boys and girls you see there?

You and your classmates might begin now to keep a record of all the accidents that occur during the next two or three weeks. See how many of the accidents are caused by bumps or falls. Suggest things that might be done to prevent the kinds of accidents that are recorded.

Watch What You Are Doing and Where You Are Going

Many falls occur because people do not look where they are going and do not keep alert for possible hazards as they move about.

For example, it is unsafe to carry so many objects that you cannot see what is in the path ahead of you but must look to the side of the objects.

You have to watch your step, too, and look ahead to see where you are going.

Another safety guide to follow is this: "Avoid leaving dresser drawers, cupboard doors, or locker doors open when they are not in use." Why is this a useful guide?

Collisions often occur in active games such as soccer, baseball, basketball, and volleyball. What are some causes of these collisions?

Sometimes, too, falls occur when people are trying to reach objects on high shelves. What do they often do instead of using a ladder?

What Do You Think?

Why might falls sometimes be caused by misuse of alcoholic drinks? (Look back at page 171 if you need help in answering this question.)

Bicycle Test of Mechanical Condition

Is your bicycle in good repair? Use these checkpoints to find out.

Warning device: Must be heard at least 100 feet away.

Seat: Adjust to proper height. Tighten.

Reflector or reflector tape: Must be visible for 300 feet.

Crank hanger: Clean and oil. Adjust bearings if necessary.

Pedals: Oil and tighten bearings. Check pedal treads for wear.

Coaster brake: Should take hold quickly and brake evenly.

Chain: Clean and oil. Have one-half inch slack in lower part of chain.

224

Handlebars: Set for proper height. Tighten. Fasten grips tightly; replace if worn.

Hand brakes: Oil and adjust if necessary. If bike has foot brakes, adjust properly.

Light: Must be visible for 500 feet.

Brake cable: Inspect for fraying.

Fork bearings: Oil. Adjust for easy steering.

Wheels: Oil and tighten bearings and lock nut.

Spokes: Replace broken ones at once.

Tires: Inflate to correct air pressure. Inspect valves for leaks.

225

What Might Cause Bumps or Falls Here?

Study the pictures on these two pages and see how many possible causes of bumps or falls you can find. What are they?

What Would You Do About These Injuries?

Suppose you got a small cut on your finger. What would you do about it?

What would you do about a splinter?

What would you do if a friend fell and you thought he had a broken leg?

What would you do about a mild burn? An unbroken blister?

Now compare your answers with the following material.

Using First-Aid Procedures

First aid is the first care that is given in case of an injury. If the injury is a small one, first aid of the right kind is usually the only care that is needed.

If the injury is serious, first aid is the care that is given until a doctor takes over.

First Aid for a Small Cut

Wash the cut with soap and water to help kill germs in and around it. Wash away from the cut instead of toward it.

Put a Band-Aid or a sterilized bandage over the cut. Press down on it to stop bleeding.

First Aid for a Splinter

Wash the skin around the splinter with soap and water and then with rubbing alcohol.

Sterilize a needle by holding it over a flame.

Use the sterilized needle to remove the splinter. Then press above the wound to clean it by causing a little bleeding.

Put on a Band-Aid or a sterile bandage.

First Aid for a Broken Bone

If you should be around when someone falls and possibly has a broken bone, follow these steps:

1. *Use a nearby telephone to call a doctor or have someone else make the call.*

Something to Do

Tell how a person might get a cut. Be ready to suggest how the cut might have been prevented.

2. *Do not move the injured person.* Leave that for the doctor or a trained adult. If the bone is broken, moving the injured person could cause even more damage.

3. *Keep the injured person warm and comfortable until a doctor comes.* Put a coat, sweater, or blanket over him if it is cool or he seems chilled.

Perhaps you wonder about what happens when a bone breaks.

Sometimes a bone is cracked but not really broken. This is called a *green-stick fracture,* and it is most likely to happen in very young children because their bones are soft.

If the bone breaks into two pieces, it is called a *simple break* or a *simple fracture.*

Sometimes the bone breaks cleanly; at other times it splinters somewhat, resulting in a number of tiny bone fragments.

If the ends of the broken bone are pushed through the muscles and skin, the break is called a *compound fracture.* This break takes the longest time to heal.

First Aid for a Mild Burn

If the burn is a mild one, without blisters, immediately put cold water or ice cubes on the burned area. This helps reduce the pain and also lessens the chance of injury to the skin.

First Aid for a Blister

Cover an unbroken blister with a bandage. The body will gradually reabsorb the fluid in the blister. If the blister should break, treat it as you would a cut to avoid infection.

Sometimes a blister is very painful, or in a critical area such as the heel, and may have to be opened. If so, a doctor, nurse, or another adult should open it.

Things to Do
1. Be ready to tell the group what you have learned about first aid in your Boy Scout or Girl Scout troop or in your Camp Fire Girl group.
2. A book about first aid that you may want to look for at the library is In Case of Emergency: What to Do Until the Doctor Arrives *by Bry Benjamin, M.D., and Annette Benjamin (Doubleday).*

229

1. Look back at the questions on page 216. How would you answer them now?

2. When a fire breaks out, what is as great a hazard as the flames?

3. What is the safe way to move through a smoke-filled room or hall?

4. What is the correct way to report a fire to the fire department?

5. What is the proper signal for a bicycle driver to give for a left turn? A right turn? A stop?

6. What are some common safety violations of bicycle drivers? Give a safety guide to avoid each violation.

7. What are some causes of falls among young people your age? How might some of these hazards be eliminated?

8. Why do you think a unit on keeping *safe* is included in a book on health?

9. Why is it helpful to press down on the bandage over a small cut?

10. How can you sterilize a needle to be used in removing a splinter?

11. What is meant by "first aid"?

12. What often causes collisions in a group game such as volleyball?

1. Think of a holiday such as Halloween, Christmas, or the Fourth of July. Prepare a list of safety guides that can help prevent accidents on these special days.

2. Fill in a second line that rhymes with the one below to make a good safety guide.

If you drive a bike at night

_____.

3. Discuss fire-safety guides used in your school, especially those for fire drills. Give some reasons for each guide.

4. When you were younger, you learned about safety with such things as the following. What safety ideas do you remember about each one?

a. ball bats	d. guns
b. bows and arrows	e. kites
c. darts	f. softballs

5. Tell what you remember about safety guides for swimming and boating.

Special Research

Make a report on what to do in the event of these disasters: electric storms and hurricanes.

Self-Help Review

Use a ruler or a strip of paper to cover the answer column at the right. Read the first item and write the missing word or words on a piece of paper. Then move your ruler or paper strip down to uncover the answer and see if you are right. Go on in the same way with each of the other items. Do not write in this book.

The numbers by the answers show the pages in this book that give information about the subject. For the items you miss, go back and review this information.

1. If you have to move through a room or hall filled with smoke, crawl along the _____; cover your _____ and _____.

floor, nose, mouth 217

2. If your house should catch on fire, you and your family should _____ at once and report the fire from a _____ home.

leave, neighbor's 218

3. When you drive a bicycle in the street, drive _____ the traffic and keep well to the _____ side of the street.

with, right 221

4. Always _____ your bicycle across busy crossings.

walk 221

5. The first thing to do with a small cut is to _____ it with _____ and _____.

wash, soap, water 228

6. Do not try to remove a splinter unless the needle you are using has been _____.

sterilized 228

7. A person with a broken bone should be moved only by a _____ or a trained adult.

doctor 229

Health Test for Unit Seven

Part I

On a piece of paper, copy each sentence below, filling in the blanks correctly. All blanks in a sentence must be filled correctly if a point is to be scored.

1. If you are in a room in a burning building, test the exit door before leaving the room to see if the door is _____.

2. If in a burning building, cover your _____ and _____ to avoid suffocation.

3. It is dangerous when you are on a bicycle to _____ rides on moving vehicles.

4. When you and others are driving bicycles together, drive _____ _____.

5. If you drive a bicycle at night, be sure there is a _____ on your bike, and wear something _____-colored.

6. Many falls are caused by _____.

7. When you are walking down a street or hall, _____ where you are going.

8. After opening a drawer or a closet or cupboard door, be sure to _____ it when you have finished what you are doing.

9. Once you are out of a burning building, do not go _____ into it.

10. You need to know guides for _____ living as well as for healthful living.

Part II

Copy each number on a piece of paper. After the number write the correct answer, *true* or *false*.

11. If you cannot leave a room in a burning building, you should stuff wet cloths at the door to keep out smoke and flames.

12. It is desirable for an adult to report a fire to the fire department.

13. Gases and smoke from fires can suffocate people.

14. Doing stunts on a bicycle is likely to cause accidents.

15. Icy pavements are safe for bicycling.

16. It is safe, while walking down the sidewalk, to turn backwards to talk to friends.

17. Collisions are a very frequent cause of accidents in sports and games.

18. A sterilized needle should be used to remove a splinter.

19. If a friend has fallen and seems to have a broken bone, you should get adult help before the injured person is moved.

20. If an injury is serious, first aid given by those nearby is not enough.

Number of Answers   20

Number Right   _____

Score (Number Right x 5)   _____

232

8 How Do You Grow Up?

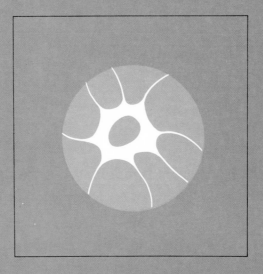

Have you ever thought about what does happen when you grow? Have you ever wondered why some boys differ in height and weight from other boys their same age? Have you thought about why girls the same age differ from each other in height and weight, especially in their preteens? Have you ever wondered about when *you* will stop growing in height? You will find answers to these questions in this unit. You will also learn about your *emotions* and how you can keep improving in learning to manage them. In fact, you will discover many ways in which you can help yourself grow into the kind of person you want to be.

233

1. What happens when you grow?

2. Why do young people stop growing at about the age of sixteen or eighteen or so?

3. Why is it important to realize that each boy or girl grows in his or her own way?

4. How can you grow in ways other than in height and weight?

5. Why is it important to study about feelings, *or* emotions, *in connection with health?*

6. What are some helpful ways of managing upset feelings?

7. How can you grow up strong and well and safe?

What Happens When You Grow?

If you were asked to tell what you are made of, you would probably name such things as fat, muscles, blood, nerves, and bones. But each of these, in turn, is made up of millions of tiny living parts. Each tiny part is called a *cell*. These cells are so very small that it takes a powerful microscope to see them.

Each cell is a "working world" in itself; it takes in food and oxygen and gives off wastes such as carbon dioxide.

In the picture on page 235 you can see how some of your cells look under a microscope. Notice that the muscle cells do not look at all like the fat cells—and that the fat cells do not look at all like the muscle or nerve cells. Of course, muscles, nerves, and fat do not look alike either. So you would not expect them to be made of the same kinds of cells.

Did You Know?

Cells are of various sizes and shapes, as you can see in the picture on page 235. It would take about 4000 averaged-sized cells, placed side by side, to make a line one inch long.

234

Many, many cells of one kind grouped together make what is called *tissue*. For example, a great many muscle cells grouped together form muscle tissue, out of which muscles are made. A great many bone cells grouped together form bone tissue, out of which bones are made. And groups of nerve cells form nerve tissue, out of which nerves are made.

These cells that are grouped together to form bone tissue, muscle tissue, and the other kinds of tissue are sometimes compared to bricks joined together one by one to make brick walls.

Unlike brick walls, however, tissues can *grow*. They can grow because each cell of the tissue can divide to make a new cell exactly like itself.

These new cells, in their turn, divide to make other new cells. Of course, when cells divide, they make more cells of the same kind. For example, when bone cells divide they always make more bone cells.

But not all these new cells are used for growing. All the time you are growing—and even after you are fully grown—some cells in your body are always wearing out. So some of the new cells are used to take the place of those that wear out or to repair cells that have been injured. This is why your body does not become worn out in a few years, as your clothes and shoes wear out.

However, in the brain and spinal cord, nerve cells are not replaced if they become injured during your lifetime. After a person is fully grown, the cells of the skeletal muscles and the cells of the heart muscle also have only slight growth through cell division. Such cells, of course, can grow in size—but the number of cells increases very little after a person reaches his full growth.

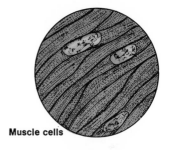

Muscle cells

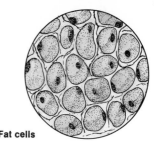

Fat cells

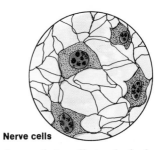

Nerve cells

Some of the cells in the body as they appear under a microscope

235

How a Cell Divides

All cells are made of a living, jellylike substance called *protoplasm*. Surrounding each cell is a *membrane*, or covering. This membrane allows materials needed by the cell to enter the cell from the blood; it also allows wastes to move out from the cell into the blood.

Within the cell, near the center, is the part called the *nucleus*. The nucleus has a membrane of its own around it. The nucleus controls many of the cell's activities, such as its growth and division. Without the nucleus, the cell would soon die. Inside the nucleus are a mass of tiny threadlike particles called *chromosomes*.

These chromosomes contain *genes* which determine which traits are passed on to you by each of your parents. These traits include the color of hair, skin, and eyes; body build; intellectual potential; general temperament; and so on.

In cell division the cell first doubles in length; then changes appear in the nucleus, and next the membrane around the nucleus disappears.

The chromosomes line up in the center of the cell and divide before the rest of the cell divides. Half of each chromosome moves to one end of the cell and half to the other. At last the cell, which has stretched into an elongated shape, breaks into two equal parts — each like the original cell. See the picture at the left.

Growth of the body, during the growing years, is made possible by this process of cell division.

Although scientists today know a great deal about human cells, the basic secrets of the cells are just beginning to be discovered. Many of the facts about just how the cells carry out their work are still a mystery.

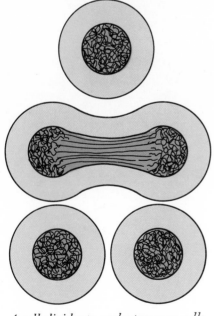

A cell divides to make two new cells, each exactly like the original cell. Here is a diagram of a bone cell dividing.

236

Your Glands and Your Growth

Perhaps you are curious to know why it is that boys and girls keep on growing and adults do not.

To understand why, you need to know about the work of certain glands inside your body. These glands are called *endocrine glands*, and they have much to do with such activities as regulating growth.

For a long time people did not know much about the endocrine glands — even doctors did not know much about them. But now it is known that these glands have much to do not only with how you grow but with how you feel and act.

The endocrine glands manufacture certain substances called *hormones*. These hormones are sent directly into your blood stream. Usually the glands

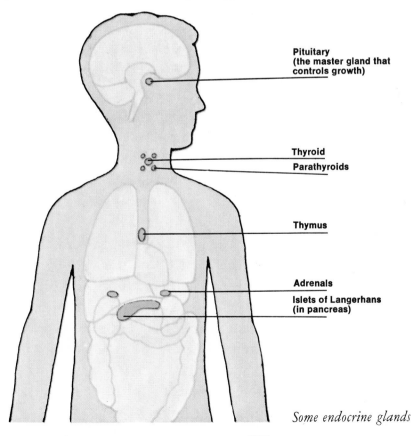

Pituitary
(the master gland that controls growth)

Thyroid
Parathyroids

Thymus

Adrenals

Islets of Langerhans
(in pancreas)

Some endocrine glands

make just the right amount of hormones to help you grow and feel able to work and play as you should. But once in a while one of these glands makes too much or too little hormone. If that should happen, a person might get too thin or too fat. Or he might feel tired or jumpy much of the time or get excited too easily. In such cases, a doctor can usually do something to regulate the amount of hormone produced.

However, in some *rare* cases one of the endocrine glands makes *far too much* or *far too little* hormone. In those rare cases where an endocrine gland is not working as it should, a very unusual thing happens. A person may grow to be very tall or a person may be as small as a dwarf. A woman may grow a beard or a man may have a very high-pitched voice. Doctors can now be of some help with these unusual cases if they can treat the person early in life.

Boys and girls sometimes become a little concerned about the way they are growing. They may wonder if a doctor can do something to help speed up or slow down their growth. Rarely would a doctor find such treatment is needed. Although a person may be growing in a way that is a little different from the way others the same age are growing, it is usually the way that is right and normal for him or her.

In the picture at the bottom of page 237 you can see the location of the various endocrine glands. Notice that there are several different glands and that they are located in different places in the body.

The gland that has the most to do with your height and growth is the *pituitary gland.* This gland is labeled in the picture on page 237. It is located on the underside of the brain and is attached by a stalk to the brain.

Something to Do

To learn more about the work of the endocrine glands, look for books like these at the school or public library:

McGovern, Ann. The Question and Answer Book About the Human Body *(Random).*

Weart, Edith L. The Story of Your Glands *(Coward). Advanced.*

The pituitary gland produces a number of hormones. One of these hormones is sent into the blood stream only during your growing-up years.

This particular hormone causes your cells to keep growing until you have reached your full size. Then the pituitary gland stops making this special growth hormone. After this you may grow fatter but you will stop growing taller.

All the glands indicated on page 237 are the same for both boys and girls. Other endocrine glands, which are different in boys and in girls, are the reproductive glands. They are the ones that help you grow up to be a man or a woman. These glands cause boys, as they grow, to become men —ready to be husbands and fathers; and these glands cause girls, as they grow, to become women —ready to be wives and mothers.

If you are a boy, these glands will someday cause a beard to grow on your face, will make your voice become deeper, and will cause your shoulders to widen. If you are a girl, these glands will cause your face to be smooth, your hips to become more womanly, and your body to round out.

Such changes start at different ages in different boys and girls. But generally the changes start in the early teens or a year or so before the teens. These growth changes usually come earlier in girls than in boys, generally from one and a half to two years earlier.

And now you know a few of the things your endocrine glands do for you. They help regulate your growth in an effort to keep you from becoming too tall or too short, too fat or too thin. They help you grow up to be a man or a woman. Also, as you learned earlier, they have much to do with how you feel and act.

Special Research
You may want to find out about some of the endocrine glands other than the pituitary gland. Look in reference books such as the encyclopedia—or books such as those mentioned on page 238—to learn more about these endocrine glands: thyroid, thymus, pancreas, adrenal.

What Is Known About Individual Growth Differences?

Differences in height and weight among young people your age are common. You have only to look around you to see that.

You may, at times, wonder why it is that a friend your age is taller than you, or why someone else your age seems to have grown up faster than you in physical size.

What you may not realize, or what you may sometimes forget, is that *each boy or girl grows in his or her own way* and that *each young person has a different pattern for growing.*

For example, some boys and girls your age may not be growing very much for a time now. Others may be starting to "shoot up" tall and to gain weight.

Then, too, there are different body builds. Some boys and girls are small-boned and do not weigh nearly so much as others their age who are large-boned. Some young people may be stocky in build and weigh more than others their age. Yet all these boys and girls may be strong and well.

So, you see, there is no *right weight* or *right height* for all boys, or for all girls, of a certain age.

You may be interested in studying the charts on page 241. The charts give normal *ranges* in weight and in height for boys and girls of different ages. It is possible for an eleven-year-old boy, for example, to fall almost anywhere within these broad ranges and still be healthy and growing quite right for him. How he grows depends, in part, upon heredity. If one or both of his parents, for instance, were "fast growers" or "slow growers," he might follow the same pattern.

What Do You Think?

Sue, age 11, noted that her sister, age 10, was taller than she was. "There must be something wrong with me," Sue thought.
Do you agree with Sue? Why or why not?

240

In looking at these charts, you should remember, too, that body build is important. Tall boys and girls are usually closer to the higher weights in the charts; short young people are usually closer to the lower weights.

As you think about growing, you may sometimes wonder, "Is there something special I ought to do to make myself grow as I should?" Of course, if you weigh much more, or much less, than the broad range for your age as shown in these charts, you should check with your doctor. But otherwise you really need not worry about growing. If you eat, sleep, play, and exercise as you should, your body will grow at the rate that is right for you.

An important thing for girls to know is that sometimes when they are between the ages of nine

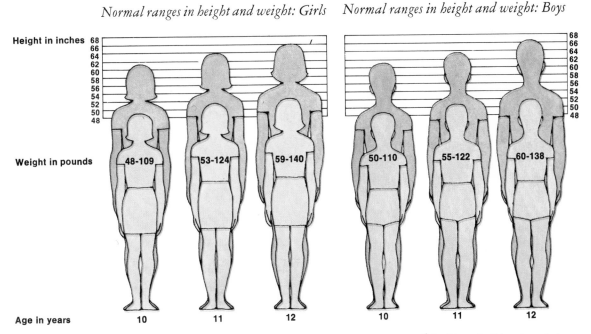

Normal ranges in height and weight: Girls *Normal ranges in height and weight: Boys*

Adapted from the Growth Charts for the Joint Committee on Health Problems in Education of the NEA and AMA (1967).

241

or ten and thirteen, they may make sudden and rather large gains in height and weight.

Ten- and eleven-year-old girls, for example, have been known to gain four or five inches in height and up to 20 pounds in weight in one year. Girls often worry about these gains and think they are much too tall or getting "too fat." They should know, however, that such gains are common in the years of rapid growing.

Often these gains are preceded or followed by periods when there is little or no gain in height or weight. And the excess fat gained in a growth spurt is not usually kept—unless the girl has developed a pattern of overeating regularly, for emotional or other reasons.

Boys, on the other hand, do not usually make such large height and weight gains in such short periods of time. Their gains are made more steadily over a longer period of years.

Until the age of nine or ten, boys may grow a little more in height than the girls their age do. Then for a few years, the girls begin to "shoot up" and often in Grades Five to Eight there are several girls who are taller than the boys. Later, the boys begin to catch up, and by the age of sixteen or so, many boys will be as tall as or taller than the girls their age. Boys may continue to grow in height until they are about twenty.

At the same time that children are growing in height and weight, their arms are growing longer and their hands larger. Because of this uneven growth of various parts of the body, there may be some awkwardness for a time. But in spite of this awkwardness, boys and girls usually find that, during these years, they are growing in the ability to move quickly and skillfully.

242

In How Many Ways Can You Grow?

Growing tall and weighing more are not the only ways in which you can grow. Each year you grow up in many different ways. And while you cannot control to any great extent how tall you will grow, for instance, there is *much* you can do about some of these other ways of growing.

Growing Up Mentally

Just stop and think of some of the ways in which you can grow up *mentally*. You can read more books than you used to; you can spend more time with newspapers and magazines. Often, nowadays, you can read some of the same things your parents are reading. You can watch for special television programs, too, that tell you about things taking place in the world around you—or about other things that are interesting to know. In what other ways do you think a person can grow mentally?

Growing Up Emotionally

You can work at growing up *emotionally*, too. In other words, you can grow in your understanding and managing of your feelings, or emotions. This includes your ability to take responsibility and to get along with others—family members, friends, and those you are around at school and elsewhere. You can grow in learning to be *considerate* of others, too. The best way to do this is to treat others as you yourself want to be treated. Can you think of other ways to grow emotionally? What are they?

You can grow in another way, too, as far as your emotions are concerned. You can grow in deciding what is right or wrong—and in doing what you believe in, no matter what "the others are doing." Why is it important to consider growth of this kind in connection with health?

Some Questions About Emotions

Here are some questions students your age often ask about emotions. Think how you would answer them now. Later come back and see if you have changed any of your answers.

1. Do all people get angry or worried or sad or shy now and then?

2. Should you try hard never to show your emotions?

3. What can you do to help yourself when you are feeling angry or unhappy or the like?

4. Should you be swayed by others to do something you do not believe in—such as experimenting with alcohol or smoking or drugs—just to go along with the crowd?

243

An important decision that may face you in the years ahead is whether or not to experiment with drugs. Drugs, of course, have proper uses to improve or cure some physical or mental ailments. When taken improperly, however, for "kicks," on a dare, or because of the need to escape from unpleasant situations, some drugs can be dangerous to a person's health.

A person who is growing in the ability to make wise decisions will consider carefully such facts as the following about certain drugs.

"Eye-openers," "pep pills," and "Bennies" are some names given to *stimulant drugs* that speed up the work of the nervous system. Such drugs, if used improperly, can make a person nervous, excited, shaky, and unable to sleep at times. While "hopped up" with pep pills taken improperly, a person may even commit a crime.

"Reds and blues," "goofballs," and "barbs" are names sometimes given to *depressant drugs*. Depressant drugs slow down the work of the nervous system. When these drugs are not used according to directions, they can be dangerous. An overdose can cause a serious slowdown in the breathing center or even death.

Use of *marijuana* — often called smoking "pot" or "grass" — is illegal. Possession of it is a crime and is punishable by a fine or a jail sentence. Research workers are still studying the effects of repeated use of marijuana on the body.

LSD is a drug that can cause a person's brain to distort the ways in which messages of sight, sound, touch, or taste come to it. Even small amounts of LSD can cause serious mental changes. It is illegal to buy, use, or sell LSD.

Did You Know?

Some chemicals such as glue, paint thinner, and lighter fluid are dangerous to sniff. Continued sniffing of such substances can cause serious damage to the brain, kidneys, liver, heart, and nervous system.

244

Why Are Emotions Important?

Your feelings, or emotions, are a part of everything you do. When you are happy, your food digests better than it does when you are worried or angry or unhappy.

When you are not emotionally upset, it is easier for your digestive system to function as it should. You sleep better and you can work and play better when you are not disturbed by upset feelings. Your heart does not have to work so hard either. In fact, all the organs of your body are able to function more smoothly.

You can concentrate on your schoolwork more easily, too, when you are relaxed and feeling good about yourself than when you are worrying, angry, or sad.

You can see, then, that learning to understand your emotions — and learning how to manage your emotions in ways that help you and do not hurt others — can aid you in growing up to be a strong and healthy person.

Everyone Has Emotions

Every human being has feelings, or emotions. And people all over the world at one time or another have the same emotions. Some of the emotions we all have can be recognized in the pictures on pages 248–249. What are some of these emotions?

Your class can carry out an interesting activity to help show that *all* of you have strong feelings at one time or another. For example, you might think of, then write about, a time when you felt angry.

Later all the papers, unsigned, might be put in a class scrapbook for class members to read. It will be very unusual if you do not find that *all* of you at

What Do You Think?

It has been said that young people who are learning to deal with their problems and their emotions successfully are not likely to misuse drugs. Why might this be true?

245

one time or another have felt angry. You may learn of instances such as these:

Once I felt very angry when my brother said I had lost his pen and I hadn't even seen it. . . .

Once I was angry when a friend left me and went off to play with someone else. . . .

I was angry when my mother wouldn't let me go to my friend's house to play. Instead I had to help. . . .

A big boy on our block took a little boy's cap and threw it in a mud puddle. That made me mad!

I was angry one day when my new pup chewed up my baseball. . . .

I was angry the day my little brother broke my ship model. . . .

A similar activity could be tried with other feelings. Thus you could write about a time when you felt *afraid*. Or you could write about a time when you felt *shy*.

It would be surprising if you did not discover that everyone in your group has felt scared at some time or other.

And you would most likely find that at one time or another *all* the students have been in situations where they felt shy or ill at ease.

Realizing that you are not the only one who has emotions is an important part of growing up. *All* human beings have emotions.

Should You Try to Hide All Your Feelings?

When you consider whether or not you should try to hide your emotions, the chances are that you are thinking of unpleasant or very strong emotions such as anger or fear.

Certainly most of us would not want people to hide their pleasant feelings! Just think what the world would be like if no one ever looked or felt happy or proud or excited.

Some Things to Do

1. Volunteers might act out some of the various emotions that human beings experience. The others can guess which emotion is being portrayed.

2. Write a paragraph that begins "Once I felt very happy when. . . ."

246

If you stop to think about it, you can see why it is a good idea for people to express their pleasant feelings. How would you feel, for example, if your parents or others who care for you looked at you with blank faces—and tried not to show their affection? How would you feel if your friends did not have a smile for you—and did not show by their facial expression that they like you?

All of us need to know that there are people like our parents and our friends who like us and show that they do.

Now perhaps you are wondering if maybe the thing to do is to try to show only your pleasant emotions—and hide the unpleasant ones. To do that, however, would offer problems at some times and in some situations.

Suppose, for example, you should see someone mistreating a dog or a cat—or a bully hurting a small child or breaking the child's playthings. Don't you think you would have a right to show anger at such times? It is perfectly natural for people to be angry at cruelty or unkindness or destructiveness. Such anger may stop mean or unkind acts.

It is quite natural, too, to get angry when you feel you are being mistreated, treated unfairly, or "left out" of things.

In general, you are likely to get angry at your parents or brothers or sisters more often than at other people. That is because you are most sensitive about those you care for.

Since we all *do* get angry now and then, we need to learn ways to manage our emotions—ways that keep us from hurting others or ourselves. As a starter, think about the pictured situations on pages 250–253. For help in ways to deal with the emotions, read pages 254–256.

Something to Do

You might like to get the book All About the Human Mind: An Introduction to Psychology for Young People *by Robert M. Goldenson (Random) from the school or public library. There is a good chapter in it called "Emotions and the Mind."*

Another good book is The Hidden You: Psychology in Your Life *by Arthur Alexander (Prentice).*

Human Emotions

Everybody has emotions! What emotions are being expressed by the girl in these pictures?

Sadness **Happiness** **Fear**

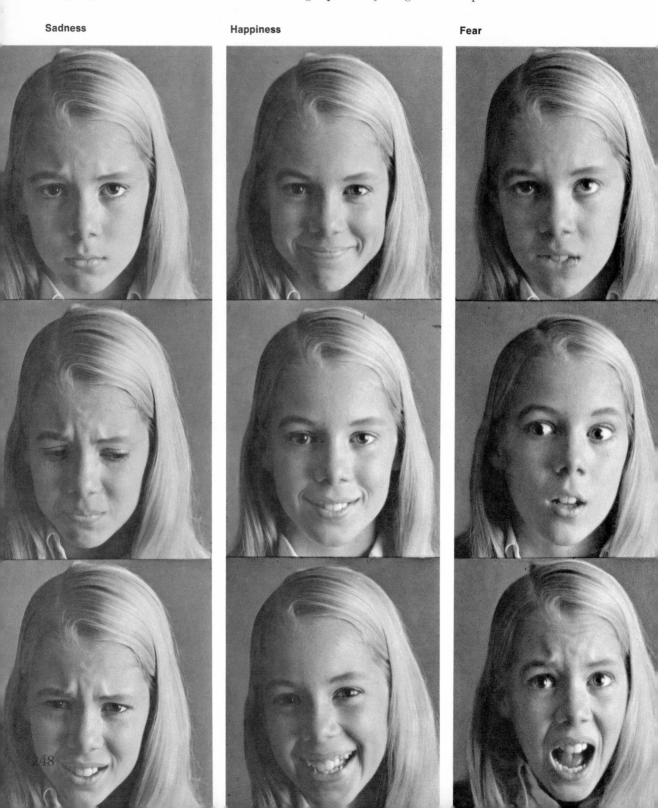

248

What might make a person feel in the different ways you see on these two pages?

Anger   **Excitement**   **Worry**

249

Tom feels left out of things and is thinking to himself: "Ray and Mike go to the Community Center all the time, but they never ask me."
What might Tom do about his problem?

Joe's family has just moved and these thoughts keep running through his mind: "I've lost all my old friends. I'll probably hate our new neighborhood."
What might make Joe feel better about his upset feelings?

Ida May is angry because her little brother has been getting into her things. She is thinking: "I'm so angry I don't know what to do. I can't keep anything around here." What might Ida May do about her feelings? What might keep the situation from happening so often?

252

Rose feels like crying. "Everything seems to be going wrong this day," she thinks. "I lost a glove at school. At supper I quarreled with my brother. And now I can't understand the problems in my homework."
What might she do to calm herself?

How Can You Manage Upset Feelings?

When you have angry feelings that stay with you for a while, it is better to let them out than it is to keep these feelings inside you. If you can talk over your feelings with your parents or some other adult you trust or with a friend or an older brother or sister, it is better for you than if you try to keep these feelings locked up inside you. For as long as the feelings are inside you, you will feel mean and unhappy. And such feelings can keep your body from working properly.

And sooner or later the feelings will come out, sometimes disguised in other ways. You may "take out" your feelings on some person or thing. Angry feelings may also come out in such ways as teasing or bullying small children or even animals—not that you have anything against the children or the animals. You are just getting rid of anger you feel toward someone else. Anger of this kind is sometimes called *displaced anger*.

The angry feelings you keep bottled up inside you may also come out in ways that cause you pain. You may find that your head aches or your stomach hurts when you are upset.

So, for these reasons, too, you should try to let out angry feelings by "talking them out" when possible. This does not mean going around and telling everyone you see about your feelings. But it does mean talking, if you can, to some older person you trust.

If there is no one around with whom you can talk over angry feelings that are bothering you, there are other things you can do. Instead of having a temper tantrum or sulking or taking out your angry feelings on a young child or a pet, try to

Things to Talk Over

1. Why are emotions treated in a book about health?

2. What example can you suggest of displaced anger?

3. What would be the disadvantages of always trying to hide your feelings?

hold off for a while. Get busy doing something. Take a long walk, play a strenuous game, clean your room or some other part of the house. Or try making something, doing something new, or doing something for others. Such activity often helps you through the angry period until you have a chance to think through your feelings.

Misunderstandings

Perhaps in your class discussion someone has mentioned *hurt feelings*. Often we get angry at people or are hurt by them because we misunderstand something they have done or said—because we do not know *why* they are behaving as they are. Suppose, for example, that a friend seems grumpy or not very talkative one day. This may make you angry or hurt your feelings. Such hurt feelings can often be avoided if you will be a little more understanding. It will help, too, if you will be more willing to think about *why* another person may be acting as he is.

Perhaps the other person is worried about something. Maybe something has gone wrong at home. Instead of getting angry or feeling hurt, you might ask in a friendly fashion if anything is wrong. Or you might just overlook for the moment the things the person is doing that are not usual behavior for him.

Or suppose a newcomer at school acts in an unfriendly way. Instead of responding by getting angry or feeling hurt, you might stop to consider why the new person may be acting this way. Maybe he or she is shy and unsure of how to start making friends. Perhaps the person has been badly treated by some others and is afraid you are going to do the same. A little *extra* friendliness on your part may be just what is needed.

Things to Talk Over

1. How can long-standing feelings of anger or the like hurt you?

2. What have you learned about sensible ways of handling angry feelings?

255

As you have just been learning, there *are* ways of dealing with anger and hurt feelings in order to make them less bothersome.

Finding Causes for Upset Feelings

Many times it is helpful to try to think of what may be causing your upset feelings.

Thinking about *why* you feel as you do can sometimes be difficult since you may not want to admit to yourself what has caused you to become angry or feel hurt. But if you can discover what is behind your upset feelings, it may be easier for you to deal with them.

When you feel that others are leaving you out of things or do not want you around, remember that you may be mistaken in thinking people feel this way about you. So, instead of keeping off by yourself, try making some friendly moves of your own. You can make friends with others outside the one special group who seem unfriendly to you. Remember, too, that people do not like all of their acquaintances equally well. Nor do people like all of their acquaintances well enough to want to be *special* friends with them.

If you frequently feel quarrelsome, stop and ask yourself, "Is it because I always want to have my own way?" If so, try giving in now and then. If you give others *their* way at times, you will find that they are more likely to "go along" with you and let you have your way at other times.

When everything seems to be wrong and you are too upset to try to figure out what to do, see if you can turn your attention to something else for a little while. Play a game, watch an interesting TV program, or work on a hobby. But be sure to come back to your problem later when you feel calm and better able to work through it.

Something to Do

You can learn a lot about feelings by reading good books that deal with boys and girls your age who meet and manage upset feelings in various ways. Look in the school or public library for such books as these:

Byars, Betsy. The Summer of the Swans *(Viking).*

Cleaver, Vera and Bill. Grover *(Lippincott).*

Shotwell, Louisa R. Roosevelt Grady *(World).*

Stolz, Mary. The Bully of Barkham Street *(Harper).*

_____. A Wonderful, Terrible Time *(Harper).*

256

How Can You Grow Up Strong and Well And Safe?

Throughout this book you have learned of the many wonders of the human body. To help keep your body functioning properly, you need to follow safe and healthful practices in your daily living.

For example, by cleanliness you can keep many harmful germs from getting inside you. That means being careful to wash your hands before handling or eating food and after going to the toilet. It means being careful to drink safe drinking water—and to avoid eating food that has spoiled because of improper storage. It also means using your own towel, washcloth, toothbrush, and drinking glass if you possibly can.

By having enough of the right kinds of foods, getting enough fresh air and exercise, and getting plenty of sleep and rest—you can work toward keeping well and strong.

If you should get sick in spite of your best efforts, you can still do things to help fight off the illness. One good way is to go to bed and get lots of rest if you have a cold. Rest is one of the surest ways of helping fight disease. If you are very sick, your parents will probably take you to a doctor or a clinic. Then you can help by doing just what the doctor tells you.

You can also try to have health checkups every few years by your family doctor or at a clinic so that any minor problems can be taken care of before they become serious.

You can try, too, to avoid illness by making sure you have been immunized against such communicable diseases as polio, diphtheria, German measles, tetanus, and whooping cough.

Polio viruses as seen under a microscope

Diphtheria bacteria as seen under a microscope

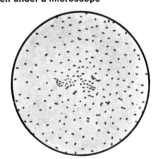

Immunization can help protect you against some communicable diseases.

257

Malaria germs as seen under a microscope

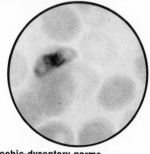

Amoebic-dysentery germs as seen under a microscope

Personal cleanliness and sanitary measures can help curb such diseases as dysentery and malaria.

Against which of these communicable diseases have you already been immunized?

Besides avoiding disease, there are other things you can do to keep your body strong and well. You can learn to work and play safely so that you will not get hurt.

In all these ways you can help prevent the needless trouble, worry, and expense that can be caused by illness and accidents.

As you have learned, your emotions affect your physical health, too. Your feelings go along with everything that you do, and they affect the way the body works.

When you are worried, for example, the worry may spoil your appetite; it may keep your food from digesting well; it may even keep your body from getting rid of wastes as it should. That is why it is important to know helpful ways of managing your emotions.

Your body, you see, is a very interesting machine; it has even been said to have a "wisdom of its own." Each part of the body has its own job to do and does it.

Yet your feelings and the way you handle them can often make the body fall down on its job. That is because you are not just a body. You are a *person*.

All parts of you work together — your body, your mind, and your feelings; and each part depends on every other part to keep the body healthy. That is what makes you what you are and what makes the subject of *you* one of the most fascinating subjects in the world.

There is much you can do, too, to help this person you are now grow into the kind of person you would like to be. How exciting it is to think of the *future* you.

Check Yourself

1. Look back at the questions on page 234. How would you answer them now?

2. How would you explain the statement, "Each body cell is a 'working world' in itself"?

3. What is your explanation of these terms?

    a. cell nucleus   c. protoplasm

    b. chromosomes   d. tissue

4. How do cells divide?

5. What glands in the body have much to do with regulating your growth?

6. Which gland, in particular, has the most to do with your growth?

7. What explanation would you give to someone who wonders why he is not growing in the same way as a friend his age?

8. What have you learned about how girls your age grow?

9. What have you learned about how boys your age grow?

10. What are some ways in which you can grow *mentally? Emotionally?*

11. How would you explain this statement, "Your feelings are a part of everything you do"?

Things to Do

1. Look back at the situations that made some boys and girls angry—as described on page 246. Then choose one of the situations and be ready to tell or write what the person might have done to manage the angry feelings in a helpful way.

2. Be ready to tell or write about a character in a book you have been reading who had some problems and some upset feelings. Tell, too, about what the character did to solve the problems and deal with the upset feelings.

3. Think back to the last time you were angry. How did you deal with your anger? What have you learned that could help you handle the situation better another time?

4. Make a list of things you have learned about growing up that you did not know or had not thought of before.

Special Research

You can learn many interesting things about the endocrine glands by looking in the encyclopedia or other reference books under such topics as these: *Endocrine Glands, Pituitary Gland, Hormones, Dwarf, Cortisone, Insulin,* and *Adrenalin.*

Self-Help Review

Use a ruler or a strip of paper to cover the answer column at the right. Read the first item and write the missing word or words on a piece of paper. Then move your ruler or paper strip down to uncover the answer and see if you are right. Go on in the same way with each of the other items. Do not write in this book.

The numbers by the answers show the pages in this book that give information about the subject. For the items you miss, go back and review this information.

1. Your nerves, bones, blood, muscles, and so on, are made up of tiny, living parts called _____.

cells 234

2. Each cell takes in food and _____ and gives off wastes.

oxygen 234

3. Many cells of one kind grouped together make up what is called _____.

tissue 235

4. When a cell divides, it makes another cell of the _____ kind.

same 235

5. All cells are made up of a living, jellylike substance called _____.

protoplasm 236

6. Glands that manufacture substances known as hormones are called _____ glands.

endocrine 237

7. The gland that has the most to do with your height and growth is the _____ gland.

pituitary 238

8. Besides growing physically, you can also grow mentally and _____.

emotionally 243

9. Every human being has feelings, or _____.

emotions 245

Health Test for Unit Eight

Part I

On a piece of paper, copy each sentence below, filling in the blanks correctly. All blanks in a sentence must be filled correctly if a point is to be scored.

1. _____ give off wastes such as carbon dioxide and take in food and oxygen.

2. Some of the emotions that all people have at times are _____, _____, _____, _____, _____, _____.

3. Many cells of the same kind grouped together are called _____.

4. You could not grow if your cells did not have the ability to _____.

5. At the center part of a cell is the _____.

6. Chromosomes contain _____ which control the traits passed on to you by each of your parents.

7. The endocrine glands send _____ into your blood stream.

8. The _____ gland has much to do with stopping your growth in height when you have reached your full size.

9. Another word for feelings is _____.

10. Cells are so tiny that in order 'to see them you have to use a _____.

Part II

Copy each number on a piece of paper. After the number write the correct answer, *true* or *false*.

11. All cells look alike under the microscope.

12. When a bone cell divides, it always makes a blood cell.

13. Some of the new cells made by your body are used to replace worn-out cells.

14. The nucleus controls many of the cell's activities.

15. Scientists have at hand all the information they need and want about the body's cells.

16. Dwarfs and giants are very common.

17. There are some endocrine glands that help you grow up to be a man if you are a boy and a woman if you are a girl.

18. There is *one* right weight for every boy of age eleven.

19. You should try hard to hide your strong emotions such as fear or anger.

20. Your emotions can affect the way your body works.

Number of Answers   _20_

Number Right   _____

Score (Number Right x 5)   _____

End-of-Book Test

Part I

Copy each number on a piece of paper. After the number, write the name for each part of the body that each of these words or phrases brings to mind.

1. camera
2. pump
3. hinges
4. shock absorbers
5. grinders
6. framework
7. computer
8. waterproof covering
9. air conditioner
10. taster

Now write a name for the things that are described in the following sentences.

11. It makes food soft and able to be swallowed more easily.

12. They keep your bones in place by holding the bones together.

13. It is another name for the food tube.

14. It is the liquid part of the blood and its name starts with the letter *p*.

15. It is the part of the tooth containing nerves and blood vessels.

16. It is the main artery that carries blood away from your heart to every part of your body.

17. Sometimes it is called the voice box.

18. Another name for it is the true skin.

19. It is the largest part of the brain and it has a grayish-pink cover.

20. It is the place where two movable bones fit together.

21. It is a thin film of sensitive nerve cells found in the eye.

22. It is a skinlike part that stretches across the auditory canal.

23. It is a little opening in the middle of the iris of your eye.

24. It has tiny bumps on it that are called papillae.

25. It is a thick nerve cord that goes down the back of you.

Number of Answers	25
Number Right	_____
Score (Number Right x 4)	_____

Part II

Copy each number on a piece of paper. After the number, write the letter that goes with the *best* answer choice.

1. Digested food substances are carried to the cells of the body by the
   a. large intestine
   b. blood
   c. saliva
2. The heart
   a. rests much of the time
   b. never rests
   c. rests between beats
3. The color of skin is due to
   a. sunburn
   b. vitamins
   c. pigment
4. The chief work of the lungs is to
   a. help you talk
   b. keep the blood supplied with oxygen
   c. warm and moisten the air you breathe
5. Digestion of food begins
   a. in the mouth
   b. in the stomach
   c. in the small intestine
6. The body's "telephone wires" are
   a. the nose
   b. the nerves
   c. the stomach
7. The "chemical senses" are the senses of
   a. seeing and hearing
   b. tasting and smelling
   c. touching and tasting
8. Body cells that can surround and "eat up" disease germs are
   a. white blood cells
   b. red blood cells
   c. blood platelets
9. The stomach's chief work is that of
   a. grinding food into pieces
   b. making bile to aid in digestion
   c. helping break down food in the body
10. Places where two bones join are
    a. tendons
    b. ligaments
    c. joints

Number of Answers   __10__

Number Right   _____

Score (Number Right x 10)   _____

Part III

Copy each number on a piece of paper. After the number, write the letter and phrase that best describes this item.

1. Heart
   a. the body's pump
   b. the body's air conditioner
   c. the body's switchboard
2. Cortex
   a. an important vitamin
   b. colorless covering over the eye
   c. the surface layer of the brain
3. Auditory nerve
   a. nerve that carries sound messages to the brain
   b. nerve that carries sight messages to the brain
   c. nerve that carries taste messages to the brain
4. Spinal cord
   a. thick nerve that goes down the back
   b. the main vocal cord
   c. an important branch of the windpipe
5. Aorta
   a. upper-right part of heart
   b. the main artery
   c. the main vein

6. Molars
   a. teeth that cut food
   b. teeth with two points
   c. teeth that grind food
7. Nutrients
   a. nourishing substances found in food
   b. food allergies
   c. harmful bacteria in food
8. Dr. William Beaumont
   a. discoverer of stethoscope
   b. doctor who studied work of the stomach
   c. doctor who discovered blood circulation
9. Dr. William Harvey
   a. scientist who studied the senses
   b. scientist who learned about blood circulation
   c. scientist who studied work of the stomach
10. Muscles you can make move
    a. voluntary muscles
    b. involuntary muscles
    c. muscle fibers

Number of Answers _____ 10 _____
Number Right _____
Score (Number Right x 10) _____

End-of-Book Summary Discussion (Safety)

Part I

1. What is the first-aid treatment for a small burn without blisters?

2. What is the safe way to treat a blister?

3. What first aid should be given in case of a small cut?

4. What is a good way to stop a cut from bleeding?

5. What are some important first-aid steps to follow in case a broken leg bone is suspected?

6. What safety suggestions can you give for a bicycle driver to follow?

7. What are some common causes of injuries to boys and girls your age in such games or sports as these?

   a. volleyball
   b. baseball
   c. racing relays

8. What is the correct way to report a fire in your own home?

9. How can you protect yourself from smoke and poisonous gases that are released by a fire?

10. What should you do if your own clothing should catch on fire?

Part II

In past years you have learned much about safety, too. Use the next questions to help you see how many of these important safety ideas you remember.

1. If you have to walk on a street or road, on which side should you walk?

2. When you walk or ride a bicycle at dusk or at night, how can you make sure you will be seen?

3. What should you always do before you get into a bathtub or shower?

4. What are some places that are never safe ones in which to play?

5. What is the correct way to put in or take out an electric plug?

6. How can you "safety-proof" darts or arrows if you are using them?

7. What are some safety guides to follow if you fly a kite?

8. What are safe places for a pedestrian to cross a street?

9. What are some important safety ideas to keep in mind if you are playing with ropes?

10. What is missing from the following safety guide? *Look both ways before you cross a street.*

Books of Information

Structure, Function, and Care of the Body

Cosgrove, Margaret. *Bone for Bone* (Dodd, Mead).

Froman, Robert. *The Many Human Senses* (Little, Brown).

Glemser, Bernard. *All About the Human Body* (Random).

Liberty, Gene. *The First Book of the Human Senses* (Watts).

McGovern, Ann. *The Question and Answer Book About the Human Body* (Random).

Madison, Arnold. *Drugs and You* (Messner).

Ravielli, Anthony. *Wonders of the Human Body* (Viking).

Schneider, Herman and Nina. *How Your Body Works* (Young Scott).

Weart, Edith L. *The Story of Your Respiratory System* (Coward).

———. *The Story of Your Skin* (Coward).

White, Anne T., and Lietz, Gerald S. *Built to Survive* (Garrard).

Zim, Herbert S. *Bones* (Morrow).

The Emotions

Alexander, Arthur. *The Hidden You: Psychology in Your Life* (Prentice-Hall).

Goldenson, Robert M. *All About the Human Mind: An Introduction to Psychology for Young People* (Random).

LeShan, Eda. *What Makes Me Feel This Way? Growing Up with Human Emotions* (Macmillan).

Limbacher, Walter J. *I'm Not Alone,* Dimensions of Personality Series (Pflaum).

Weart, Edith L. *The Story of Your Glands* (Coward).

Advances in Science and Environmental Education

Chester, Michael. *Let's Go to Stop Air Pollution* (Putnam).

DeGering, Etta. *Seeing Fingers: The Story of Louis Braille* (McKay).

Kavaler, Lucy. *Dangerous Air* (John Day).

Pringle, Laurence P. *The Only Earth We Have* (Macmillan).

Nutrition and Meal Planning

McDonald, Barbara G. *Casserole Cooking Fun* (Walck).

Paul, Aileen, and Hawkins, Arthur. *Kids Cooking* (Doubleday).

Riedman, Sarah R. *Food for People* (Abelard-Schuman).

First Aid

The American National Red Cross. *Basic First Aid: Books 1, 2, 3, 4* (Doubleday).

———. *First Aid Textbook* (Doubleday).

Books to "Grow On"

Understanding Problems of Growing Up

Bloch, Marie Halun. *Aunt America* (Atheneum). When her aunt visits from America, Lesya — who lives in modern Ukraine — learns some things about freedom.

Bragdon, Elspeth. *That Jud!* (Viking). An orphan boy learns to understand himself and to find a place for himself.

Calhoun, Mary. *Depend on Katie John* (Harper). A fifth-grade girl has to adjust to a new school and to the fact that her family home has been turned into a rooming house.

Canfield, Dorothy. *Understood Betsy* (Holt). How shy Betsy's whole life and personality changes when she moves to Vermont makes a story that girls will enjoy.

Cleaver, Vera and Bill. *Grover* (Lippincott). Ten-year-old Grover must face the hard reality of his mother's death and his father's illness.

Clymer, Eleanor. *My Brother Stevie* (Holt). An older sister in an inner-city neighborhood worries about her younger brother and learns that he may get into trouble.

De Angeli, Marguerite. *The Door in the Wall* (Doubleday). Robin, a cripple, proves his courage in thirteenth-century London.

Fenner, Phyllis R., Editor. *Crack of the Bat: Stories of Baseball* (Knopf). These fast-paced baseball stories provide many examples of good sportsmanship "in action."

Heide, Florence Parry. *The Key* (Atheneum). Three stories in which children have to face and work through difficult situations.

Konigsburg, Elaine L. *Altogether, One at a Time* (Atheneum). Four short stories that deal with young people's emotions.

Lenski, Lois. *Shoo-Fly Girl* (Lippincott). Shoo-Fly, one of nine children, is an Amish girl who lives in Pennsylvania Dutch country.

Robinson, Veronica. *David in Silence* (Lippincott). A deaf boy learns to share the fun and activities of children who can hear.

Seredy, Kate. *The Good Master* (Viking). Kate goes to live on her uncle's farm. There she learns to love and respect others.

Snyder, Zilpha K. *The Velvet Room* (Atheneum). Robin tries to escape the problems that go with a sharecropper's life; in so doing, she gains new understandings.

Whitney, Phyllis. *Nobody Likes Trina* (Westminster). Whether to be "popular" or to be kind to a lonely new girl is the problem posed in this book.

Glossary

Full Pronunciation Key

The pronunciation of each word is shown just after the word, in this way: **ab bre vi ate** (ə brē′vē āt). The letters and signs used are pronounced as in the words at the right. The mark ′ is placed after a syllable with primary or heavy accent, as in the example above. The mark ′ after a syllable shows a secondary or lighter accent, as in **ab bre vi a tion** (ə brē′vē ā′shən).

Foreign Sound: H as in German ach. Pronounce k without closing the breath passage.

a	hat, cap	o	hot, rock
ā	age, face	ō	open, go
ä	father, far	ô	order, all
		oi	oil, voice
b	bad, rob	ou	house, out
ch	child, much		
d	did, red	p	paper, cup
		r	run, try
e	let, best	s	say, yes
ē	equal, be	sh	she, rush
ėr	term, learn	t	tell, it
		th	thin, both
f	fat, if	ŦH	then, smooth
g	go, bag		
h	he, how	u	cup, butter
		u̇	full, put
i	it, pin	ü	rule, move
ī	ice, five		
		v	very, save
j	jam, enjoy	w	will, woman
k	kind, seek	y	young, yet
l	land, coal	z	zero, breeze
m	me, am	zh	measure, seizure
n	no, in		
ng	long, bring		

ə represents:
a in about
e in taken
i in April
o in lemon
u in circus

ər represents:
er in mother
ur in pursuit

This pronunciation key is from *Thorndike-Barnhart Intermediate Dictionary* (Scott, Foresman and Company).

268

ab do men (ab′də mən), the part of the body containing the stomach, the intestines, and certain other important organs; belly.

ab scess (ab′ ses), a collection of pus in the tissues of some part of the body. An abscess results from an infection and is usually painful: *an abscess of a tooth.*

ac id (as′id), 1. sour; sharp or biting to the taste: *Lemons are an acid fruit.* 2. a sour chemical substance. The acids caused by fermentation of sweet foods in the mouth can cause cavities if these foods are not removed by brushing the teeth.

al bi no (al bī′nō), person or animal that from birth has a pale, milky skin, very light hair, and pink eyes.

al ler gy (al′ər jē), *pl.* **al ler gies,** unusual sensitiveness to certain substances, such as a particular kind of pollen, food, hair, or cloth. Hay fever, asthma, headaches, or hives are common signs of allergy.

an ti bod y (an′ti bod′ē), *pl.* **an ti bod ies,** substance produced in the blood or tissues of the body that can destroy or weaken bacteria or neutralize poisons produced by them.

a or ta (ā ôr′tə), *pl.* **a or tas** or **a or tae** (-tē), main artery of the body, leading out of the left side of the heart to smaller arteries all over the body, except for the lungs.

ar ter y (är′tər ē), *pl.* **ar ter ies,** any of the blood vessels or tubes that carry blood away from the heart to various parts of the body.

ar thri tis (är thrī′tis), inflammation of a joint or joints of the body.

a stig ma tism (ə stig′mə tiz′əm), unequal curvature in the cornea or lens of an eye that makes objects look blurred.

au di to ry ca nal (ô′də tô′rē or ô′də tō′rē kə nal′), tube or passageway that leads from the outer ear to the middle ear.

au di to ry nerve (ô′də tô′rē or ô′də tō′rē nèrv′), hearing nerve that carries messages of sound to the hearing center of the brain.

au ri cle (ô′rə kəl), either of the two upper chambers of the heart that receive blood from the veins.

au to nom ic nerv ous sys tem (ô′tə nom′ik nèr′vəs sis′təm), the ganglia and nerves of the nervous system of vertebrates that control digestive, reproductive, and other involuntary reactions.

bac ter i a (bak tir′ē ə), microscopic living plants. Some kinds of harmful bacteria cause diseases such as pneumonia and typhoid fever. Some helpful bacteria are those that turn milk into cheese and cider into vinegar.

Beau mont (bō′mont), **William,** 1785–1853, American surgeon who made some important observations on digestion while watching a man's stomach at work.

bi cus pid (bī kus′pid), tooth having two cusps, or pointed ends, that tears and grinds food. An adult has eight bicuspids.

blood (blud), the red liquid in the veins, arteries, and capillaries; the red liquid that flows from a cut. Blood is circulated by the heart and carries oxygen and digested food to all parts of the body and takes away waste materials.

blood ves sel (blud′ ves′əl), any tube in the body through which the blood circulates. An artery, vein, or capillary is a blood vessel.

bone (bōn), the hard substance forming the skeleton of the body.

bow el (bou′əl), tube in the body into which food passes from the stomach; one of the divisions of the intestines.

brain (brān), part of the central nervous system in Man and other vertebrates that is enclosed in the skull or head and consists of a soft mass of nerve cells. The brain controls almost all the functions of the body, and with it we can learn, think, remember.

brain stem (brān′ stem′), lower portion of the brain, where functions such as breathing and circulation are controlled; the extension upward from the spinal cord.

bron chi al tube (brong′kē əl tüb′ or tyüb′), either of the two main branches of the windpipe leading into the lungs.

can cer (kan′sər), a very harmful growth in the body that tends to spread and destroy healthy tissues and organs; malignant tumor. There are many different kinds of cancer.

cap il lar y (kap′ə ler′ē), *pl.* **cap il lar ies,** a blood vessel with a slender, hairlike opening. Capillaries join the end of an artery to the beginning of a vein.

car bo hy drate (kär′bō hī′drāt), substance made from carbon dioxide and water by green plants in sunlight, composed of carbon, oxygen, and hydrogen. Carbohydrates in food furnish heat and energy for the body. Sugar and starch are carbohydrates.

car bon di ox ide (kär′bən dī ok′sīd), a heavy, colorless, odorless gas. It is formed in body tissues as a waste product and is excreted by the lungs.

car ti lage (kär′tl ij), gristle; the firm, elastic, flexible substance forming parts of the skeleton.

cav i ty (kav′ə tē), *pl.* **cav i ties,** hole; hollow place. Cavities in teeth are caused by decay.

cell (sel), basic structural unit, or building block, of living matter. Animals and plants are made of cells.

ce men tum (sə men′təm), the hard, thin substance covering the roots of a tooth.

cer e bel lum (ser′ə bel′əm), the part of the brain that controls the automatic coördination of the muscles.

cer e bral cor tex (sə rē′brəl or ser′ə brəl kôr′teks), the outer layer of gray matter of the cerebrum.

cer e brum (sə rē′brəm or ser′ə brəm), the part of the human brain that controls thought and voluntary muscular movements.

chem i cal (kem′ə kəl), any simple substance that is used to cause changes in other substances. Sulfuric acid, bicarbonate of soda, chlorine, and borax are chemicals.

chro mo some (krō′mə sōm), any of the microscopic threadlike particles that appear in the cell nucleus during cell division and that contain genes which determine heredity.

chyme (kīm), a pulpy, semiliquid mass into which food is changed by the action of the stomach. Chyme passes from the stomach into the small intestine.

coc cyx (kok′siks), a small triangular bone—usually several vertebrae fused together—at the lower end of the spinal column.

coch le a (kok′lē ə), a snail-shaped cavity of the inner ear, containing the nerve endings that transmit sound impulses along the auditory nerve.

com put er (kəm pūt′ ər), a machine that computes, especially an electronic machine that solves complex mathematical problems when given coded information.

con nec tive tis sue (kə nek′tiv tish′ü), tissue made up of an interlaced mass of tough, elastic cells that connects, supports, or encloses other tissues and organs in the body.

con tact lens (kon′takt lenz′), a very small, thin plastic lens fitted on the front of the eyeball or only over the cornea.

cor ne a (kôr′nē ə), the transparent "window" of the eye that covers the iris and the pupil.

cor tex (kôr′teks), the layer of gray matter that covers most of the surface of the brain.

cra ni um (krā′nē əm), 1. skull of a vertebrate. 2. part of the skull enclosing the brain.

crown (kroun), part of a tooth that appears beyond the gum, or an artificial substitute for it.

cus pid (kus′pid), tooth having one cusp, or pointed end, and used especially for tearing food. There are four cuspids in a full set of permanent teeth.

den tal car ies (den′tl ker′ēz or kar′ēz), decay of dental tissues; tooth decay; cavity.

den tin (den′tən), the hard, bony material beneath the enamel of a tooth, forming the main part of a tooth.

de pres sant drug (di pres′ ənt drug), substance that slows or reduces mental and physical function.

der mis (dėr′mis), the sensitive layer of skin beneath the outer skin in which are located many blood vessels and nerve endings.

di a phragm (dī′ə fram), a partition of muscles and tendons separating the cavity of the chest from the cavity of the abdomen.

di ges tion (də jes′ chən or dī jes′chən), the changing or breaking down of food in the mouth, stomach, and intestines so that the body can absorb it.

di ges tive juice (də jes′tiv jüs′), any liquid secretion made by the body that aids in the digestion of food. Saliva and gastric juice are digestive juices.

dis solve (di zolv′), change from a solid or gas to a liquid; form into a solution in a liquid: *Salt or sugar will dissolve in water.*

duct (dukt), tube in the body for carrying a bodily fluid: *tear ducts.*

e lec tron mi cro scope (i lek′tron mī′krə skōp), microscope that uses beams of electrons instead of beams of light to enlarge images, and that has much higher power than any ordinary light microscope.

EEG, *see* **electroencephalogram.**

e lec tro en ceph a lo gram (i lek′ trō en sef′ ə lə-gram), tracings of brain waves made by the electro-encephalograph machine. *Abbrev.:* EEG.

e lec tro en ceph a lo graph (i lek′ trō en sef′ ə lə-graf), instrument that measures and records the brain's electrical activity.

em phy se ma (em′fə sē′mə), respiratory disease in which the lungs become expanded and inefficient in supplying oxygen to and removing carbon dioxide from the blood. Cigarette smoking can cause emphysema.

e nam el (i nam′əl), smooth, hard, glossy, outer layer of the teeth.

en do crine gland (en′dō krən or en′dō krīn gland′), any of various glands, such as the thyroid gland, that produce secretions which pass directly into the blood stream or lymph instead of into a duct.

ep i der mis (ep′ə der′mis), the thin outer layer of the skin.

ep i glot tis (ep′ə glot′is), a thin triangular plate of cartilage that covers the entrance to the windpipe during swallowing.

e soph a gus (ē sof′ə gəs), tube for the passage of food from the mouth to the stomach; it is also called the food tube.

Eus ta chi an tube (yü stā′kē ən or yü stā′shən tüb′ or tyüb′), a slender canal between the throat and the middle ear. It equalizes the air pressure on the two sides of the eardrum.

far-sight ed (fär′sīt′id), seeing distant things more clearly than near ones.

fats (fats), a class of nutrients essential in our diet; they build fatty tissues and serve as a source of energy.

first aid (ferst′ ād′), emergency treatment given to an injured or sick person before a doctor comes.

fluor i da tion (flür′ə dā′shən), process of adding minute amounts of a fluoride to drinking water.

flu o ride (flü′ə rīd′), fluorine compound that may be added to drinking water in small amounts or applied by a dentist directly to the teeth to help prevent tooth decay.

fo cus (fō′kəs), adjust a lens, the eye, and so on, to make a clear image: *A near-sighted person cannot focus accurately on distant objects.*

frac ture (frak′chər), break; crack: *The boy fell from a tree and fractured his arm.*

gall blad der (gôl′ blad′ər), pearshaped sac attached to the liver in which bile is stored until needed for digestion.

gas tric juice (gas′trik jüs′), the digestive fluid secreted by glands in the lining of the stomach. It helps break down foods, particularly proteins.

gene (jēn), a minute part of a chromosome that influences the inheritance and development of some characteristic.

gland (gland), organ in the body that separates materials from the blood and changes them into some secretion for use in the body, or into a product to be

---

hat, āge, fär;   let, bē, tėrm;   it, īce;   hot, gō, ôrder;   oil′, out;   cup, pùt, rüle;   takən, mothər

discharged from the body. The liver, kidneys, pancreas, and thyroid are glands.

growth plate (grōth′ plāt′), the middle section of growing bones, consisting of cartilage, which joins the ends and shafts of the long bones. As bone cells come up from the shaft, cartilage cells withdraw to the ends of the bones, and the bone becomes longer.

Harvey (här′vē), **William**, 1578–1657, English doctor who discovered the circulation of the blood.

heart (härt), a hollow, muscular organ that pumps the blood throughout the body.

he mo glo bin (hē′mə glō′bən or hem′ə glō′bən), the red substance in the red blood cells made up of iron and protein that carries oxygen from the lungs to the tissues.

Hip poc ra tes (hi pok′rə tēz), 460?–357? B.C., a Greek physician, called "the father of medicine."

hor mone (hôr′mōn), chemical substance formed in the endocrine glands that enters the blood stream and affects or controls the activity of some organ or tissue. Adrenalin and insulin are hormones.

im mu nize (im′yə nīz), make resistant to disease, poison, and so on: *Vaccination immunizes people against smallpox.*

in ci sor (in sī′zər), tooth having a sharp edge for cutting; one of the front teeth. We have eight incisors in all.

in fec tion (in fek′shən), 1. a causing of disease in people, animals, and plants by the introduction of germs. Air, water, clothing, and insects may all be means of infection. 2. disease that can be spread from one person to another.

in ner ear (in′ər ēr′), innermost part of the ear. Sound waves traveling through the liquid in and around the snail-shaped part cause the nerve cells to send messages of sound to the brain. The inner ear also contains organs concerned with balance.

in vol un tar y (in vol′ən ter′ē), not controlled by the will: *Breathing is mainly involuntary.*

i ris (ī′ris), the colored part of the eye around the pupil.

joint (joint), part in an animal where two bones join, allowing motion, and the way those bones are fitted together.

kid ney (kid′nē), one of the pair of glands in the body that separates wastes from the blood and passes them off through the urinary bladder as urine.

Laën nec (lā nek′), **Re né** (rə nā′), 1781–1826, French doctor who made the first stethoscope.

large in tes tine (lärj′ in tes′tən), lower part of the intestines into which the small intestine discharges food that has been digested.

lar ynx (lar′ingks), upper end of the windpipe, where the vocal cords are and where the voice is produced.

lens (lenz), 1. a curved piece of glass or other transparent material which brings closer together or sends wider apart the rays of light passing through it. 2. the part of the eye that directs light rays upon the retina.

lig a ment (lig′ə mənt), a band of strong tissue that connects bones or holds organs of the body in place.

lit mus pa per (lit′məs pā′pər), paper treated with litmus, a blue dye used as a chemical indicator. It turns red when put into acid solutions and back to blue when put into alkaline solutions.

liv er (liv′ər), the large, reddish-brown gland in vertebrate animals that makes bile, aids in the body's use of food, and stores glycogen.

LSD, drug that causes the brain to distort messages from the senses. It has highly dangerous properties and cannot be bought, used, or sold legally in the United States.

lung (lung), either one of a pair of saclike, spongy organs found in the chest of vertebrates that breathe air. The lungs absorb oxygen from the air, give the blood the oxygen it needs, and relieve the blood of carbon dioxide.

Mal pi ghi (mäl pē'gē), **Mar cel lo** (mär chel'ō), 1628–1694, Italian doctor who discovered how blood gets from the arteries to the veins.

mar i jua na (mar'ə wä'na), the dried flowering tops and leaves of the Indian hemp plant. It is commonly called "pot."

mar row (mar'ō), the soft tissue that fills the hollow central part of most bones. Blood cells are formed in the marrow.

me dul la ob lon ga ta (mi dul'ə ob'long gä'tə or ob'long gā'tə), the lowest part of the brain stem, at the top end of the spinal cord, containing the nerve centers that control breathing and other involuntary functions.

mem brane (mem'brān), 1. a thin, soft sheet or layer of animal tissue lining or covering some part of the body. 2. a similar layer of vegetable tissue.

men tal health (men'tl helth'), a person has good mental health when he can manage upset feelings in ways that help him but do not hurt others.

mi cro scope (mī'krə skōp), an instrument with a lens or combination of lenses for making small things look larger.

mid dle ear (mid'l ēr'), a hollow space between the eardrum and the inner ear that contains three small bones which carry sound waves from the eardrum to the inner ear.

min er al (min'ər əl or min'rəl), any substance that is neither plant nor animal, but which often occurs in tiny amounts in foods such as meats and vegetables. Minerals are important in the diet to provide material for body growth and repair and to help regulate body activities.

mo lar (mō'lər), 1. adapted for grinding. 2. a tooth with a broad surface for grinding. A person's back teeth are molars.

mol e cule (mol'ə kyül), the smallest particle into which an element or compound can be divided without changing its chemical properties.

mo tor nerve (mo'tər nėrv'), bundle of nerve fibers that arouse muscles to action. When you want to walk or talk, motor nerves carry these messages from the brain or spinal cord to the right muscles.

mu cus (myü'kəs), a slimy substance that is secreted by and moistens the linings of the body. A cold in the head causes a discharge of mucus from the nose.

mus cle (mus'əl), the tissue in the bodies of people and animals that can be tightened or loosened to make the body move.

near-sight ed (nir'sī'tid), not able to see far; seeing distinctly at a short distance only.

nerve (nėrv), a fiber or bundle of fibers through which impulses pass between the brain or spinal cord and the eyes, ears, muscles, glands, and so on.

nerve end ing (nėrv' en'ding), the end of a nerve fiber, where stimulation of the nerve occurs.

nu cle us (nü'klē əs or nyü'klē əs), mass of specialized protoplasm found in most plant and animal cells, without which the cell cannot grow and divide.

nu tri ent (nü'trē ənt or nyü'trē ənt), nourishing substance found in foods, having specific functions in maintaining the body. Vitamins and proteins are nutrients.

nu tri tion (nü trish'ən or nyü trish'ən), 1. food; nourishment. 2. series of processes by which food is used by animals and plants for growth, energy, and so on.

ol fac tor y (ol fak'tər ē), having to do with smelling; of smell. The nose is an olfactory organ.

oph thal mol o gist (of'thal mol'ə jist), doctor who specializes in the treatment of all diseases, defects, and injuries of the eye.

op tic nerve (op'tik nėrv'), nerve that goes from the eye to the brain.

op tom e trist (op tom'ə trist), a person who specializes in correcting visual defects by means of glasses and eye exercises.

---

hat, āge, fär;   let, bē, tėrm;   it, īce;   hot, gō, ôrder;   oil, out;   cup, pùt, rüle;   takən, mothər

out er ear (out'ər ēr'), the visible curved flap of the ear and the short passageway that goes to the middle ear. The outer ear directs sound waves into the inner parts of the ear.

pan cre as (pan'krē əs), gland near the stomach that empties several secretions into the small intestine to aid digestion. Within the pancreas are cells called islets of Langerhans which secrete insulin.

pa pil la (pə pil'ə), *pl.* **pa pil lae** (-ē), a small nipple-like projection concerned with the senses of touch, taste, or smell: *the papillae on the tongue.*

pel vis (pel'vis), *pl.* **pel vis es,** the basin-shaped cavity formed by the hipbones and the end of the backbone.

Pen field (pen'fēld), **Wilder,** 1897– , a Canadian doctor, born in the United States, who made important discoveries about areas in the brain where memories are stored.

per i stal sis (per'ə stal'sis), movement in the wall of a hollow organ by which it propels its contents onward; especially, the wavelike circular contractions of the alimentary canal.

per ma nent teeth (per'mə nənt tēth'), the second set of teeth (of which there are 32) which start to come in when the primary teeth begin to fall out. They are intended to last a lifetime.

pig ment (pig'mənt), substance that occurs in and colors the tissues of an animal or plant. The color of a person's hair, skin, and eyes is due to pigment in the cells of the body.

pi tu i tar y gland (pə tü'ə ter'ē or pə tyü'ə ter'ē gland'), a small, oval endocrine gland situated at the base of the brain. It produces several hormones that promote growth, stimulate other glands, and regulate many bodily functions.

plaque (plak), thin, transparent film composed of saliva, bacteria, and food debris that is constantly being formed on the surfaces of the teeth.

plas ma (plaz'mə), the clear, almost colorless, liquid part of blood or lymph, in which blood or lymph cells float. Plasma consists of water, salts, proteins, and other substances, and it makes up the largest part of the blood.

plate let (plāt'lit), one of many small disks which float in the blood plasma, and are involved in clotting of the blood.

po li o my e li tis (pō'lē ō mī'ə lī'tis) or **polio,** an acute, infectious, virus disease that destroys nervous tissue in the spinal cord, causing fever, paralysis of various muscles, and often death. It is caused by three different viruses. Vaccines are available.

pol lu tion (pə lü'shən), polluting; defiling; uncleanness; for example, air pollution.

pos ture (pos'chər), position of the body; way of holding the body.

pri mar y teeth (prī'mer'ē or prī'mə rē tēth'), the first set of teeth (of which there are 20) which are later replaced by the permanent teeth.

pro tein (prō'tēn), one of the substances containing nitrogen which are a necessary part of the cells of animals and plants. Meat, milk, cheese, eggs, and beans contain protein.

pro to plasm (prō'tə plaz əm), a colorless substance somewhat like soft jelly or egg white that is the living matter of all plant and animal cells; the substance that is the physical basis of life.

pul mo nar y ar ter y (pul'mə ner'ē är'tər ē), blood vessel that carries "used" blood from the right side of the heart to the lungs where the blood gets rid of carbon dioxide and picks up oxygen.

pul mo nar y vein (pul'mə ner'ē vān'), blood vessel that carries oxygen-rich blood from the lungs to the left side of the heart. This blood is then pumped to all parts of the body.

pulp (pulp), the soft inner part of a tooth containing blood vessels and nerves.

pulse (puls), the regular beating of the arteries caused by the rush of blood into them after each contraction of the heart.

pu pil (pyü'pl), the opening in the center of the iris of the eye, which looks like a black spot. The pupil, which is the only place where light can enter the eye, expands and contracts, thus controlling the amount of light that strikes the retina.

Ré au mur (rā'ə myur), **Re né de** (rə nā də), 1683 – 1757, French scientist who studied the work of the stomach. He found that gastric juice was present in the stomach of animals.

red blood cells (red' blud' selz'), cells that with the white blood cells form a large part of blood. Red blood cells contain hemoglobin, which gives them their color. They carry oxygen from the lungs to various parts of the body.

res pir a to ry sys tem (res'pər ə tôr'ē sis'təm), system having to do with or used for breathing. The lungs are organs of the respiratory system.

ret i na (ret' n ə), layer of cells at the back of the eyeball that is sensitive to light and receives images of things looked at.

rick ets (rik'its), disease of childhood caused by a vitamin D deficiency and resulting in softening, and sometimes bending, of the bones.

root (rüt), the part of a tooth that is covered by the gums and cannot be seen.

rough age (ruf'ij), 1. rough or coarse materials. 2. the coarser parts or kinds of food which stimulate the movement of food and waste products through the intestines.

sa crum (sā'krəm), bone at the lower end of the spine, which is formed by the joining of several vertebrae and which forms the back of the pelvis.

St. Mar tin (sānt mär'tən), **A lex is** (ə lek'səs), American trader who permitted studies by Dr. William Beaumont on his stomach after it had been opened in an accident (1822).

sa li va (sə lī'və), liquid that the salivary glands secrete into the mouth to keep it moist, aid in chewing, and start digestion.

sal i var y gland (sal'ə ver'ē gland'), any of the various glands that empty their secretions into the mouth.

scler a (sklir'ə) or **scle rot ic coat** (sklə rot'ik kōt'), strong, white outer membrane covering the eyeball; the "white of the eye."

se crete (si krēt'), make; produce and discharge: *Glands in the mouth secrete saliva.*

sem i cir cu lar ca nal (sem'ē sèr'kyə lər kə nal'), any of the three curved, tubelike canals in the inner ear that help us keep our balance.

sense (sens), power of the mind to know what happens outside itself. Sight, hearing, touch, taste, and smell are the five main senses.

sen sor y nerve (sen'sə rē nèrv'), bundle of nerve fibers that carry messages or sensations from all parts of the body to the brain. Pain, temperature, touch, sight, smell, sound, and taste are conveyed by sensory nerves.

shock (shok), weakness of the body or mind caused by some severe wound, blow, or disturbance of the nervous system.

skel e tal mus cle (skel'ə təl mus'əl), any of the more than 600 muscles that are attached to and cover the skeleton. They make up what is commonly called the flesh of the body.

skel e ton (skel'ə tən), the bones of a body, fitted together in their natural places. The skeleton is a frame that supports the muscles, organs, and so on.

small in tes tine (smôl' in tes'tən), slender part of the intestines, extending from the stomach to the large intestine; it is about 21 feet long in adults.

Spal lan za ni (spä'län zä'nē), **La za ro** (lä zä' rō), 1729 – 1799, Italian scientist who studied digestion.

spi nal cord (spī'nl kôrd'), the thick, whitish cord of nerve tissue in the backbone which extends from the brain down through most of the backbone, and from which nerves to various parts of the body branch off.

spine (spīn), the backbone.

---

hat, āge, fär;   let, bē, tèrm;   it, īce;   hot, gō, ôrder;   oil, out;   cup, pùt, rüle;   takən, mothər

starch (stärch), a white, tasteless food substance; one of the carbohydrates. Potatoes contain much starch.

ster ile (ster'əl), free from living germs.

steth o scope (steth'ə skōp), instrument used by doctors to hear the sounds produced in the lungs, heart, and so forth.

stim u lant drug (stim'yə lənt drug'), a substance which temporarily speeds up the action of the nervous system.

stom ach (stum'ək), the large muscular bag in the body which receives, mixes the food, and digests some of it before passing it on into the intestines.

syn thet ic (sin thet'ik), made artificially.

taste bud (tāst' bud'), any of certain small groups of cells in the lining of the tongue or mouth that are sense organs of taste.

ten don (ten'dən), a tough, strong band or cord of tissue that joins a muscle to a bone.

tet a nus (tet'n əs), disease caused by certain bacteria usually entering the body through wounds. The disease is characterized by violent spasms, stiffness of many muscles, and even death; it is also called lockjaw.

tis sue (tish'ü), substance forming the parts of the human body, animals, and plants; a mass of similar cells which performs a particular function.

tra che a (trā'kē ə), pl. **tra che ae** (-ē). See **windpipe.**

trans fu sion (tran sfyü'zhən), transfer of blood from one person or animal to another.

ur i nar y blad der (yùr'ə ner'ē blad'ər), saclike structure that stores and discharges urine.

ur ine (yùr'ən), the fluid that is excreted from the kidneys as a waste product of the body. Urine goes to the urinary bladder and is then discharged from the body.

valve (valv), 1. movable part that controls the flow of a liquid or gas through a pipe by opening and closing the passage. 2. membrane that works similarly. The heart valves control the flow of blood.

vein (vān), one of the blood vessels or tubes that carry blood to the heart from all parts of the body.

ve na ca va (vē'nə kā'və), pl. **ve nae** (-ē) **ca vae** (-ē), either of two large veins that return blood to the right side of the heart.

ven tri cle (ven'trə kəl), either of the two lower chambers of the heart.

ver te bra (ver'tə brə), pl. **ver te brae** (ver'tə brē) **ver te bras** (ver'tə brəz), any of the bones of the spinal column, or backbone.

vil li (vil'ī), tiny hairlike parts growing out of the lining of the small intestine. The villi absorb certain substances.

vi ta min (vī'tə min), any of certain special substances required for the normal growth and nourishment of the body.

vo cal cords (vō'kəl kôrdz'), two pairs of membranes in the larynx. The lower pair can be pulled tight or let loose to help make the sounds of the voice.

voice box (vois'boks'). See **larynx.**

vol un tar y (vol'ən ter'ē), 1. acting of one's own free will or choice. 2. deliberately intended; done on purpose. 3. controlled by the will: *Talking is voluntary; breathing is only partly so.*

white blood cells (hwīt' blud' selz'), cells that float in the blood and lymph. Some of them destroy disease germs.

wind pipe (wind' pīp'), passageway from the throat (pharynx) to the bronchial tubes; the trachea.

X ray (eks' rā'), 1. ray which penetrates substances that light cannot penetrate. X rays are used to locate breaks in bones and cavities in teeth and to diagnose and treat certain diseases. 2. picture made by means of X rays.

---

hat, āge, fär; let, bē, tėrm; it, īce; hot, gō, ôrder; oil, out; cup, pùt, rüle; takən, mothər

Index

About the Book

A Health Program for Ten- to Eleven-Year-Olds

The special health needs, interests, and curiosities of ten- and eleven-year-old pupils form the basis for the content for *Book Five* of the HEALTH AND GROWTH Program.[1]

Boys and girls this age have pronounced interest in their bodies and how they work. These youngsters seek broad and basic information about how they look inside, what happens when they eat and breathe, how they grow, how they see and hear, what the brain does, and so on.

These children also—if given the opportunity—raise such provocative health questions as "What does it mean to be color-blind? What are freckles? What are allergies? Do smart people have bigger brains than other people? What is the harm in smoking?"

Problems of mental and emotional health loom large at times, too, as boys and girls work at coping with strong emotions such as fear and anger. For this reason mental and emotional understandings are important strands in the text. Children learn how body and mind and emotions work together to make them what they are—and to make the study of themselves one of the most fascinating pursuits in the world.

Crucial health problems of the community—such as that of air pollution—also evoke some curiosity and concern.

This book contains a wealth of information, verbal and pictorial, about ways to keep the body strong and safe and healthy. Vivid four-color drawings throughout every unit show, often in minute detail, the structure of various parts of the body. These drawings, made by a well-known medical illustrator, help enrich the text and clarify concepts about the body's structure and function.

This text, then, is in the main a junior physiology planned to satisfy the major health and safety queries—and the intriguing minor ones—of youngsters who are "going on eleven" or so.

Teaching aids in both the pupil's text and the accompanying Teacher's Edition are planned to give youngsters guidance in reading in the content field of health and safety—with emphasis on the use of basic reading skills to fully interpret factual material presented through text, pictures, charts, and diagrams.

Readability

The vocabulary of this book has been checked with readability scales and the book itself has been tried out in manuscript form with fifth-graders. It is suitable for use with most boys and girls at this age level.

---

[1]The HEALTH AND GROWTH Program includes *Off to a Good Start* (Junior Primer Activity Sheets), and *Book One* through *Book Eight*, with accompanying *Teachers' Editions*. Also available is a preprimary health program, *Health and Safety Highlights: Pictures and Songs for Young Children.*

Index of Health and Safety Ideas[1]

---

[1]Selected behavioral objectives for this level are given in the *Resource Book*, pages 27-28.

Credits

Cover: Photograph by Ray Komorski.

Unit 1: 9, 10—Drawings by George Suyeoka. 12—Photograph from The Bettmann Archive, Inc. 15—Drawing by George Suyeoka. 17-21—Anatomical art by Lou Barlow, AMI. 22-24—Photographs from International Business Machines Corporation. 25—Photographs courtesy of the Clinical Neurophysiology Laboratory of the Section of Neurology, University of Chicago.

Unit 2: 36-38—Anatomical art by Lou Barlow, AMI. 39, 40—Drawings by George Suyeoka. 41-43—Anatomical art by Lou Barlow, AMI. 44-46—Photographs by Stef Leinwohl. 49—Drawing by George Suyeoka. 50—Photograph from Richard A. Buckingham, M.D., Department of Otolaryngology, University of Illinois at the Medical Center, Chicago, Illinois. 52-54, 56-59, 61-63—Anatomical art by Lou Barlow, AMI. 64—From American Optical Corporation.

Unit 3: 73—Photograph by Lyle Mayer. 75—Drawing by George Suyeoka. 77-79—Anatomical art by Lou Barlow, AMI. 80-81—Photographs by Lyle Mayer. 82—Photographs from Federal Bureau of Investigation, U.S. Department of Justice, Washington, D.C. 84—Anatomical art by Lou Barlow, AMI. 86—Photographs from The Bettmann Archive, Inc. 89—Photographs from Dermatology Department, Northwestern University Medical School. 92—Anatomical art by Lou Barlow, AMI.

Unit 4: 99-102—Anatomical art by Lou Barlow, AMI. 104-105—Photograph by Lyle Mayer. 106-113, 115, 116, 118-123—Anatomical art by Lou Barlow, AMI. 125—Drawing by George Suyeoka. 129, 130—Anatomical art by Lou Barlow, AMI.

Unit 5: 137, 139, 141—Photographs from The Bettmann Archive, Inc. 142-148—Anatomical art by Lou Barlow, AMI. 149—X ray from X-ray Department, Children's Memorial Hospital, Chicago, Illinois. 150-151—Drawing by George Suyeoka. 152—Anatomical art by Lou Barlow, AMI. 153-155—Photographs by Ray Komorski. 156—Photograph from American Hospital Supply Corporation. 157, 158, 160, 161—Anatomical art by Lou Barlow, AMI. 162—Photographs from Captain Gordon H. Rovelstad, United States Navy, Naval Dental Research Institute, Naval Training Center, Great Lakes, Illinois. 165, 171-173—Drawings by George Suyeoka.

Unit 6: 179, 180—Photographs from The Bettmann Archive, Inc. 181—Drawing by George Suyeoka. 186, 187—Anatomical art by Lou Barlow, AMI. 188-189—Drawing by George Suyeoka. 190, 191—Photographs by Ray Komorski. 192, 193—Anatomical art by Lou Barlow, AMI. 194—Photograph courtesy of Clay Adams, Division of Becton, Dickinson and Company. 196-198—Anatomical art by Lou Barlow, AMI. 199—Drawing by George Suyeoka. 200, 201—Photographs by Ray Komorski. 202-203—Drawing by George Suyeoka. 204—Photograph by Ray Komorski. 207—Anatomical art by Lou Barlow, AMI. 209—Drawing by Cynthia Fujii. 211—Drawing by George Suyeoka.

Unit 7: 218-221—Drawings by George Suyeoka. 224-227—Photographs by Myles DeRussy.

Unit 8: 235, 236—Anatomical art by Lou Barlow, AMI. 237, 241—Drawings by George Suyeoka. 248-253—Photographs by Ralph Cowan. 257 (Top) Courtesy A. R. Taylor, Ph.D., Laboratory Director of Virus Research, Parke, Davis & Co. 257 (Bottom)—Photograph from USPHS, Center for Disease Control. 258—Courtesy S. Stanley Schneierson, M.D., and Abbott Laboratories.